IN A BLACK SE...
a young Russian ...
an executioner pumps bullets into his body.

IN WASHINGTON'S KENNEDY CENTER,
the Yugoslav ambassador suddenly slumps
in his seat, dead.

IN THE WRECKAGE OF A GEORGETOWN
TOWNHOUSE,
a shattered man uses his last breath to gasp out
a message too shocking to believe.

THROUGHOUT THE WORLD,
human pawns are toppling, and bloody pieces are
falling into place, shaping a plot that only a
computer could comprehend...and only a holo-
caust can stop!

"ANOTHER MASTER TALE...EXCITING!"
—Indianapolis News

MASTERSTROKE

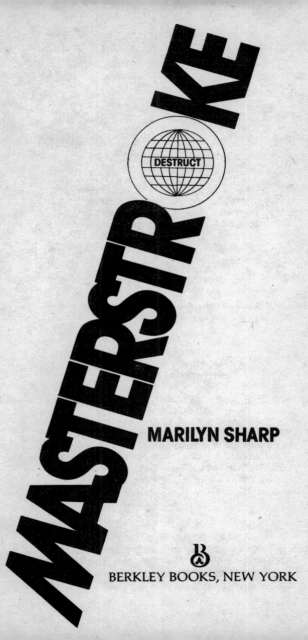

MASTERSTROKE

DESTRUCT

MARILYN SHARP

BERKLEY BOOKS, NEW YORK

This Berkley book contains the complete
text of the original hardcover edition.
It has been completely reset in a type face
designed for easy reading, and was printed
from new film.

MASTERSTROKE

A Berkley Book / published by arrangement with
Richard Marek Publishers

PRINTING HISTORY
Richard Marek edition / May 1981
Berkley edition / February 1982

ISBN: 0-425-05201-X

A BERKLEY BOOK ® TM 757,375
Berkley Books are published by Berkley Publishing Corporation,
200 Madison Avenue, New York, New York 10016.
PRINTED IN THE UNITED STATES OF AMERICA

To Mother

1

YURI DANCHENKO STOPPED and looked back the way he had come. His breathing was labored but silent, his bones sharply prominent under sallow, ill-nourished skin. His forehead creased into a frown over his dark eyes, but his face showed no hint of fear. Curiosity was all the emotion he could register.

He stood still, listening.

He had heard a sound, a sliding of rock, perhaps a foot slipping in the dense forest behind him. He stared up the slope of the mountain, but he saw nothing. No movement, no sign of life beyond the luxuriant growth emerging deep green in the dawn. Oak and pine forest had given way here to magnolia and eucalyptus, to cypress and palm. Sharp air had turned soft and warm, even now, on this last day of September.

Or was it the first of October? Yuri couldn't remember, nor did he much care. The sun rose and set; days blended together, each like another except for one thing—every sunset brought him one day closer to freedom. And Gena.

Snow capped the mountains that rose in the distance, above and behind the slope where Yuri stood. The Caucasus—rugged peaks, some taller than the Alps—a natural line of defense against invading armies, an impassable range at times to all but the skilled local guides. And yet it was over those mountains that Yuri Danchenko had come, alone, in borrowed clothes that rightly belonged in a rag bin, in a pair of shoes that were bound together by cord. No course was impassable when it was the only way home.

Home! Yuri gave a silent, sardonic laugh. He *had* no home. Certainly not Moscow, where he lived all but one of his thirty-seven years. Not the university where he earned his degree, nor the institute where he worked. Not even the flat in Lenin Prospekt where he had lived with Gena. Any sentiment he felt for the places that had been home had faded in a Moscow courtroom, had vanished in a camp called Perm. Life at hard labor was not life at all. It was time spent in a vacuum, where only the body functioned, where brain and heart quickly atrophied from disuse.

He pushed on, one step at a time—slowly, heavily, silently. Caution came as instinct now. He was weary beyond exhaustion, numbed to pain, unable to think of anything but the one unwavering purpose that had kept him going till now. Escape. Then he rounded a curve in the path, and without warning the view opened up before him—the green slope of mountain descending to a narrow strip of beach, to orange and lemon groves, to tea and tobacco plantations, all thriving in the subtropical climate of the Black Sea, at the edge of the Soviet world.

For a moment Yuri felt nothing but profound shock. At last, the end was in sight. Then tears came up in his eyes. He and Gena had honeymooned here, up the coast road at Sochi. They had promised themselves they'd come back. Now Yuri had returned, in rags, hungry and frail to the point of illness—not to Sochi, but Gagra, at the gate of the ancient Colchis, where Jason had sailed in search of the Golden Fleece.

Yuri stared out over the sea. Home was out there somewhere, in the gray mist, beyond the dark water, beyond the far shore of Turkey. He would spend one last day in Russia, one more day as a fugitive for a crime that defied all sense. Tonight, under cover of darkness, he would leave his homeland forever. Tomorrow he would be free.

Exhaustion lifted with new hope. Yuri walked more quickly as he continued on down the path, but his instinct for caution sharpened. If anything, he was in more danger here than ever—here, now, in calling distance of friends. Friends, though he'd never seen them and didn't know them by name. They shared something far more intimate than names: a common purpose. They offered something far more urgent: food and shelter, rest, false papers, and passage to a new world.

Yes, friends were here, but so too was the enemy.

Gagra was a health resort where the Soviet elite came to bathe away their ills in the warm mineral springs. And autumn was the height of the season. While temperatures plunged below freezing in other parts of Russia, the climate here remained balmy well into November. Rooftops dotted the green slope that rose up from the beach below, but the houses beneath them were concealed by trees. They were rest homes and sanatoriums, each isolated from the next by design, because some ailments were better treated in private.

Three of the roofs were more isolated than the rest. They sat above the others and could not be seen unless someone came from the mountain peaks behind them. Yuri paused for a moment as a map appeared in his mind, a map scratched out crudely on paper, weeks ago, memorized and burned. He could see it now as clearly as he had when he held it in his hand.

And he smiled. His escape would shock the Kremlin for more reasons than one. These mountains were combed with ravines and caverns and hidden underground streams. But Yuri's friends weren't waiting in a mountain cave or a hidden ravine. Their plan was far more audacious. They had taken over a house in that uppermost tier—not a rest home or sanatorium, but a villa owned by the government and operated solely for the pleasure of its *crème de la crème*.

Yuri followed the map in his mind, moving carefully behind cover, making sure his approach could not be seen from within. There was still time for retreat if the sign was not in place, as he had been told it would be when the underground took control. He moved cautiously, approaching the house from the rear.

It was a big white frame house with large windows above and below the roof of a wide veranda, Victorian by design, like the seaside homes Yuri had seen in pictures of Cape Cod and Cornwall. An old house, untouched by the new brand of progress that came with the Revolution. An old house, but with its own modern touches: a rooftop TV antenna and, beside it, a smaller device for sending and receiving radio signals to and from Moscow.

Yuri smiled to himself. Any radio equipment inside the house was no doubt sitting idle. The present occupants were hardly likely to be in touch with the Kremlin. The sign was in place, in a window on the upper floor—a white candle, fat and misshapen, leaning drunkenly to one side, as if melted by the sun. It pointed west, toward the future. Yuri stepped out into the open; he moved quickly across the back lawn. The sign was in place; it was safe to enter the house.

A servant opened the door. He was a blank-faced man in a coarse, ill-fitting suit, and he stared at Yuri with impassive eyes, like the *stukachi* who worked as servants in every government house and were paid by the KGB. Yuri felt a stab of fear—fear of the man and the cold look of the eyes. His voice failed; he hadn't used it for days, for weeks, not since he departed from other friends who arranged this escape, who had seen him off on this long journey south, through rain and snow and treacherous terrain. He had spoken to no one in the meantime; he had taken pains to avoid any human contact. But now, here, he needed help once again.

He heard himself speaking the code he had memorized.

A hint of a smile appeared in the servant's eyes. He replied—he gave the *correct* reply—and stepped back to let Yuri enter.

Yuri stumbled past him into a large room where drapes were drawn against daylight. Relief swept over him as he heard the door shut behind him and a bolt lock slide into place. Then exhaustion returned with overwhelming force. He dropped into a comfortable chair. His throat was dry, his body aching for food, but those needs would have to wait. His eyes closed and he slept.

For a moment? An hour? A day? All sense of time had vanished. There was only a voice calling urgently: "Yuri! Yuri, wake up!"

Yuri struggled to open his eyes. He focused slowly. A man stood over him, smiling; three others stood just behind.

"Yuri, have you brought the tape?"

Yuri's lips tried to form an answer, but words wouldn't come. He felt drugged, secure in the presence of friends, reluctant to rouse himself from the soft edges of sleep. He raised one hand and gestured toward a pocket inside his jacket.

The man leaned forward, reached into the pocket, extracted a reel of tape small enough to enclose in one hand. He studied it for a moment, then glanced back at Yuri, still smiling. He gave a silent nod. Behind him, the three men moved apart, and a new man came forward.

No, he didn't come forward. He *advanced*, his arms before him. In his hands he carried a Czech-made submachine gun.

Yuri came awake with a start. His eyes turned cold, but not from fear. It was too late for that. The truth swept over him in a rush of shock, in an instant of realization. He had been betrayed! These were not friends, but *cheka*! KGB!

The man with the gun raised the stock to his shoulder, lowered his face against the black metal, closed one eye, lined up his target with the other. Yuri went rigid in the chair. There was no time for self-pity, as there was no time for fear. He thought about Gena; he wondered when she would know. He thought about the others who escaped with him; he wondered where they were now. And he thought about the friends who planned the escape. Friends? Hardly! Someone, at least, thrice worse than Judas! He had been betrayed *by his friends*!

His eyes shifted from the gun to the man with the tape, who came, no doubt, from Mokrie Dela, KGB's assassination bureau, the dreaded Department V. The man's smile remained fixed in place, but he no longer tried to feign kindness. The smile was smug, full of pleasure. The bastard was *enjoying* himself!

He did not look away, merely gave another small nod.

Yuri heard a sharp click, then a high burping sound and the light tinkle of brass casings hitting the floor. His consciousness lasted no more than a second, as the room exploded in gunfire, as round after round of bullets was fired into his chest—but his eyes remained on the man from Department V, on the smug bastard who was, this once, too sure of his own success. In that last moment, Yuri returned the smile. He died with a sense of victory. His betrayers had failed. The *cheka* had failed.

The tape on the reel was blank.

2

PETER WAS HAVING a nightmare.

There were no voices in the dream, only heavy footsteps—leather boots marching in the ominous silence of the broad marble corridor just beyond the door. The sound of them pierced the bright morning, as sharp and precise as the crack of a rifle, as thundering as the roar of artillery in another part of the war. It set off waves of fear, hollow terror, a ringing in the ears—like the echo of the ocean in a seashell, incomprehensibly threatening for its infinite scope.

In his dream, Peter's small fingers gripped the rosary beads in his pocket, but he found no comfort there. He was barely six, but he already knew that life had little to offer beyond his own resourcefulness. There was no one to pray to, *no* comfort; these things had ceased to exist before he knew what they were. There were only the soldiers and the sharp, mocking sound of their boots, against which even the sisters scarcely dared to breathe.

The other children waited in silence; their faces, like his, repressed fear. They waited with calm acceptance, sure of only one thing—some among them were hated, and though they didn't know why, they had learned all too well what hate was. Some were hated and hunted. And by the time the noon bells rang in the abbey, one or more of them would be gone.

Peter was one of the hunted. The soldiers had been here before and they would come back, again and again. He knew they would never give up. He knew they were after *him*.

Bootsteps. A sharp sound, the latch of the door. Bright morning shadows shifted, and movement entered the room. Peter couldn't breathe. He was trapped there.

Hail Mary, Mother of God. Blessed Virgin. Blessed Savior. *Mama* . . . !

Mama, *help* me!

The cry rang out in silence, unheard except inside Peter's heart. Then anger rose up to replace it, for promises broken— for mother and father, for saints and guardian angels, for the sisters' loving God who watched over this earth. Anger because they were *not* there, and because they never had been. Peter wanted them, how he *wanted* them to be real, but he knew inside they were not.

He was trapped, and he was alone.

Then suddenly he was awake. His hands and face were damp with perspiration, like the sheet that lay twisted across his pounding chest. Lean muscles had tensed for action. He was ready to kill or to die.

An old reflex, learned years ago in that time of genuine danger—no longer needed, but impossible to shake off. A defensive, reflexive action, as instinctive to Peter as life.

He sat up slowly and shook his head to clear the lingering fear. Then his eyes swept the room. They studied each mundane object—the dresser where he dropped his wallet and keys when he came in the night before; the chair where he tossed his shirt; the rug where he kicked off his shoes; the cartons of books he had dragged from one foreign post to another, still unpacked for want of a bookcase. Eventually he might furnish this place with more than just what he needed. In the meantime, it was his. Real and safe. Familiar.

Sounds repeated themselves: a garbage truck, having paused on the street below, roared on to another stop. Wind swept under the partially open window, encountered resistance, retreated, leaving the louvered blind to fall sharply back into place. Movement recurred as patterns of pale sunlight shifted across the wall. It was morning. There was no danger here. This was Washington, not Paris; his apartment, not the orphanage. The nightmare was gone, more than thirty years past.

Peter got up and crossed the room to the dresser where he'd left his cigarettes, took one and held his lighter to it. Then he looked at his face in the mirror, as if trying to prove that the passage of time was real. The boy of the dream was going on forty now. New gray showed in his dark hair. New lines were clear in the fading summer tan of his skin. But old shadows darkened his eyes. The face in the mirror was still the boy of the dream. Peter hadn't forgotten. Old feelings stirred inside. Hatred. Injustice. The inequity of the world. *Children*, for Christ's sake! It made no sense. Even now, it made no sense.

But that was all a long time ago. What mattered was now, justice now. Too many people were still trapped, by poverty and political oppression. Peter returned to the bed and leaned back against the pillows, smoking in silence, his long legs stretched out before him. He had no illusions. His own life had been like a patchwork quilt without formal design—born in Amsterdam, raised in Paris and New York, born a Jew but guided and taught mostly by nuns and priests. He spoke English now with no trace of an accent, though his first language was French, and he never had learned to speak his native Dutch.

For a long time he didn't know who or what he was, who or what he *ought* to be. His home in Amsterdam was gone when the war was over. His parents were gone, too. He no longer remembered them, or the night they sent him away. But he remembered the stranger they had handed him to, the stranger who carried him across two borders—from Holland into Belgium, from Belgium into France. He remembered Paris, and the iron gates of the orphanage that marked off the edge of his life. Beyond the gates lay unspeakable terror, the Nazis, but he hated those gates and ran from the orphanage as soon as the Nazis fled. He escaped to the streets, a child alone in a city emerging from war. He escaped to become what he had never been, a child finally free.

And he remembered that the same stranger who had smuggled him into Paris found him when he was starving, fed him, clothed him, became his mentor and his friend. Arthur Compton. Now the Secretary of State—and still his friend and benefactor. Arthur Compton, who had sponsored him at Harvard, given him a job in his law firm, brought him to Washington, made him Assistant Secretary of State for Human Rights.

He closed his eyes, rubbing his face with both hands. Morning was his vulnerable time, the moment when he could be caught defenseless against his own bad dreams. It had been a while since the past had come back to terrify him, and he wondered why it had chosen to come back now.

Now, when life was so good. When the Korcula summit—his brainchild, his consuming passion, his ultimate goal—was about to take place.

The Soviets had agreed to his idea, transmitted to them by Compton, of a summit conference on human rights. Of course, they had agreed to human rights conferences before. But this time they promised major concessions, to negotiate freedom in a spirit of cooperation that went far beyond Helsinki, at the highest levels, with the President and the Premier. Broad outlines of the agreement had been worked out already between Compton and the Soviet Foreign minister; when announced, they would come as a bombshell. Relaxed immigration policies. Reduced travel restrictions. Increased freedom of speech. And, as a show of sincerity, the release of two hundred political prisoners, including six world-famous dissidents, from the Soviet labor camps. That much, and then, if it all worked out, still further concessions, another level of freedom. It was staggering to think about. And it was his idea, made possible through Compton's backing.

The Russians were ready to open the Iron Curtain. From the inside.

Peter could almost bring himself to believe that it was a miracle, but he knew it wasn't. There was no magic here, only work and determination. Injustice would not be wiped out. But the Korcula pact would be an enormous first step. Freedom, established on trust between two international giants. The rest of the world would not dare to object.

Peter drew on his cigarette. Then the telephone rang beside him. He glanced at his watch. Who the devil would be calling him at this hour? Nicole, maybe—either that or one hell of a crisis somewhere in the world.

He picked it up. "Hello?"

"Peter Lucas, you *are* a son of a bitch!"

Peter smiled as Nicole's sweet face came to life in his

mind—blond hair, soft curls, gentle blue eyes. The kind of woman, he thought the first time he met her, who might have inspired Fragonard or Watteau. The kind of woman for whom fainting couches were made.

Except Nicole, the expert on ancient history, didn't care for "modern" rococo painters, and she wouldn't notice a fainting couch unless it belonged to Cassandra or Nefertiti. World crises, to her, were mere current events if they had not happened B.C.

"I gather I've done something to displease you," he said.

"Indeed you have. You promised me dinner tonight—dinner for two at your place, with wine and candlelight. And *no one* to entertain."

So that was the problem.

"And now," she said, "here's a note from Daddy. It seems we're all off to the President's box instead."

"I guess I forgot to tell you."

"With that *Hungarian*."

Peter laughed. Nicole knew very well who Jovan Kersnik was—not Hungarian, but Yugoslavian, the ambassador at that. She even liked him—but not, it seemed, for tonight.

Peter understood why. He'd been so damn busy with Korcula lately that they'd had almost no time alone. He longed for her touch, to hold her, without having to rush away. Time alone. He had let it become too rare.

Nicole had been busy too. She had taken a leave from her work as an archaeologist to come home and get an advanced degree at Georgetown; she was busy trying to finish her dissertation. But she was also a busy Washington hostess—for her father, Arthur Compton, the Secretary of State. And that job, so sought by some women, was far more of an effort for her than the most grueling expedition, because social Washington wasn't Nicole's way of life, any more than it was Peter's.

He glanced at the picture on his bedside table. No studio portrait with love and kisses penned across a draped shoulder—this was Nicole as she saw herself and wanted Peter to see her, in jeans and a bandanna, face streaked with dust, eyes squinting against a desert sun. He didn't know where the picture had been taken—at a Hittite palace, an Etruscan grave, or the tomb of an unknown pharaoh—but there was no mistaking the triumph on her face. Weeks and months of hard work had paid off—the scraping, layer by layer, the patient, painstaking search. Nicole had found yet another link between this world and the past.

The *ancient* past—Nicole's passion, like her father's quest for peace.

So different, those two, Peter thought, like a twin-headed Janus with one pair of eyes on the future while the other looked to the past, neither one of them quite here. So different, and so alike.

"At least you'll be glad to know it's the opera," he told her. "The Met's in town. They're doing *Turandot*. And we can have dinner anyway. The curtain is early. We can come back here when it's over."

There was silence at the other end of the phone. Peter waited a moment, then asked, "Am I forgiven?"

Nicole dismissed the question with an easy laugh. "Never mind. There's nothing to forgive, beyond a small lapse of memory, of course, but I've grown used to that. I know where I stand with you and Daddy—just after Bolivia, right before Senegal."

"I don't know about that. There's been trouble in Senegal . . ."

"Never *mind*. I'll see you tonight."

"Good."

"And, Peter . . ."

"Yes?"

"I love you anyway."

Peter hung up the phone, still smiling. Life *was* good.

The Korcula conference was set to begin next week, on October 7. Its agenda was predetermined. More importantly, so was its outcome. It *would* succeed. The man who saved his life, Arthur Compton, had seen to that.

The nightmare was in the past.

3

PETER LOOKED UP as Arthur Compton entered the Adams Drawing Room on the top floor of the State Department. Not only Peter; every face in the room turned toward him, as if he had been announced. Bodies shifted slightly in a physical show of respect. Eyes acknowledged his presence. Conversation ceased for the briefest of moments before it resumed in somewhat more hushed tones. The reception went on. Nothing had changed, but a current had passed through the room. It was not just a man, but power that walked through the door, and everyone there knew it.

Peter smiled. He had observed the reaction so many times, in so many different settings. The *effect* of Arthur Compton was always the same—subtle, but profound. It was and it always had been.

"And now let the party begin," someone behind Peter said.

Peter chuckled and turned to the sound of the voice. Jonathan Kimbal's gaunt face and serious dark eyes seemed inconsistent with the sense of humor. Kimbal was the British Foreign Secretary, a man of considerable stature on his own, but he knew his shadow paled beside the one cast by Compton. He knew and accepted, even made it a joke: nothing of any importance ever began without Compton.

Peter shrugged. "At least we didn't hold the food until he

12

arrived," he said. Brunch had been served, in three courses, in the Jefferson Dining Room.

"I daresay that's only because the good secretary has eaten." Peter chuckled again, but he didn't contest the point.

It was October 1, Indian summer in Washington, a bright, clear, perfect autumn day. Sunshine sharpened the edge of gold on the trees outside the building and turned the Potomac River a deep shade of blue. The streets below were snarled with traffic, the air outside full of city noise. But here people lingered over coffee, in an elegant room full of Hepplewhite and Chippendale, with light glowing softly from crystal sconces mounted against the warm cream-colored walls.

A State Department reception, at the end of a NATO conference, the largest gathering of foreign officials in Washington since the funeral of JFK. The conference was over today, at the end of this farewell reception. Compton, as usual, had timed his appearance precisely.

"I'd like to see him," Kimbal said.

Peter studied the other man's face. He knew that Compton would never leave the reception without seeking out the British Foreign Secretary, but he sensed something in Kimbal's quiet request, an edge of concern, a tone of implied importance. He caught Compton's eye, raised his hand in a signaling gesture. Compton joined them, smiling at the Foreign Secretary, and putting his arm around Peter's shoulder. "Is something wrong?" he asked.

Kimbal hesitated a moment, then acknowledged the question with a nod. "Overall, I'm very pleased with the work we've done here," he said. "But I'm troubled by one decision. Cerebrus 77."

"The reinforcement of Norway."

"Precisely. I don't think we should cancel the exercise, this year or any other."

"I see."

Peter took a cup of coffee from a passing waiter, tasted it, and put it down on a table nearby. Like everything else in the room, the table was a museum piece, an artifact, the desk on which the final Treaty of Paris was signed in 1783. He looked back at Kimbal. Relations with Britain had improved somewhat in the meantime.

"I understand the difficulties your President faces," Kimbal was saying. "The American people are hell-bent on cutting back spending, and a practice defense of Norway seems a highly expendable item. An exercise staged by NATO, of course, but funded by U.S. tax dollars."

Compton smiled. "You state the problem precisely. We could use you on Capitol Hill."

"I have my own problems with Parliament," Kimbal replied. For a moment his eyes brightened with a shared sense of appreciation for the dilemma of democratic government; group decisions were never easily made. Then his face grew serious again. "Nevertheless, I'm deeply concerned about Norway and the increasing Soviet presence off the coast of the Finmark province."

Peter knew what Kimbal was talking about; this had all been hashed over before. Soviet ships, ostensibly civilian, had been trespassing in the arctic waters off Norway's northernmost coast. They made all sorts of excuses—mechanical difficulties, sick or injured crew, vague storm threats. At least one of the ships had been boarded by Norwegian Navy, who later reported seeing the kind of equipment one scarcely needed on a civilian freighter.

Oslo filed complaints with Moscow, to no avail, and raised the issue with the NATO command at Brussels. And here again at the conference. Norway's supporters had argued that this was hardly the time to cancel Cerebrus 77. Warn the Soviets, they said: Trespassers will be tolerated to a point, but Norway is not without friends. To probe too deeply, to press too far, is to risk confrontation with NATO. With the military might of the United States.

"You know our position," Compton said. "The Soviets maintain their largest concentration of military force on the Kola peninsula, near their border with Norway. They're extremely defensive about the close proximity of a NATO nation. The situation bears watching—"

"—but is not, at this time, a cause for real concern." Kimbal smiled. "Yes, I know the U.S. position. What I want to know is whether there's any chance that position might be changed."

"I'm afraid not," Compton replied. "The President has committed himself to a tighter budget. Of course, if the Soviets start playing rough . . ."

Peter knew that expense was not the primary reason Cerebrus 77 had been canceled. The Korcula summit was the President's top priority, and until the pact was signed, the U.S. would do nothing to aggravate tensions with the USSR. Kimbal, of course, had no way of knowing just how much was at stake. The Soviet Premier had insisted that no details of the agenda for the Korcula meeting be disclosed in advance, for internal political reasons of his own. The President had no objection, and so the preliminary agreements had been worked out in secret, between Compton and the Soviet Foreign Minister, at an undisclosed location, with maximum security and minimum personnel—excluding even Peter, who had learned the dramatic results only after Compton came home.

The Secretary of State had lowered his voice, and his eyes suggested a secret about to be shared. "Frankly," he told Kimbal, "I'm just not worried about what the Soviets are doing. I think there's nothing more than a flexing of muscle—a reminder to us, as it were, that NATO does not control the world. I have reason to believe it won't come to anything."

"You've discussed it with Moscow?"

"With Premier Sukhov himself." His gaze shifted past Kimbal to an aide who was hurrying toward him across the room.

"Mr. Secretary, the White House has called. The President wants to see you. I've ordered your car."

There was nothing in Compton's face to reveal what was in his mind. A White House summons, routine or unexpected? Or was the aide from the scheduling office and merely concerned about time?

Compton turned back to Kimbal. "I'm sorry," he said. "We'll have to take this up later."

"Of course."

"Safe journey home." Compton shook Kimbal's hand. He nodded to Peter. Then he turned and walked out of the room.

4

PETER'S DESK WAS positioned near a window looking over the trees on Independence Avenue to the Potomac River. He had two armchairs and a leather couch, regulation for an assistant secretary, and a coffee table strewn with news magazines from half a dozen countries. He was sitting behind his desk, studying the poster on the wall before him. A stark black-and-white lithograph—frightened faces, barbed wire, armed guards. And a message: *Save the Soviet Six*. Peter had never taken the poster down, even after every attempt to free them had failed. He left it there as a reminder, so he would never forget the faces, the names. So he would never forget the importance of six human lives.

But now those names were at the top of a list. Altogether, two hundred political prisoners to be released as soon as the Korcula pact was signed. First among them would be the Soviet Six.

"Do you have a few minutes, Peter?"

Peter glanced up at the sound of the voice. He smiled. "Sure, Dan. Come on in."

Daniel Ravage dropped into a chair and looked at Peter across the top of the desk. He was about fifty, a tall man, lean and fit, with brown hair and a strong, open face that testified to his Polish ancestry. He was an academician with a penchant for practical problems, a Soviet scholar who came to the State Department on a temporary work-study assignment from Columbia University, where he taught international relations. That was six years ago; now Ravage was here to stay.

"What's on your mind?" Peter asked.

"This just came over my desk." Ravage handed Paul a piece of paper, a cable from the embassy in Berlin. "It's a routine part of a minor but nasty incident," he said. "The Soviets have buzzed a Lufthansa flight, a passenger plane, that strayed to the edge of the Berlin corridor."

Peter read the cable quickly. "An accident, with apologies all around. Hardly worth State Department attention."

"An accident, right." Ravage nodded. "It probably was."

"Probably?"

Ravage leaned back in his chair. "That's only the latest in a series of incidents related to Berlin," he said. "Soviet patrols in the west, for example. Granted, there's nothing new about that, but they're coming more often lately, jeeploads of Soviet soldiers—not once a day, sometimes three or four times, and not just to the American sector, but the British and the French. *Why*?"

Ravage had answered his own question. Soviet patrols in West Berlin were as old as the quadrapartheid agreement. A few more now and then suggested nothing more menacing than harassment or the vagaries of military whim.

But there was more than a suggestion of worry on Ravage's face. Peter dropped the cable on his desk. "Obviously you think there's more to it," he said.

"A lot more, and I'm very concerned about it." Ravage leaned forward, elbows on knees, rubbing his hands together, averting his eyes. "I've been wanting to talk to you for a couple of weeks, but I've been reluctant to—frankly, because you're such good friends with the Secretary."

Peter frowned. "You're worried about Compton?"

"What I'm worried about is Korcula."

Peter glanced at the map under the glass on his desk. Yugoslavia. Korcula. The site of the meeting. A tiny sunlit island in the Adriatic Sea. Then his eyes shifted to the poster on the wall behind Ravage's chair. Ravage, too, was no stranger to the pain of political oppression. He had been in Poland when

the Nazis attacked. He too had been trapped, like Peter—first
by the war, and then by the Iron Curtain. He was as committed
to Korcula as Peter was. He had asked for a transfer from the
Soviet desk to the Human Rights Department, to take on the
task of supervising the arrangements for the conference—a
ticklish job—and Peter was glad to have him. But now Ravage
was worried. Peter thought it was only pressure, building to
a high point as the start of the conference grew near. He guessed
that Ravage only needed to talk, to get something off his chest.
Peter lit a cigarette, leaned back in his chair. "Why are you
worried?" he asked.

Ravage shook his head. "I don't know. Maybe I'm only
imagining things."

"Maybe you are, but why don't you tell me about it."

Ravage sat there a moment. Then he got up and crossed the
room to the window, looked out, turned back to Peter. "I don't
have to tell you where we started with this," he said. "Before
Compton negotiated the Korcula meeting, Soviet-American
relations were deteriorating badly. Angola. Ethiopia. Cambodia
and Vietnam. New Soviet bases in Latin America. And finally,
Iran and Afghanistan—the world almost at war over oil sup-
plies and control of the Persian Gulf."

Ravage looked back at Peter, then started to pace the room.
The professor embarked on a lecture from notes he knew by
heart. His face was quietly thoughtful, but the worry still
showed in his eyes. "Then Compton intervened," he said. "He
figured the Soviets didn't want confrontation any more than
we did, and they were only acting out of their own need for
self-preservation in an explosive world. He offered a bold alternative. Korcula. The restoration of detente at a new level,
deemphasizing ideological differences, concentrating on the
mutual burdens and responsibilities of superpower status in the
nuclear age. He chose the arena of human rights—no little
thanks to you—not only for its own importance, but for its
symbolic value, a clear sign to the world that major change
has occurred, that we're on a new footing here, that the U.S.
and the USSR are united in the cause of peace."

Peter drew on his cigarette. No, he didn't need to be reminded how close to the edge of disaster the world had come.

He didn't need to be told the importance of the Korcula meeting. But he did wonder what Ravage was building to.

"You're complaining?" he asked.

"Hell, no, I'm not complaining! It's a masterstroke, wrought by the great God Compton, and I'm not being facetious. He's convinced the Russians to *trust* us, for Christ's sake. No one else could have done it. No one else would have dared."

"And yet . . . ?"

"And yet, there's a little voice telling me it's not going to happen that way. There are funny things going on in the world, and I can't figure them out. It's the balance of power, Peter. Spheres of influence. I know, the world is always in a state of flux, but it's happening too fast lately, and too much for our side. Look at the changes that have taken place in the last year alone. We signed a defense pact with China; that's a clear shift of power to our side. And what did the Soviets do? Nothing. Oh, sure, they objected—"

"And negotiated their own deal with India," Peter reminded him. "Now they've got China damn near surrounded, and full use of India's ocean ports."

"China for India?" Ravage laughed dryly. "That's hardly an even exchange. And anyway, India has been more theirs than ours ever since the British left. The new agreement only formalized a long-standing relationship."

"And opened the doors to an actual Soviet presence on the Indian subcontinent, right next door to the Middle East and the world oil supply." Peter shrugged. "All the more reason why both sides need to make Korcula work."

"Maybe so," Ravage said, "but the Russians can't think they came out even on that one. And then there's Cuba. An internal revolt backed by exiles in the United States. Sure it was! No one will ever prove it, but you know as well as I do, those 'exiles' came straight from the CIA."

Peter nodded. No one would ever prove it: no one had to. Cuba was a *fait accompli* and back in the U.S. fold.

"The Russians know that too," Ravage said. "Of course they know. But what did they do? Nothing—except move their own troops into Angola once the Cubans withdrew. Again, hardly a fair trade."

Peter sighed. "Look, Dan, I understand why you're worried. This is a critical time. In another few days we're going to have an agreement that will put an end to the very fears you're talking about. At least it will be a first step. That's the promise of Korcula. But it's only a promise. We don't have an agreement yet, and until we do, it's going to be business as usual."

"The usual hostilities," Ravage said. "But we're supposed to be in a period of mutual nonhostility. And if so, what about Berlin?"

"What *about* Berlin?"

"If the Soviets were serious about mutual nonhostility, or even just the appearance of it, Berlin is the last place where they should be causing trouble. Unless it's Norway. That's hardly business as usual."

Peter shrugged. "You're the Soviet expert. And anyway, you said it yourself—there's nothing going on in Berlin that hasn't been going on for years. As for Norway, if it will make you feel better, I just left Compton, and I assure you he's well aware of what's going on there. He's aware, and not worried about it."

"That's precisely what does worry me," Ravage said. "The fact that he *isn't* worried. You know Compton better than anyone here. What do you think? Is it possible he's blinded himself? Is he too committed to making Korcula work? Could he be playing into the Russians' hands?"

"Jesus, Dan! What are you getting at?"

"I don't know. Retaliation, maybe. For China. For Cuba."

"In Berlin? Good God, in *Norway*?"

Ravage sighed heavily. He seemed tired. "I don't mean to be melodramatic, but believe me, I can feel it. There's something wrong, something very wrong. I'm beginning to think it's all too good to be true."

Peter stared at him. Compton blinded to the reality of the world? Impossible! He was nursed on reality, the man and the boy. He was not so easily fooled. "What the hell did you have for breakfast?" he asked.

"I don't remember."

"It's just as well!" Peter laughed gently to take the edge off the tension that was building between them. "You professors are always looking for something that isn't there," he said.

"You're just like the political columnists. Things can't be the way they appear to be on the surface. You've got to have a conspiracy."

Ravage smiled. "Maybe you're right."

"This time, I think I am. You know how it is, Dan. The Soviets are in the same position we are. They've got to hold this thing together back home. They have to deal from strength; they can't go to the table unless it looks like they're giving and not being pushed. Internal politics, touchy at this point—or maybe they've got a good case of last-minute butterflies."

Peter's cigarette suddenly tasted bitter. He put it out. Butterflies in ample supply, enough to go around. Then he glanced up as a flurry of tweed and silk rushed past his door. His assistant was back from lunch.

"*Mary . . . ?*"

Her head appeared in the doorway. Dark curls and dark-framed glasses. Eyes wide with excitement. And concern. "Did you hear the news?" she asked.

"What news?"

"The Syrians have seized an American ship. I just heard it at the Golden Table."

"*What*? Why, for God's sake? When did it happen?"

"I don't know, but I'll see what I can find out."

Mary disappeared, heading for her own office, and Peter turned slowly back to Ravage. The two men exchanged a long, silent look. Syria. A Soviet client state. And a nation with a long history of human-rights violations.

"That's what I call a definable hostility," Ravage said.

Peter didn't reply.

Ravage got up to go. Then, at the door, he turned back. "You see what I mean?" he added without a trace of emotion. "Korcula may be too good to be true."

"I want to know what's going on," the President said.

He was standing by his desk, framed by the thick curve of bullet-proof windows behind him. He had clearly been pacing the room before Compton arrived; an excess of nervous energy charged the air in the Oval Office.

"You *know* what this is," he said. "It's an open act of war!"

"Yes, I know."

Compton's voice was calm, his attitude professional. There was no outward sign of the way he was feeling inside. He was stunned. And he was disturbed.

He glanced down at the Navy Department memo in his hand. It was just that clear, that outrageous. An American destroyer, the USS *Richmond*, on routine patrol in the Mediterranean, had been seized by Syria and forced into port at Latakia, where the captain and crew were under arrest. The ship had been seized in international waters, without warning or provocation. An act of war. Outrageous and unexpected. More threatening for the shock it caused in this room.

"I know what it is," Compton said, "but I don't know what it means."

The President eyed him coldly. "Korcula has its head on the block, that's what it means."

Compton hardly needed to hear it. The implications were clear: the blatant seizure of the American ship by a Soviet client state did not fit into the pattern. Soviet interest in Norway was not unexpected. Berlin and Turkey would fall into place again. China, the Middle East, Cuba—they were all where they should be now. A world constantly changing. Understandable. Predictable.

Until now.

The *Richmond* didn't fit the pattern; it defied the pattern. It was an extraordinary incident that had little to do with the fate of the captain or crew, but everything to do with the fate of the Korcula meeting.

The President moved around his desk and sat down. "I don't see much room for conjecture," he said. "It's got to be one of two explanations. The Syrians have found out about the preliminary agreements and are trying to wreck the conference. Either that or the Soviets want out."

"They've picked a hell of a way to tell us," Compton said. He shook his head. "No, it's neither of those. If the Soviets want out of Korcula, they only have to say so. What could we do about it? There's nothing to bind them until the pact is signed."

"All right, then the Syrians have found out what we're doing."

"If the Syrians knew, they wouldn't take it out on us; they'd go after Russia. And in any case, there's no way they could have found out."

"How can you be so sure?"

"Because *I* have the tape."

The President shrugged. "I didn't say they had proof. You can know something without being able to prove it."

Compton conceded the point. "But they would still go after the Russians," he said.

"Unless they're afraid of the Russians. Unless they think we're such pushovers they can do it and we won't mind."

Compton shook his head again.

"All right." The President raised his hands in a gesture of frustration. "Then what *is* going on?"

"I told you, I don't know. And I won't make a hasty assessment. Where Korcula is concerned, we have to move very cautiously."

"Well, someone better do something, and soon, or there won't *be* any Korcula. I've already got the Defense Department on my back, and the press will be right behind them. You know what that means. This is the kind of incident that the public takes hard. They'll want revenge. Or a valid explanation."

Compton nodded. Trust, where it never existed, was a difficult thing to establish. "Some people are already asking questions," he said.

"That's what I mean. The people and then the Congress. I'll have senators telling me I can't talk to the Soviet bullies. They'll be telling me I can't *go* to Korcula."

"It won't come to that," Compton assured him. "I don't know what's going on, but I intend to find out. I'm going to talk to Voloshin."

Andrei Voloshin, the Soviet ambassador to the United States.

"Do it soon."

"I'll call him now."

"And make sure he understands how I feel about this. If the seizure of the *Richmond* was an independent action by Syria, then the Russians had better damn well straighten it out. And they'd better do it *before* it triggers the kind of public reaction that will prevent Korcula under any circumstances."

Compton nodded.

"If it's *not* an independent action by Syria . . ." The President stopped mid-sentence; his thought needed no further expression.

Syria acting on orders from the Soviet Union? Impossible. Unthinkable. *More* than threatening, because it would mean the Soviets never meant for Korcula to take place.

A question appeared in the President's eyes, unspoken. Compton stared back at him. Then he shook his head sadly. He understood the question, but he didn't have an answer.

He didn't know if Korcula could be saved.

5

Boris Levitsky was alone in the backseat of the polished black Volga that made its way through the northern suburbs of Moscow toward the open country ahead. He was a thick-faced man, nearly fifty, a true Slav, with narrow eyes over wide cheekbones, under a mass of gray hair. He was wearing a heavy coat against the chill of winter. A black hat, fur-trimmed, lay on the seat beside his attaché case. His bare hands were square, thick and strong, resting lightly against the harsh wool of his coat. His face was a blank as he gazed unseeing past the driver in the front seat. His thoughts were elsewhere, remembering warm autumn days in Washington, D.C., where October brought fall color to the trees in front of the Soviet Embassy six blocks north of the White House. In Moscow today, the trees were outlined by a fine white edge of snow, the first snowfall of many in a long, bleak winter ahead.

Levitsky missed those days in America. He enjoyed the privileges that came with his new power as Chairman of the Committee for State Security, the head of the KGB, but he envied men like Dmitri who were still enjoying the milder climate of America's capital city, who were still enjoying the excitement of clandestine lives.

Levitsky had worked for the KGB all of his adult life, some thirty-odd years. The embassy jobs in Washington, and in London and Paris before that, had been real enough, with the usual diplomatic chores. But they had existed primarily to cover the nature of his true work. Dmitri was something else. An illegal. A deep-cover agent, planted on U.S. soil to bloom and flourish as an authentic American, avoiding controversy and establishing a reputation that was beyond reproach, until, free and clear of suspicion, he was ready to go to work.

The time had come. Dmitri was perfectly placed for the job that had to be done.

Levitsky glanced at the attaché case lying on the seat beside him. His mind ran through the report he had to give. It was no accident that Miloslavsky had decided to spend a few days at his dacha northeast of Moscow, away from the electronic ears that picked up the merest whisper at the Kremlin. It was no inconvenience that Levitsky had to meet him there. Miloslavsky had left Moscow on purpose, because the operation he had ordered Levitsky to carry out had the highest priority, the most secret possible classification.

Levitsky's glance connected now with the world beyond the car windows. His eyes made a broad sweep of the scene around him—the huge gray buildings of flats, edged by gray sidewalks and streets, all of it blending into a dull, gray, overcast day. He smiled as he thought about what lay ahead. The sun might be shining in Washington, but there on the cold streets of Moscow Levitsky felt a warm glow of anticipation. He was back where the excitement was, and that made him feel good.

A maid took Levitsky's coat and showed him to a room at the rear of the house where Yevgeni Miloslavsky, the Soviet Foreign Minister, stood motionless by a large window, the inevitable glass of vodka in one well-manicured hand.

Miloslavsky was a tall, slender man in elegant pin stripes—purchased, no doubt, in London, where he visited a tailor regularly every year. His shirt collar was starched and pressed to perfection, and the handkerchief in his pocket was folded to a neat point. His hair was white, his face thin and aristocratic. He had aged gracefully; he was now eighty-one, but he looked fifteen years younger. He was vichyssoise to Levitsky's cabbage soup.

He was also rare among modern Soviet bureaucrats—the son of a wealthy land-owning family, a man who remembered the way things were before the Revolution.

Miloslavsky rejected the old class structure with the fervor of one who had seen its injustice firsthand, like the young middle-class Americans of the sixties. But he had not mellowed with another decade. His Marxist zeal was as strong as it ever had been—stronger, perhaps, for surviving the cycles of change from Lenin to Stalin and Khrushchev, and on into the age of détente.

He turned a pair of cold blue eyes to Levitsky as the younger man entered the room. Then his face creased into a smile. "Ah, Boris, you've come. I was just beginning to worry. Have you brought good news?"

"Good and bad."

Miloslavsky nodded.

Levitsky laid his attaché case on a table as Miloslavsky moved away from the window. The snow was heavier here in the north, blanketing the hills outside with a cover of white, against which old trees stood out as dark skeletons. Inside, two comfortable chairs were drawn up by the stone fireplace, where a blazing log drew the chill from the air. A table between the two chairs was spread with *zakuska*—black Beluga caviar with toast and butter, smoked salmon, cold sturgeon in aspic, a selection of cheeses and bread, and a tray of *vareniky*, the sweet fruit-filled dumplings Levitsky found irresistible. He popped one into his mouth as Miloslavsky poured him a drink, then freshened his own.

Miloslavsky raised his glass. "Welcome, comrade. *Nazdorovie*."

"*Nazdorovie*," Levitsky repeated. Their glasses touched, and they drank. Then they sat down across from each other.

Miloslavsky gestured to the table as he settled himself in the chair, and it occurred to Levitsky that this small feast was not for his benefit. Miloslavsky had not known precisely when to expect him. *Zakuska* was simply his custom, like the British habit of tea.

Levitsky sampled the caviar. "Some good Bolshevik you are," he said.

Miloslavsky accepted the gibe with good humor; Levitsky was an old friend. "I am merely a worker who enjoys good food," he replied with a small smile. "Served with some flair, I grant you. Besides, I'm not that old. My father might have been a Bolshevik."

"Apologies."

"Accepted. He wouldn't have been, in any case. Beyond raising a whip on the peasants who worked his land, my dear father, I fear, rarely strained himself." His face turned serious once more. "What do you have to report?"

Levitsky took a drink of his vodka. It was *ryabinovka*, a special brew flavored with ashberries. He took in a breath, prepared himself for the reaction he knew his bad news was bound to produce.

"Danchenko did not have the tape."

Miloslavsky's blue eyes turned to ice. His jaw tightened, his knuckles whitened against the arm of the chair. Shock was released in a gasp of air, a mixture of anger and fear. "He did *not* have the *tape*?"

"He had *a* tape," Levitsky explained. "It was blank."

"He *erased* it?" Miloslavsky's shock gave way to disbelief.

"No, no, I don't think so. He would sooner have given it up. As a matter of fact, I suspect that's just what he did."

Miloslavsky said nothing for a moment, but the strong emotion began to fade from his eyes. Emotion only immobilized the brain cells. He was starting to think again. "He would not have passed it to the CIA."

"No. There was no way he could have done it, even if he wanted to."

"That's too bad. Then to one of his colleagues?"

"Inevitably. And a wise move, I must say, given the persistence of Department V."

"Department V—those dogs! But effective." Miloslavsky brought his hands together; he closed his eyes as the new set of circumstances fell into place in his mind. "One of the five who are left," he said. "We have only to find out which one." His eyes opened abruptly. "Who's next on the list?"

Levitsky consulted a paper he took from his pocket. "Maria Petrovskaya at Khvalinsk."

"Ah, the Volga to the Caspian Sea."

Levitsky nodded. "If she doesn't have the tape, then we move on to"—he consulted his paper—"Nicolai Pinsky at Tallin, across the Baltic from Stockholm. And the others, each in their turn."

"We have the locations?"

"Yes, and approximate dates."

"Good. We will manage."

"I believe so."

"No, comrade, you *know* so. That tape was entrusted to me. We must have it back before it is lost forever. We must not fail."

"We won't."

"I expect no less." Miloslavsky sipped at his drink. "Now, for the rest," he said. "That tape has no value whatever without its other half. What's the status of our Washington operation?"

Levitsky cleared his throat. The Washington operation was Dmitri's domain, and the news from Washington was little better than the news from Gagra. It was better only because Dmitri had an alternate plan. "The Washington operation," he said, "is more sensitive, and riskier, because, as you know, it requires direct penetration to the Secretary of State."

"You're convinced Compton kept the other half of the tape?"

"He would trust it to no one else."

Miloslavsky nodded his agreement.

"However," Levitsky went on, "there's a problem in Washington. The man named Stephen Katz."

Miloslavsky frowned. "What sort of problem?"

Levitsky took another drink of his vodka and leaned back in the chair. "Well, as you know, Katz works for Freedom International—"

"A subversive organization."

"Yes, from our point of view. Some Americans distrust it, too, as they distrust anything that shakes up the status quo. But Katz was an ideal choice at the start. There could be no doubt that he would come down on our side, once he knew the truth. Dmitri approached him, gave him the scent, fed him pieces of information, got him started on the right track. Then Dmitri left him alone to discover what he would by himself. The point, of course, was to achieve credibility. It would not have done to make the job easy for Katz."

"I know all of that," Miloslavsky said with an impatient gesture. "What's the problem?"

"Katz took the scent too effectively. He has learned too much. He has even been to see Compton, and apparently he intends to go back again."

Miloslavsky was openly alarmed. "What has he told Compton?"

"Don't worry. Whatever he said, Compton didn't believe him. But Katz intends to see him again soon."

"We can't permit that!"

"Of course not. Dmitri will make sure it doesn't happen."

"How?"

"The only possible way. He will eliminate Katz."

Miloslavsky set his glass down hard on the table. "That's wonderful," he said. "Here we are, seven days from the start of the conference, and Dmitri wants to remove our only link with the Washington tape."

"Not quite," Levitsky said. "He only wants to make a substitution."

"There's no time for a substitution."

"I believe there is." Levitsky got up and opened his attaché case. He removed a manila file and gave it to Miloslavsky, who glanced through it quickly and looked up again.

"As you see," Levitsky said, "this man is ideally placed for our purposes. He will take over the job Katz was to perform. He is far better suited for it psychologically, and more important, if we give him the right incentive, he can get us the tape himself."

Miloslavsky remained skeptical. "And how do we provide incentive at this stage?"

"We don't. We let Katz do it for us."

"I don't understand. Explain it."

Levitsky sat down again. "We do it as follows. Dmitri has given Katz one last piece of information. Katz will know—I daresay he already knows—he can no longer sit on the information he has. He will go to the one man he can trust, a ranking

U.S. official, a personal friend. *This* man, who is also *Compton's* friend, can get his hands on that tape."

Miloslavsky glanced at the name on the file. "Lucas," he said.

Levitsky smiled. "That's right. Peter Lucas. With Dmitri's help, he will find that he has no choice."

6

PETER PICKED UP the telephone and dialed an inside number.
A woman answered at the other end. "May I help you?"

"This is Peter Lucas. Is the Secretary in?"

"He is," the woman told him, "but he has someone with
him." She paused significantly, then added, "It's Ambassador
Voloshin." In other words, interruptions were out of the question. "May I give him a message?" she asked.

"No, thanks," Peter said. "I'll be seeing him tonight."

Tonight would be soon enough.

Peter dropped the phone back in place. He wanted to know
what was happening in Syria. Compton obviously did, too; he
had summoned the Soviet ambassador. He no doubt had his
hands full with finding out for himself. This was not the time
for Peter to start raising questions.

Anyway, he didn't like to impose on his friendship with
Compton. He rarely asked for information that wasn't his routinely. But this was different. This was Korcula. This *was* his.

What if something *were* wrong?

Dan Ravage's questions reasserted themselves. Compton
was committed to success at the Korcula meeting. Was he
committed to a fault? *Had* he blinded himself? Was he unconsciously ignoring danger signals in Berlin, in Norway, in
Syria? Was there a chance that what Ravage thought was true?

Because if there was even that, just a chance . . .

No! Peter brought his hand down hard on the desk. Nothing, not even Korcula, could cause Compton to deceive himself so badly. There was, as he said, nothing new in Norway; the Soviets had always been touchy about their military base at Murmansk. There was nothing new in Berlin, either, only more of what had been for years. As for Syria, that remained to be seen. But Compton was not ignoring the seizure of the ship. He had called in the Soviet ambassador, which is exactly what he should have done.

There was nothing wrong with Korcula.

Peter smiled at his own foolish doubts. Then the telephone rang, and his smile quickly faded.

There was tension from the first words: "Peter, this is Steve. I've got to see you."

Peter leaned forward. "What's the matter? You sound—"

"I've got to see you tonight."

"Why? What's wrong?"

"I can't tell you now. I want you to come here, to my place."

Steve Katz was an old friend—next to Compton, Peter's oldest. They were schoolboys together in New York. Then they each went their separate ways—separate colleges, separate careers. Peter went into the Foreign Service; he joined the establishment to work from the inside out. But Steve had taken a different route. He was a freedom fighter who worked out of an office, an adversary to government delay. He didn't want to hear why a thing couldn't happen; he wanted to show why it must happen, and now.

Separate directions, spanned by a long-standing friendship. They kept in touch. And now life had brought them together again. Steve was director of the Washington office of Freedom International, an organization that made war on oppression anywhere in the world, militant but nonviolent. Like Steve.

A gentle man. Radical, yes, and unreasonable at times, but there was no questioning his immense dedication to his work. He and Peter shared more than friendship; they shared a common goal.

"I've got plans tonight," Peter said.

"Cancel them."

"I can't, but I can probably get away this afternoon. If it's that important to you, I will."

"That's no good; it's too soon. I'm putting something together I want to show you. It's got to be tonight." Steve was silent a moment. Then he said, "You can see Nicole anytime, but you don't often get a chance to prevent a major international disaster."

Peter glanced at the phone in his hand, startled by the urgency of Steve's words. "For Christ's sake, what are you talking about?"

"I can't tell you now, but it's that important. I'm serious."

Peter didn't doubt it. Steve was not an alarmist. "I can't change my plans," he said. "It's not just Nicole; it's the Secretary and the Yugoslavian ambassador. I've got to go to the opera with them. But I could come see you after that."

"All right, that will have to do. Come as soon as you can."

"I'll be there," Peter said, "but can't you give me a clue?"

"Not on the phone. I'll just tell you this: I'm sitting on something bigger than you can imagine." Steve's voice cracked, as if he were close to tears. "I need your help," he said. "You're the only person I trust."

"But Steve . . . *Steve?*"

Peter stared at the phone, but the line had gone dead in his hand.

Andrei Voloshin was a big man with a fringe of soft hair and a belly laugh that was dangerously contagious. He was the dean of the diplomatic corps; he had been in Washington longer than any other ambassador, and for a reason: he was good at his job.

In a city full of professional charmers, Voloshin was number one. He put people at ease by poking good-natured fun at himself and the Soviet Union. He told amusing stories about red tape and bungling behind the scenes at the Kremlin. About his young grandson who hoped they would not be recalled because there were no fast-food hamburgers in Russia. About Khrushchev raging at his agricultural ministers when he discovered they had failed him, while a bumper crop of corn was flourishing in the backyard of the American embassy in Moscow.

Amusing stories, but harmless. They served Voloshin well. They underscored human problems, the same the world over, and helped take the edge off more serious points of dispute.

Compton got up as Voloshin was ushered into his office and extended his hand across the top of his desk.

"Mr. Ambassador."

"Mr. Secretary."

"It's good of you to come on such short notice."

Voloshin shrugged. "When have I not come?"

Compton smiled and let the point go by without challenge. He gestured to a chair, flipped open a box of cigarettes he kept on his desk for visitors. The Russian declined and lit one of his own with a Florentine gold lighter.

"From the *beryozka*?" Compton asked, nodding at the lighter. The *beryozka* were shops in Moscow where ranking Soviets could purchase imported items; officially they didn't exist.

Voloshin chuckled. "A gift from my wife. I believe it's from Cartier."

"I see. The jewelers of America thank you."

Voloshin's belly shook with a ripple of laughter. He held up the lighter. "I wonder how much profit found its way to the artisan's pocket," he said. Then he dismissed the question and put the lighter away. "I don't suppose you called me here for a chat."

"No. Though I'd like that."

"So would I." Voloshin cleared his throat. "The Syrian matter?"

Compton nodded. He swung his chair around, got up, walked the length of the room and back. There was no sense of urgency in his movement, only thoughtfulness in his eyes. He sat back on the edge of his desk and looked down at the Russian. "We've been friends for a long time," he said.

"So we have."

"We've been through many a crisis and still managed to stay friends."

Voloshin nodded.

Then Compton got up and moved back around to his chair. He sat down, eyeing Voloshin cautiously. "The Syrian matter," he said. "I want you to tell me the truth, or tell me nothing at all." Then he leaned forward. "If you people have so much as one finger in this, then Korcula is off. Period. And there's going to be hell to pay. Now, tell me, what's going on?"

Voloshin very nearly smiled. "I believe this is what we call a direct diplomatic encounter. And I will be equally honest—if, perhaps, less terse."

Compton said nothing.

"My government," Voloshin went on, "has instructed me to tell you that the seizure of the *Richmond* was accomplished without our knowledge and most certainly without our approval. We are as disturbed by the action as you are. Furthermore, my government—"

"Screw your government," Compton broke in. "I want to know what *you* think."

Voloshin drew on his cigarette. "I think you should accept the assurances of my government."

"Where does Korcula stand?"

"Precisely where it has stood. Premier Sukhov is committed to the success of the meeting. As you know, I am too."

Yes. Voloshin had been Compton's most ardent supporter when he first broached the matter of the Korcula-conference to the Soviet side.

"We are of one mind, on this subject at least," Voloshin said. "You can count on what I say. Syria has nothing to do with Korcula, beyond the threat it poses. We're as anxious to clear the air as you are."

Compton's face didn't change, but he leaned back in his chair as relief eased the tension and softened the edge of concern. Relief, yes, but tempered by reality. He believed Voloshin, but it was too soon to make a final judgment. "Syria is your client state," he said. "How are you prepared to resolve the problem?"

"Are you asking me or my government?"

Compton smiled.

"Contrary to what the American right wing believes," Voloshin said, "our clients don't always jump when we snap our fingers. However, we're prepared to do all we can, as long as we don't have to come out in the open. We will certainly make our views known to Damascus."

"That's all?"

"We want to help, but I can't guarantee military assistance. We know you can't go to Korcula unless this is resolved; we can't either. But we don't need a rearguard action at home because we've taken sides against our own client. That would destroy Korcula as surely as anything."

Compton nodded. Internal politics, a sticky problem on both sides of the world. "Let's hope it won't come to that," he said. "At the moment, of course, we're in the process of contacting Damascus through channels. We'll try to negotiate and hope it works. In the meantime, I have only one thing to say. This threat must be resolved immediately. If you can't do it, we will."

"I understand."

"And if we have to do it," Compton said, "we'll need one more assurance."

"Yes?"

"That when we go in, you'll stay out."

Voloshin stubbed out his cigarette in the ashtray. "I'm sorry," he said. "I don't know if I can guarantee that."

Neal Stefan looked around the garage and observed that everything seemed to be under control. The limousine had been checked by the mechanic; its fuel tank was full. The chauffeur was standing by upstairs. Stefan glanced at his watch. He added a margin for Washington rush-hour traffic. Thirty minutes at best; he could wait no longer.

He turned and made his way into a small adjacent room, where he filled an old teakettle, switched on the hot plate, and measured instant coffee into a cracked ceramic mug. Then he removed a pack of cigarettes from his pocket. They were British-made, Dunhills, a fresh, unopened box. Stefan studied the wrapper carefully—cellophane, folded envelope-style at each end, with a narrow strip of gold dots to facilitate the unwrapping. He was careful not to touch the gold strip.

He waited until the teakettle came to life, rattling against the hot plate. The water inside had reached a boil; steam poured out through the spout. Stefan held one end of the box into the steam, using his body to hide what he was doing from anyone in the garage. He counted off thirty seconds. Then carefully he ran a table knife under the cellophane flap. The wrapper came open easily. Stefan pocketed the cigarette box, poured water into his cup, tasted the coffee routinely, and turned away toward the bathroom.

Inside, he locked the door and began to move more quickly. He removed a roll of paper towels from its holder next to the sink, reached into the cardboard tube and withdrew a small leather pouch. In it were a tube of glue, a glass vial, and a disposable syringe. He inserted the needle into the vial and drew out the liquid inside. Then he opened the cigarettes, slipping the box smoothly out of its wrapper without marring the cellophane. He raised the cardboard lid, took the third cigarette from the left, picked up the syringe once again.

In a moment, he was finished. The cigarette was back in place, third from the left, the box rewrapped and sealed with two drops of glue. Stefan dropped the cigarettes into one pocket, the leather pouch into the other. There would be plenty of time when his shift was finished; he would dispose of the pouch and its contents somewhere beyond the beltway, a long way from here.

The chauffeur had arrived and was checking the interior of the car as Stefan returned to the garage, carrying only·his coffee cup.

The chauffeur glanced up. "There are no cigarettes," he said coldly. "There is always to be a fresh box."

"I'm sorry," Stefan replied. "Just a moment, I will get them."

7

THE PRESIDENTIAL SEAL was missing. All that was left was a round impression in the red plush wall where the seal had been—that, and two white holes where someone had yanked the screws right out of the plaster. Someone, apparently, had stolen the seal from the President's box in the Opera House at Kennedy Center.

Peter wasn't greatly surprised. There were always those, even among the President's guests, who couldn't resist the lure of a rare souvenir. He was only surprised that the seal had not been replaced.

He looked around the reception room that adjoined the box—red carpeting, wall-to-wall and floor-to-ceiling, with a crystal starburst chandelier set into a dome overhead. Four chairs in subdued stripes. A chinoiserie table and a beige telephone, to which a tiny high-intensity lamp was attached. To pick up the phone was to make contact with the Army Signal Corps, which maintained White House phone lines everywhere outside the White House.

There were doors all around the room—to the boxes on each side of this one, for those occasions when a large crowd gathered here; to the outer corridor, where an usher in a red jacket headed off anyone who tried to come too near; to a private bath and a cloakroom with a small refrigerator; and to the theater box itself, where eight red plush chairs were arranged in two rows overlooking the orchestra seats and the stage.

This was where the President sat when he came to the Opera House. The tickets were reserved for his use at every performance. He used it himself a few times a year. Otherwise the tickets were a gift from the White House, doled out as thanks for support given on critical issues, or encouragement for support needed—to members of Congress, Cabinet secretaries, foreign diplomats, press, and ranking White House staff. Or to people like Peter and Nicole because they were suitable companions for the guest of honor.

The box was full tonight; eight guests sipped champagne as they waited for the first curtain. Arthur Compton, looking relaxed, as if he had nothing more pressing on his mind than last-minute cast changes for the performance. Senator Elizabeth Harvey of Connecticut, fortyish, auburn-haired, casually dressed; she had probably come here straight from the hill. Her husband, Michael Baker, a professor at Yale. Jovan Kersnik, the Yugoslavian ambassador, informal in a dark suit, and Madame Kersnik, dramatic in vibrant red. An aide from the Yugoslavian embassy who was introduced as the ambassador's military adjutant but was clearly something more like a bodyguard. Peter himself, and Nicole.

Peter caught her eye. She smiled. She was bearing up bravely. But then, he hadn't yet told her that dinner after the opera was off for tonight. He hadn't yet found the nerve.

"I'm delighted you could be with us," Compton was saying to the Kersniks.

"No more delighted than we are," the ambassador replied. "Your Metropolitan Opera is one of the world's great treasures."

Compton acknowledged the compliment with a proprietary nod, as if the opera were federal property.

Conversational initiatives, Peter thought—not unlike the start of official talks. Inconsequential now, on a social level—except these were not just two men, but two nations, coming together in their off hours. Neither Compton nor Kersnik had finished his working day. Neither one could take off the professional veneer; they were not permitted the luxury of casual conversation. Offhand remarks, lightly meant, could be mis-construed and blown out of shape. The sparks that ignited the fire; the small incidents that launched war. Like the murder of an archduke. Or the sinking of the battleship *Maine*.

Or the seizure of the USS *Richmond*.

The *Richmond* was headline news by now, the main topic of conversation from here to Capitol Hill. Conversation and conjecture. There was talk of the PLO and a new bid for power by the terrorists. There was talk of renewed conflict in the Middle East. In some quarters, there was indifference: a single ship seized by a tiny nation, smaller than the state of Utah. In others, deep fear: U.S. forces in the Mediterranean were on alert for action. So, too, was the Soviet Mediterranean Fleet.

Everyone was talking about the *Richmond*, but no one out-side the President's inner circle knew anything beyond the official line. Negotiations were under way with Damascus. The official line; there was nothing more to know.

And Compton, of course, would reveal nothing here. Peter intended to catch a moment with him in private, but there had been no chance for that yet.

He turned to Madame Kersnik. "Are you going to be with us at Korcula?"

The ambassador's wife smiled warmly. She was a large woman, as heavy as her husband and almost as tall. "Not until later," she said. "I plan to come for the signing."

"Very wise of you."

Very wise indeed, Peter thought. Selective scheduling: avoid the nuts-and-bolts work of the early part of the conference, while the two delegations hammered out the details; arrive in time for the fanfare and celebration, with the President and the Premier. For someone not involved in the negotiations, staying home was the best plan. The first few days would be a round of meetings, too much coffee and too many cigarettes, disagreement couched in polite diplomatic terms. Not much fun for someone on the outside waiting. Not very interesting, either.

Madame Kersnik turned to Nicole. "And you, my dear? Are you planning to go?"

No one had ever accused Nicole of opting for the best plan. "I'd sit on the beach and count pebbles just to be there," she said.

And, Peter thought, she would probably find an ancient fossil among them.

"Have you been to Dalmatia before?" Madame Kersnik asked her.

"Not to Korcula, but I have been to Split, to see Diocletian's Palace."

Madame Kersnik warmed to her subject, the glories of the Adriatic coast, Yugoslavia's tourist mecca.

Peter noticed that Kersnik was watching his wife, and the expression on his face was something more than polite interest. Then his eyes shifted to Peter, and a flicker of emotion passed through them. It disappeared as quickly.

Peter felt vaguely uncomfortable. He wasn't sure what it was he had seen, or if he had really seen anything, but he found himself scanning back over the plans for the summit. Had they done something, or overlooked something, that might have offended the Yugoslavian government? Nothing that came to him now. The arrangements had been extraordinarily smooth, and largely because of Kersnik.

That's why they were all here tonight. Compton was still courting the ambassador, because Kersnik had solved the first stumbling block, a place for the meeting. Yugoslavia, a communist country and acceptable to the Russians, but suitable to the United States as well. Yugoslavia insisted on its independence from Moscow and was a powerful force among the nonaligned Third World nations. An ideal place for the meeting. It was Kersnik who volunteered Korcula and argued the case back home. Because of him, the meeting would take place.

Kersnik had his own stake in this, Peter thought. Perhaps he had butterflies too.

The ambassador turned away to light a cigarette, and Peter escaped to the cloakroom to refill his empty glass. He looked up as Senator Harvey's husband followed him into the room. "You're dry too, I see," he said, and produced a new bottle of champagne.

Baker's blue eyes twinkled. His hair was blond and curly, his expression almost elfin——not at all what Peter expected. It was hard to believe this kind-looking man could advocate what he did.

In some circles, Dr. Michael Baker was as well known as

his wife. He headed an on-going research project at Yale—analysis of long-term social problems based on computer modeling—and the results, at least as Peter knew them, were not designed to win friends among people who cared about human rights. Because Baker, like his computers, was too damn cold-blooded.

"I've read about your work," he said as he refilled their glasses.

Baker's expression changed slightly. He turned wary. Or was he amused? "And what do you think?" he asked.

Peter shrugged. "I'm not an expert."

"Ah, the polite demurral. Very diplomatic, I'm sure. I gather you don't like what you've read."

Peter smiled to take the edge off. This was not the time or place for an argument. Nor was there much point in trying to solve differences as old as civilization before the first curtain went up. "I'm not convinced," he said lightly, "but I'm always willing to listen."

Baker's face brightened as the elfin smile reappeared. "And I'm always willing to defend my reputation. What, exactly, have you found unconvincing?"

What hadn't he found unconvincing was more to the point, but Peter didn't say so. He would be polite, not for Baker, but for Kersnik and Korcula. He wasn't even sure why Baker was here. Ah, of course, his wife! Senator Harvey was a member of the Committee on Foreign Relations, a pro-Korcula member. Peter resolved to be nice. "What about federal housing assistance?" he asked.

One Baker study had claimed to show that government-financed low-income housing only created more need for low-income housing and should thus be scrapped. The theory was that cheap housing enticed rural poor to seek relief in urban ghettos and lulled those already there into being content with their lot. Baker might have a point, Peter thought. Snatch the roof away, and let people live in the streets. Let whole families *freeze* in the streets. There would be fewer people to house again next winter.

"Federal housing assistance," Baker said. "I know what you're probably thinking. It sounds harsh."

"It *is* harsh."

"Perhaps, but I try to solve problems on a long-range basis. Based on current projections, the number of people living in ghetto conditions will double in the next ten years. Poverty grows in geometric proportions. I'm only saying that we've got to reverse that trend, for those people ten years from now, for society as a whole. *Some* people may have to be sacrificed for the long-term good of *all* people. Mine is still a humanist position in the end."

Sacrifice! Christ, he was talking about human *lives*! Living people versus people not even born. The specific versus the abstract. The rights of the individual subordinate to the system. Maybe this was what happened when a man lost his wife to Washington. Maybe Baker should have come here too. Maybe he'd been alone too long with no one but his computers.

Baker was standing in the doorway. Peter looked past him; he tried to catch Nicole's eye, but she was turned away. There was no escape for the moment. He was stuck here. He didn't want to argue with Baker. He didn't want to talk to him, either.

"In any case," Baker said, "it's not up to me to end federal housing assistance. I merely suggest alternatives."

"Of course," Peter said. "*Computer* alternatives. What can machines know about the subtleties of human feelings?"

"Heartless machines," Baker conceded. "That's precisely their value. Computers don't flinch from the truth when it hurts, as you would. Or I would." He took a drink of champagne. "Whatever you think of my machines, as you call them, *I'm* still a human being. Heartlessness isn't contagious."

"Isn't it?"

Peter asked the question rhetorically. He didn't expect an answer; he didn't even want one. He had already learned the answer, a long time ago.

There was movement behind Baker. The Senator was coming to join them. "How does your wife manage the conflicts between your work and hers?" Peter asked.

"Mostly by ignoring mine." Baker grinned good-naturedly and moved aside as his wife appeared in the door.

"What are you saying?" she asked. "Are you maligning my name?"

"Never that." His arm went around her shoulders as his eyes

brightly met hers. Their relationship was clearly a good one—easy, comfortable, even loving. Peter wondered how that was possible.

"To tell you the truth," Baker said, "Elizabeth has always supported my work, even if she doesn't agree with it. But when I talk about issues like federal housing assistance, she's quick to remind me her area is foreign affairs."

Senator Harvey laughed gently. She was an attractive woman with alert, intelligent eyes. Peter knew that her gentle manner should not be mistaken for weakness.

"Actually, I don't see a conflict in our work," she said. "My husband has the right to say what he thinks, right or wrong. That's the strength of our democratic system—dissidence, conflicting opinion, controversy. Out of that, we eventually stumble on truth."

Peter smiled. He liked Senator Harvey as much as he disliked her husband. Besides, she was right. Conformity, not dissent, was the great foe of humanity. Disagreement, however outrageous, was a stabilizing force. To hear was not to accept.

Peter raised his glass and started to edge out of the room. "As someone once said, the best way to kill an idea is to bring it up at the PTA; let them discuss it to death. But tell them they can't talk about it, and you've got a *cause célèbre*." Someone had opened the door into the theater, where the lights were already dimmed. "On that note," Peter said, "I think it's time for the curtain."

For a moment, everyone was occupied putting out cigarettes, finishing drinks, looking for purses or programs, getting ready to enter the box. Peter seized the chance to draw Compton aside for a private question. He lowered his voice. "Is there any news from Damascus?"

Compton dropped his voice, too. "Not yet. I'm expecting to hear something this evening."

"Does it mean trouble for Korcula?"

"No. The Soviets had nothing to do with what happened."

"There's no doubt of that?"

"None at all. As a matter of fact, they're doing what they can to help us." Compton studied Peter's face for a moment. "Trust me," he said. "There's nothing to worry about. Every-

thing is under control." Then he smiled as he turned away.
"Madame Kersnik?" He offered his arm and escorted her to her
seat.

Peter was relieved. The seizure of the ship was a problem,
a very grave problem, but it wasn't his problem. It wasn't
related to Korcula. That was what he wanted to know.

He looked around for a place to put down his glass. Jovan
Kersnik was standing behind him. His eyes had turned cold;
the professional mask had dropped away, exposing something
like anger. Yes, *anger*. Peter caught his breath as their eyes
met. What the hell, was Kersnik angry with him?

Or was it Compton?

It was over in the briefest of moments. Kersnik's face turned
genial again. He put out his cigarette, nodded to his aide, and
strode past Peter into the theater.

Peter shook off the feeling that lingered after Kersnik had
passed by. He knew he had not imagined the look on the
ambassador's face. But anger? Nonsense!

He probably had indigestion.

The opera was building to the climax of the first act, the
entrance of Turandot, whose beauty enticed all manner of men,
including the tenor prince, to risk their lives in futile bid for
her hand. Arthur Compton watched with approval. The theme
was hardly a new one, even in Puccini's day. There always
had been a handful of people who were willing to risk all they
had to make their dreams come true. God willing, there always
would be.

Then a soft light came on in the railing at the front of the
box. The telephone light. Compton had taken a rear aisle seat
on purpose. He was out of his chair and had the door closed
behind him before anyone else could wonder who should answer the phone.

He identified himself to the Signal Corps operator and
waited while the White House connection was made.

The President came on. "Yes?"

"I have the Secretary of State for you, sir."

"Thank you." The operator cut himself out. "Arthur?"

"Yes, Mr. President."

"The Premier has requested time on the Hot Line."

Compton's hand gripped the telephone harder. This couldn't be good news. The Premier himself would not be calling unless the crisis had grown worse.

"How fast can you be here?" the President asked.

Compton glanced at his watch. "I'll be there in ten minutes."

Outside on the stage, Turandot made her entrance, and the tenor prince dropped to his knees. The chorus begged him to turn away; no prize was worth such risk. But the tenor paid the warning no heed.

His decision was inevitable, his fate sealed. He called out Turandot's name.

Ambassador Kersnik touched Nicole's arm. She bent her head toward him, her eyes still on the stage, her attention absorbed by the tenor, by the final aria of the first act.

Kersnik said something, but Nicole didn't quite hear it.

She turned to him now. "I beg your pardon?"

Kersnik's eyes remained on the stage, remained *fixed* on the stage. He was as absorbed as she was.

His voice was thick-sounding, tired. "*Sprechi Korculu,*" he said.

Nicole looked back at him, puzzled, but Kersnik said nothing more. An offhand remark, it seemed. Of no special importance. Nicole nodded politely and gave herself back to the opera.

The curtain fell to a burst of applause; the performers were taking their bows. Nicole turned to Kersnik.

"I'm sorry," she said. "I didn't . . ."

She stopped mid-sentence, and her face broke into a smile. Peter was sitting behind her. "What should I do?" she whispered.

Peter glanced at Kersnik and shrugged. Nicole didn't have much choice. The ambassador was sleeping!

Gently she touched his arm. "Mr. Ambassador?"

But Kersnik didn't move. His hands were folded together in his lap. His head rested against the back of the seat. His eyes were closed, his mouth partly open, his face entirely peaceful.

Nicole pressed harder, got no response. Then she took hold of his arm, shook his shoulder. Her voice dropped, turned urgent. "Mr. Ambassador!"

Kersnik moved. He fell sideways, just as the houselights came up.

Nicole froze in a moment of total shock as Kersnik's head fell against her shoulder. Instinct suppressed the scream that rose in her throat. She looked around, saw faces. Madame Kersnik, eyes bulging, caught between understanding and disbelief. Peter, leaning over the seat, grimly calm as he felt for a pulse or a heartbeat. And Kersnik himself, eyes closed, face peaceful.

Nicole knew before anyone told her. The man whose head lay heavily on her shoulder was not asleep.

He was dead.

8

Peter picked up the Signal Corps phone and barked out an order without regard for courtesy: "Send an ambulance over here on the double," he said. "It's Ambassador Kersnik. I think he's had a heart attack."

"Right away, sir."

Peter hung up the phone and looked around for Compton, but the rooms in the box were empty. The usher outside finally told him Compton had left a few minutes ago and had not said where he was going. Terrific. That left Peter in charge.

There was no time to worry about it. "The ambassador is ill," he said. "I've phoned for an ambulance. Make sure there's no delay."

The usher stared back for a moment—this sort of thing never *happened* in the President's box—then hurried off to tell her superiors.

"And see if there's a doctor around," Peter called after her.

He turned back just as the ambassador's aide and Baker, between them, carried Kersnik into the room. There was no couch, only the four chairs; they put him down on the floor. He lay there, his face pale and cold under the glow of the starburst chandelier.

Madame Kersnik dropped to her knees beside him, stroking his cheek with her fingers, whispering soft words of comfort.

She was calm but terribly frightened, her eyes wide and dark, harsh against ashen skin. Her bright dress suddenly seemed irreverent. So did the red plush room.

For a moment, no one moved. Then Senator Harvey knelt down beside her. She said nothing, just touched Madame Kersnik's arm, but in the touch there was meaning. It said: you are not alone.

"I've called for help," Peter said. Madame Kersnik didn't look up. He turned to the aide. "Would you like for me to call the embassy?"

The man shook his head. "Not yet. We'll wait until we know which hospital it's going to be."

They were still hoping; they had to *know* it was true.

Peter nodded. Then he crossed the room and closed the door into the theater. He had never been briefed for this kind of emergency, but State Department policy generally favored a low profile in sensitive situations. Besides, there seemed to be nothing else he could do.

He turned to Nicole, who was almost as pale as Madame Kersnik. This had been a shock for her, too. He took her arm, led her gently but firmly to a chair. Then he glanced up at Baker. "Check the cloakroom," he said. "Maybe there's some brandy."

Nicole raised a hand to protest, but Peter silenced her before she could say anything. He took her hand; her fingers tightened on his.

"I think I should go to the hospital," he said.

"Yes, of course. You must." Her face brightened. "Do you mean . . . ?"

Peter glanced at Kersnik and shook his head. He didn't think he was wrong; he felt sure Kersnik was dead. "I'm going to ask Senator Harvey to go along," he said. "Dr. Baker can take you home."

Nicole lowered her voice. "If you don't mind," she said, "I'd just as soon take a cab."

Peter smiled and squeezed her hand. "I'll come by to see you later."

He said nothing more, nor did anyone else. The room fell into silence. The silence deepened. The steady buzz from the theater faded as the houselights dimmed on the other side of the door. In the pit, the conductor raised his baton. On the stage, *Turandot* resumed.

The music rose muted into the President's box. Still no one spoke; no one moved. Then the corridor doors burst open. White uniforms, a stretcher. It had been only minutes since Peter had picked up the phone. Now, aeons later, help was here.

The President read the Premier's message and handed it to Compton. "The Soviets have held up their side of the bargain," he said, "but the Syrians are being damned pig-headed."

Compton looked at the large type on the page. The hot line was not a telephone, but a bank of teletype machines, half of them manufactured in the United States, the rest in the Soviet Union. They transmitted written copy instantaneously in both English and Russian. An aide was standing by outside the Oval Office. The machines were only temporarily idle. The aide was waiting for the President's reply.

Compton read the message for himself. The Soviets had intervened with Damascus. They had expressed their disapproval in the strongest possible language. They made themselves very clear: the seizure of the ship in neutral waters was a violation of international law and intolerable to the world community. They expected fullest cooperation from the Syrian government. They expected nothing less than the immediate release of the *Richmond* and its crew.

But the Syrians were insisting that the *Richmond* was a spy ship, an allegation that Compton knew was entirely false—and beside the point, since the U.S. would never admit it if it were. What mattered was that the Syrians refused to be bullied by either side. They would not release the ship voluntarily.

"What do you think?" the President asked.

Compton looked up. "I think we should set a deadline."

"What kind of deadline?"

"Twenty-four hours. No more."

"And if nothing happens in that time?"

"Then we go in and take back what's ours."

The President said nothing.

"It's your decision, of course," Compton said.

"Yes, I know that." He leaned back in his chair and stared

up at the ceiling. His face was calm, his expression merely thoughtful. Then suddenly he leaned forward and pressed a button in the panel on his desk. His secretary's voice emerged from a hidden speaker. "Yes, sir?"

"I'm ready to send a reply to the Premier," he said. "Then I want you to find the Secretary of Defense and the Chairman of the Joint Chiefs of Staff. Tell them I want to see them again."

"Yes, sir. When?"

"Now. Within the hour."

It was close to midnight when Peter pulled into the driveway of Compton's town house in Georgetown. Mrs. Ross, the housekeeper, let him in and showed him to the library at the back of the house.

Peter poured himself a brandy and dropped into the corner of the brown leather couch. He stretched his feet out, leaned back, and closed his eyes. He was not tired, but weary, emotionally spent. For him Kersnik's death was a minor diplomatic problem, a matter for handling, of being there. But for Madame Kersnik and the embassy staff who had gathered at the hospital, it was far more than that—a personal tragedy, the same in any country, at any level of life. Peter was glad he had been able to facilitate unfamiliar foreign procedures, but it hadn't exactly been a pleasant evening.

The weather outside had turned damp and cold. Rain spattered a window set between built-in bookshelves at one end of the room. A fire was blazing in the hearth under a carved walnut mantel. Peter glanced at the painting hanging over the mantel, a seascape done in oils. He pressed a button in the table beside the couch. The painting moved; the wall panel swung forward; the TV behind it came on. Peter pressed another button to change channels. Then he looked at his watch and realized that it was too late for the news. He shut the set off again, and the panel clicked back into place.

Peter tasted his drink. This house was full of gadgets, from the built-in appliances in the sleek kitchen upstairs to the secret staircase hidden behind these bookshelves and leading down to Compton's private domain—his wine cellar, his exercise room and sauna, his private study, where no one was allowed to enter except the technicians who came to check his telephone for surveillance once a week, and then only with Compton present. There were two other TV sets hidden behind secret panels in other rooms upstairs. There was a temperature-controlled greenhouse attached to the main house at the second floor. There was, no doubt, a wall safe—maybe more than one—and a security system that probably rivaled the White House's.

There was also the electric train, its track built into the walnut molding that ran around the top of the library walls. More buttons—forward, reverse, a train whistle, real steam. Arthur Compton was a man of many dimensions.

Peter pressed one of the buttons, expecting the train to come roaring out of the tunnel that ran across one end of the room, but nothing happened. The train must be broken, he thought, or out for repairs. Or maybe the wires that worked all of Compton's gadgets had finally become hopelessly crossed. He'd probably just set off the sprinkler system in the garden at the back of the house.

Peter got up as Nicole walked into the room. She had changed her clothes, was in jeans and a sweater—blue, the same shade as her eyes. There was color again in her face. The shock of what had happened tonight was starting to wear off.

For Peter, too. Tension left him as she came into his arms, and he held her, stroking her hair, feeling the warmth of her face against his, the softness of her touch. Tension faded, leaving only a sense of sadness that had to do with his own fears about love and death. Tonight was a reminder; Nicole made him vulnerable again. But she also lifted the mists surrounding the nightmare. She healed his scars. She defied his fears and made him welcome the risk.

Neither one of them spoke for a moment, but then Nicole leaned back and looked up into his eyes. "Is he dead?" she asked.

"Yes." The doctors had only confirmed what Peter already knew. Kersnik's death was instantaneous.

A look passed through Nicole's eyes. "I'm so sorry for Madame Kersnik. Was she all right?"

"She will be," Peter said.

Nicole touched his face. "And are you all right?"

"Me? It's you I'm worried about."

She smiled gently. "I'm fine. I just need a good night's sleep."

"Well, I won't stay long."

"Don't go yet."

Peter sat down again and drew Nicole down beside him, wanting to forget the sadness of the evening, wanting only to be with her. But Nicole, of course, wanted to know more.

"Was it a heart attack?"

Peter nodded. "They're sure it was, though there's some confusion about an autopsy. The doctors want to do one here before they release his body, but Madame Kersnik wants to take him home."

"I don't blame her. Will they let her?"

"He's a foreign ambassador. They'll have to accede to her wishes. It just has to be worked out."

And it wasn't Peter's problem now. He had routed the Undersecretary for Eastern European Affairs out of a dinner party and dumped the whole thing on him, where it belonged.

"This won't affect Korcula, will it?" Nicole asked him.

The question had occurred to Peter already. "I don't see why it would. Kersnik would be the last person to want the meeting delayed. He was committed to Korcula."

Nicole was leaning against him, her head on his shoulder. Now, suddenly, she sat forward. "*That's* what he said. Of course!"

Peter picked up his drink. "That's what who said?"

"The ambassador. He said something to me before he died."

"Oh? What?"

"That's just it, I don't know. Or I didn't. I think he was speaking Serbo-Croatian. I didn't understand when he said it. But it was something *Korcula.*" Nicole closed her eyes, trying to remember. "It was during the last aria," she said, "just before the curtain. Two words, maybe three words. *Spray* something. Spray *key*? Spray key Korcula? Does that mean anything to you?"

Peter took a drink of his brandy, which felt warm going

down. The glow of the fire was warming, too. He was starting to feel drowsy. But the words meant nothing. "I have no idea what it means," he said.

"It can't matter now. I doubt if we'll ever know."

Nicole nodded and leaned back against the couch, but her eyes were still thoughtful, remembering.

"Can I get you a drink?" Peter asked.

"Yes, please."

"Brandy?"

She nodded.

Peter got up and crossed the room to the bar. He was thinking about the anger he had seen in Kersnik's face. Now he knew that it hadn't been anger, and hardly indigestion. If only they'd known then how sick he was, they might have gotten a doctor in time to save him. Life was like that too often. Tragedy came without warning, without time for preparation. Or prevention. He picked up the bottle of brandy.

Then he set it down hard as a memory flashed through his mind. Prevention!

"*Damn*!"

Nicole looked up, startled. "What's the matter?" she asked.

But Peter was already moving toward the door. "I've got to go."

"Peter! *Why*?" She got up from the couch and hurried after him.

Peter stopped and took a deep breath. He hadn't meant to alarm her. "I'm sorry," he said. "Nothing's wrong. I just told a friend I would stop by to see him tonight."

"*Now*? It's after midnight!"

"I know, but I said I would do it."

Nicole looked at him, her expression a mixture of confusion and worry.

Peter kissed her. "Get some sleep," he said.

He tried to make his voice sound calm, but inside he was coldly angry, cursing himself. He'd been so damn busy with Kersnik, he'd completely forgotten Steve Katz!

Steve parted the curtains just enough to look out. The street was dark under a heavy rainfall. Streetlights burned dimly at wide intervals, casting vague reflections against the wet pavement. There were a few lights on in the houses across the way, but no one on the sidewalk, no traffic passing by. Capitol Hill after-hours, after Congress had gone home; there was nothing but darkness and the steady sound of the rain.

Where was Peter?

Steve closed the curtains carefully, then turned on a light again. The door at the end of the room opened onto an outer corridor, the only direct point of access to the apartment. Curtains covered all the windows; there was only the one lamp. And yet Steve was anxious. More than that, he was afraid.

He picked up the revolver lying on his desk and checked, again, to make sure it was loaded. The feel of it only increased his anxiety. He had never fired a gun; he'd rarely handled one. He wasn't sure he could use it now if he had to.

Or if he would have the chance.

The thought made him laugh. It was *almost* funny, the vision of himself, alone with a gun, fending off the kind of people who handled weapons the way he handled his toothbrush. The gun would be no defense. He wondered why he bothered to have it.

Amusement vanished, replaced by fear. Could they know he had contacted Peter? Would they stop him from coming here?

Had they stopped him?

Steve put the gun down and quickly picked up the phone, berating himself for not giving Peter more warning. He let it ring ten times or more, but Peter still didn't answer. He hadn't gone home. Where *was* he?

Steve dropped down into his desk chair and passed a weary hand across his eyes. There was no point in calling Kennedy Center again. The Opera House stage had been dark for over an hour, plenty of time for Peter to get home. Plenty of time to take Nicole home first. Had he stayed at Nicole's? Steve couldn't call her. He didn't have the unlisted number.

Fear began to give way to despair. What could Peter do if he were here? What could anyone do?

Steve got up and went to the kitchen to make a pot of coffee. Anything to keep his hands busy, his mind from succumbing to the fear that he might yet fail. He returned to his desk and reached for a pile of newspaper clippings; the dates covered nearly two years. He glanced through them, separating some from the rest. Then he lined them up together, overlapping, so that only the headlines showed.

These were the bones of the story, just an outline. Alone, they meant nothing, but combined with the rest of what Steve had compiled, they were frightening beyond belief.

It began with the Soviet Six:

SOVIETS ARREST DANCHENKO, FIVE OTHERS, ON
ESPIONAGE CHARGES
WHITE HOUSE SUSPENDS SALT TALKS TO PROTEST SOVIET
ARRESTS
KREMLIN SILENT ON SALT SUSPENSION
U.S. LEADS WORLD PRESSURE TO FREE THE SOVIET SIX
PRESIDENT SOFTENS STAND AGAINST SOVIET HUMAN-
RIGHTS POLICY
SALT TALKS RESUME IN GENEVA
MOSCOW BEGINS TRIAL OF DANCHENKO, FIVE OTHERS
COMPTON: SALT TALKS MUST CONTINUE
SOVIET SIX GUILTY, SENTENCED TO LIFE AT HARD LABOR

It began there and went on:

REBELS OVERTHROW CASTRO
SOVIET TROOPS INVADE ANGOLA
SINO-AMERICAN DEFENSE TREATY SIGNED

Steve never got all the way through them. His body tensed as reflex to sound and sensation. His hand reached out for the gun, but his mind rejected the move as futile. There was a definite sound, a deep roaring eruption, vague, distant, as if it were happening somewhere else in the world.

Thoughts raced through Steve's mind in chaos, in an instant of time that was over as it began. Then chaos was all around him: a blast of sound so intense that it broke his eardrums, a wave of heat, a flash of incredible brightness. Sudden movement. Heat and pressure lifted him out of the chair.

Then pain and heat vanished. He was watching it all from a place apart, slow-motion, without sound. The walls of the house were cracking, crumbling, collapsing into the rain. The floor fell away. Dust and smoke. Bits of newspaper caught fire, curled, blackened, floated past him.

Steve saw himself suspended, then falling through darkness. And then he saw nothing more.

9

PETER STARED THROUGH streaks of rain as he cut across town, bypassing the White House and skirting the edge of the Federal Triangle, heading for Capitol Hill. His hands gripped the steering wheel hard; his foot alternated between the gas pedal and brake. He was driving too fast on wet pavement, because he had promised. Because he forgot.

The Capitol loomed up ahead, a white shadow in the darkness of rain and night. Its dome lights were doused, not by rain, but because of the hour. It was past midnight. He had told Steve he'd be there tonight. He'd forgotten. And now tonight was tomorrow.

The dome lights were out, but the sky behind the Capitol glowed dimly through the rain. Peter hardly noticed. He was thinking of Steve, remembering the tone of Steve's voice, the threat of a few words spoken by a gentle, rational man.

You don't often get the chance to prevent a major international disaster. And the implied prerequisite, that such a disaster was pending.

Had Steve gone mad? Peter would have preferred to believe that, but he didn't. Steve had meant what he said. Whatever it was, right or wrong, it was that important.

And Peter was the only person he trusted. He stepped down on the gas once again.

Steve lived on East Capitol Street, behind the Library of Congress. Peter turned in front of the Capitol and drove around it. Then suddenly he slammed on the brakes and brought the car to a stop.

A police barricade blocked the pavement. Patrol cars and fire trucks were jammed into the street at odd angles, like huge toys left out for the night. Crowds of onlookers pressed the barricade, jockeying for a good view. Smoke thickened the blur of rain. Fire brightened the night sky.

Peter stared through his windshield. A row of town houses was burning on the right side of the street. Where *Steve* lived. Three, four houses, maybe more. One was hardly a house anymore. Its front wall was gone; inside, it was an inferno. Peter's breath caught in his throat. It was *Steve's* house!

Something inside Peter snapped. Something fell into place. He jumped out of the car and pushed his way into the crowd. Pushing, shoving, filled with a sense of urgency like nothing he had felt since Paris. He *had* to get through, for reasons that went beyond friendship. He sensed it: Steve was there and waiting. Steve had something to say. He had to get through to see Steve.

The air was sharp with the acrid odor of water-soaked, burned timber, like a morning hearth and dead ashes. The heat was intense, but the rain soaked him through. He felt numb with cold, a man operating on reflex. His muscles had tensed. He had sprung into action. *He was ready to kill.*

A man blocked his way. Peter pushed him aside, got an expletive in reply. A sharp comment from a woman behind him. She couldn't *see*. Inconvenience! Peter paid no attention. He pushed on, reached the barricade, ducked under.

The scene he found there was pandemonium. A nightmare. Burning buildings. A fire out of control, so intense it could not be put out—not by man and not by nature. And a familiar smell: it filled Peter's nostrils, his mind. Blasting powder. Bombs! Not Paris, but Amsterdam. The start of a nightmare. *The* nightmare.

A policeman in a black slicker grabbed Peter's arm, pushed him back.

"I've got to get in there—"

"Not now, you don't."

Anger surged up inside. Old anger, old feelings. Policeman and soldier merged in Peter's mind. A barricade. Iron gates. Authority, cold and heartless, immune to reason. To argue against it was futile. Human need didn't count.

Peter took a deep breath and brought himself back to the present. This was not the same. The policeman's face was firm, but it wasn't unkind. He was doing his job, and his job was to keep people out. For their own sake. For the sake of the effort going on beyond the barricade. Peter's anger began to fade, but the urgency stayed with him.

He had only his own resources.

"I'm here on official business," he said, and produced his wallet, his government I.D.

The policeman glanced at the card but wasn't impressed. The State Department carried no weight here. He shook his head.

"Damn it, I said *official* business!"

"I heard you, mister, but we've got a small disaster here and a few dozen people injured. If you're not emergency personnel, I can't let you through."

"Who can?"

"The captain, maybe, but I can't leave my post to go ask him."

"Then I'll ask him. You can let me through to do that."

The policeman looked at the card again, then handed it back to Peter. "All right, go see Captain Wanley. He's the gray-haired man over there."

Peter nodded his thanks and moved on before the policeman had time to change his mind.

The house where Steve lived was a pile of burning rubble. It was *gone*, collapsed into the inferno. Urgency sharpened. Peter had to find Steve.

But where?

He hurried through the rain, across thick lines of fire hose, past more black slickers and fire hats, past soot-smudged faces that paid no attention to him. Orders were shouted, the fire hose repositioned; strong sprays of water shot off in new directions as the fire scattered flame onto neighboring rooftops. A nightmare. Then a siren pierced the air as an ambulance sped off in another direction. Peter followed the sound of the siren, past the fire, past patrol cars and fire trucks, to the far end of the street.

A hospital tent had been thrown up as protection against the rain. The shouting was blunted here by other, more pressing sounds—moans of pain, anguished cries from relatives and friends. There were bodies on stretchers laid out on the ground—bodies everywhere. Some were conscious, some were clearly beyond help. Men and women in white jackets moved among them, doing their work in haste and yet with incredible calm. They were trained for disaster, as Peter was trained, by experience.

Peter entered the tent. He moved quickly along the rows of stretchers, scanning faces, looking for Steve. Soon he found him—Steve, lying on a white sheet stained pink by blood and water, his eyes closed against cheeks that were crusted with blood and blackened by fire. A nurse knelt beside him. She tucked a blanket around him, leaving his hands and arms free, but her eyes were flat, without hope. She got up and moved on.

Peter stood where he was, paralyzed. He had come too late! He stepped forward and dropped to his knees.

"*Steve . . . ?*"

The eyelids moved.

"It's Peter. Christ, I'm sorry . . ."

Steve's eyes opened. He tried to focus on Peter, his concentration intense. His lips moved to speak.

"Take it easy," Peter said. "Don't talk. We'll talk later."

Steve's eyes opened wide. They stared at Peter and past him. His voice was a whisper, but each word was etched with terror: "Get away! Run from here! They got me, and they'll get you!"

He was delirious. Peter reached for his hand, and a look of pain crossed his own face. The hand was black, badly burned. Peter touched his shoulder instead, tried to calm him.

But Steve would not be calmed. "Get away! *Hurry!* They won't *let* you stop them. They'll *kill* you!"

"*Steve!*"

Steve's eyes stared at him wildly. Then slowly they came into focus. His face softened to a frown. "Peter . . . ?"

"It's all right. I'm here, and I'm all right. No one is going to kill me."

"Oh, God." A soft cry of futility. Steve's eyes turned away.

"You're going to be all right, too," Peter said. "Just take it easy."

"No!" Steve turned back. "You've got to stop them. You can't let them succeed."

"They? *Who*?"

Steve's attention faded, in and out. He was here and gone. Here again.

Peter leaned in closer.

Steve struggled to find words. It was a physical struggle, but Peter sensed something more. There were people all around them—the medical workers, the injured, people like Peter who sought familiar features among faces blackened by fire. He got the message: there were too many people. He leaned closer still.

Steve's voice was barely audible over the sounds of pain, of sirens coming and going, of rain and fire. Only two words were clear.

"*Marco Polo*."

A chill ran through Peter's body, an involuntary spasm that had nothing to with the damp clothes or night air. *Marco Polo*. The words had no meaning, and yet they elicited fear.

No, not the words. The look on Steve's face. Peter knew what it meant. Steve was dying. Good God, he was *dying*!

Peter no longer doubted, if he'd ever doubted at all. An international disaster. It was that important. He leaned closer. His own voice dropped to a whisper. "What *about* Marco Polo?"

Steve was growing weaker, his attention fading again. "Remember the Soviet Six," he said.

Marco Polo? And the *Soviet Six*? It still made no sense to Peter. History, long ago and recent. The past and the present, all mixed up into one.

"I don't understand," he said.

"You must understand."

"Then *help* me."

Steve shook his head. "It's too late."

"It's not too late. I'm here. Tell me. *Make* me understand."

Steve's eyes closed. He lay silently, unmoving.

Peter's breath caught. But then there was pressure against his arm. Steve's hand moved, the burned, blackened hand. His face had gone white under blood and soot. His jaw tensed. His eyes were full of pain. He was making a massive effort, one more effort to say what he meant. He summoned his last reserves, his last strength.

"Investigate Marco Polo," he whispered. He paused, his eyes intent on Peter, "Investigate *the origins* of Marco Polo. Avoid the obvious. And remember the Soviet Six."

His eyes closed.

The rain on the overhead awning beat a gentle counterpoint to the cacophony behind. Peter sat back against the wet pavement; he was trembling inside and out. Steve was dead. Peter knew, as he'd known with Kersnik. He felt numb, but not from the cold.

The nightmare was real, all around him. Fire. Burning buildings. Sirens and emergency personnel. Lives torn apart, lives destroyed. One more friend lost forever. Words came to him, past and present, from Steve, from behind, from all sides. *Marco Polo.* An explosion. *You must stop them. You can't let them succeed.* A familiar smell, burning timber. Dead ashes and bombs. An explosion. . . .

"A *deliberate* explosion?"

"I heard a policeman say so. He said it was a bomb."

"Really!"

Peter heard the words clearly behind him. He turned around. Two white jackets were talking, two women, about the fire. About the *cause* of the fire.

"It's hard to believe someone would do this on purpose," one said.

"But that's what I heard," said the other. "They think the bomb was planted in the cellar, in that middle house. That's where it started."

Peter followed the white jacket's gesture to the house at the heart of the fire, to the pile of burning rubble where Steve's apartment had been. Oh, my God! Someone had *killed* him! A bomb. A deliberate explosion. Steve didn't die. He was murdered!

They got me, and they'll get you.

Peter turned back to Steve, as if the closed eyes could deny what he was thinking. A man in a brown raincoat had appeared from somewhere and was bending over Steve's body. Peter acted from instinct; his arm lashed out in anger, struck the man's chest, sent him reeling back onto the ground. He lay there staring at Peter, rubbing his hand with a clenched fist, more stunned than frightened. Peter stared back at him for a moment. Then he held out his hand. "I'm sorry," he said. "I don't know why I did that. Forgive me."

The man's gaze shifted from Peter to Steve, and back to Peter again. "It's all right," he said. "I understand. I have friends here, myself." He accepted Peter's hand and pulled himself up. Then he shoved his hands in his pockets and walked away.

Peter watched the man go, shaken by the violence of his own feelings. Then he stepped back to make way for a new stretcher being rushed into the tent. On it lay a young woman, her condition obviously critical.

Because someone wanted *Steve* dead.

The trembling stopped as suddenly as it had started; Peter felt coldly outraged. None of this was possible! And yet it was happening. It was all too familiar. Someone had *caused* this destruction, this suffering. Someone with no regard whatever for human life. To kill one man was bad enough, but to take so many with him . . .

It was all too familiar.

Someone had killed Steve and had to have a reason. What reason? An international disaster. Marco Polo and the Soviet Six. A nonsense message from the lips of a dying friend designed to prevent others from understanding, but equally unclear to Peter. And yet in it, somewhere, meaning.

Peter looked down at Steve's face, where lines of pain lingered on even now that the pain was gone. Whatever Steve meant, he was going to find out. He had to do it, to prevent a disaster.

He had to do it for Steve.

The man in the brown raincoat emerged from the tent and stopped briefly to speak with a policeman. There was no one he knew by name. Some he could identify as people who lived on the block, but that was all. He didn't know who they were.

The policeman thanked him and sent him on his way.

The man moved back through the crowd, still rubbing his chest. His face showed the strain of what he had just seen. Fragile life, sudden death. He stepped into a building across from the fire, near Grubb's Pharmacy, and unlocked the inside door.

The strain on his face vanished. His pace quickened as he walked up to the third floor. The apartment he'd rented was furnished. It was strictly impersonal. Nothing in it spoke of the man. A few clothes bought off the rack, a razor and toothbrush. Nothing to trace back to him.

Except for the heavy suitcase lying flat on the floor. The man bent down and unlocked it. A tape recorder was still running inside. He shut it off, ran the tape back through, and pressed the button to play it.

The recorder was connected by radio receiver to a tiny directional microphone now in the brown raincoat pocket, where the man had dropped it after Peter Lucas hit him. His chest was still sore, but the job had been done. Voices came from the tape.

Investigate the origins of Marco Polo. Avoid the obvious. And remember the Soviet Six.

The man smiled as he turned off the tape and began to assemble the parts of his shortwave set. The words were clear, sufficient; the message was passed. He had to report to Dmitri. Moscow would want to know.

10

COMPTON WAS ALREADY on his way out when Nicole came downstairs the next morning. He was in the hall, taking his coat from the closet, and on his face was a look of deep anxiety.

Nicole frowned. She was startled by the intensity of the look; it was so unlike her father. She almost felt she was intruding on him.

"Daddy . . . ?"

He didn't hear her. His face didn't change.

"Daddy, what's wrong?"

Compton looked up and saw her. Anxiety faded. A flicker of annoyance passed through his eyes.

"I'm sorry," she said. "Did I interrupt something?"

"No, I was only thinking. I'm running late. I've got to get to the office."

Nicole helped him on with his coat. "Have you heard what happened after you left last night?" she asked.

"You'll have to tell me later."

"But it's—"

"I told you, I'm late," Compton snapped back. "I don't have time for it now." He turned and walked out of the door.

Nicole stared after him, wondering what in the world had gotten under his skin. He didn't seem to know about Kersnik, but it had to be something more than the *Richmond*. She had grown up in the shadow of crises far worse, but she didn't remember him ever cutting her off, not having time to hear what she had to say.

Obviously there was something terribly wrong. Nicole stood where she was for a moment. Then she shrugged and turned away.

Mary had to go to the archives for the files on the Soviet Six.

"Not only that," she told Peter, "but Archives had them filed under *inactive*, as if they were past tense. It's sad, isn't it?"

Sad, yes, Peter thought, but more than that, symptomatic. It was hard to keep anyone interested in prisoners of conscience after they dropped out of sight in the Soviet labor camps.

It was morning now, but Peter hadn't slept much during the night. His body demanded rest, but his mind rejected the plea. He had hashed and rehashed what had happened: sudden death, twice in one night. Now, in the familiarity of his own office, with the sun shining once more and the normal sounds of traffic seeping in under the windows, it was hard to believe last night ever happened. Especially Steve. Murdered? Impossible! But nothing else would account for the dull ache that had been there when Peter awakened this morning and was still with him now. The weight of grief; it hurt.

He took the files. Six human lives filed under "inactive." Stashed away for subsequent removal to deeper storage when the magic number of months and years had passed. In the meantime, forgotten. But not by Steve.

Peter knew the dissidents' story as well as he knew his own. They had been his major concern from Danchenko's arrest until all efforts to free them had failed. He knew their story by heart, but he took the files and read through them again on the chance that there might be something he didn't remember, or had overlooked—something to unlock the mystery of Steve's message.

The Soviet Six: a diverse group, ranging in age from twenty-four to seventy-one. A scientist, a novelist, a professor of economics at the University of Moscow. A physician, a university student, a young composer and pianist. Among them a Nobel Prize-winner, a Lenin Scholar, a Tchaikovsky medalist, and a Hero of the Soviet Union.

Six distinguished Soviet citizens who had at least two things in common: they had all requested permission to immigrate to Israel, and now they were all life inmates of the labor camp called Perm.

Peter took a drink of his coffee and looked up at the poster on his wall. Then he read on:

Yuri Danchenko: thirty-seven, married, no children. A research chemist, the Nobel Prize-winner, and, until his conviction, a member of the prestigious Soviet Academy of Sciences.

Danchenko was the group's spokesman, the best-known of the six. Like the others, he had no history of radical politics; his reasons for wanting to emigrate were entirely personal. He had gotten married, and he wanted his children to breathe their first air in Israel.

And so he applied for a permit to take his wife and leave the Soviet Union; permission was denied. Two weeks later, his apartment was invaded by the secret police, who seized a cache of "Anti-Soviet literature"—a Hebrew-language textbook, a Bible, a book on the Six-Day War, biographies of David Ben Gurion and Golda Meir.

Gena Danchenko, his wife, was allowed to leave the country; indeed, she had no choice. But Yuri was arrested, tried on propaganda charges, and sentenced to a year at hard labor. He served only thirty days. Under pressure from the west, the Soviets freed him, but his record stood firm. He was expelled from the academy and fired from his job. He had no work and could find none. He was allowed to go home, but his wife was no longer there.

He applied once again for permission to emigrate. This time, there was no denial, only an endless morass of red tape. The point became clear: there would be no denial; there would be no permission either. He would not see Gena again.

Then, and only then, did he begin to dissent.

Peter read quickly through the rest: Maria Petrovskaya, Nicolai Pinsky, Fyodor Subolev, Nina Kovalyova, Vladimir Levitan. Their stories were alike except for the small details, and even those added up to the same thing. Six loyal Soviet citizens who wanted to live somewhere else, all arrested on manufactured charges. Six people, chosen by the state to stave off a growing tide of emigration, to serve as a harsh lesson to others with the same goal. Warning: Dangerous waters. Swim at your own risk.

Under Danchenko's leadership, the six began meeting together. They staged formal protests and drew others into their cause. They attracted the attention of the Western press, who dubbed them the Soviet Six. No one in the West believed they were really in danger; they were far too distinguished for that. But Western observers were wrong. The six were arrested again in a single raid by the secret police. This time the charge was more serious. Espionage. Passing secrets through friendly journalists to the enemy. The charge, of course, was ridiculous, but they were tried and found guilty. Their sentence, life at hard labor, had stunned the free world.

Inevitably there had been a rash of popular demonstrations in the West. The harsh sentence set off parliamentary debate all around the world. Western leaders made a strong show of protest. Charges and accusations. But in the end, they did nothing. The Soviets had thrown out an audacious challenge and had gotten away with it. It was too audacious to touch. Serious purpose could not be mistaken: if the Soviets cared what the world thought of the sentence, there never would have been a trial to start with. Protest died of its own futility. The Soviet Six disappeared and had not been heard from again.

Until now.

Peter pushed himself up from his desk and began to pace his office. What *had* Steve known? That the charges were less than flimsy? The trial a mockery? Hardly startling news. Had he found some kind of proof? Possibly, but so what? What good would proof do? Who, among those who could reverse the sentence, would ever bother to listen? Why would they, when they already knew?

Damn it, Steve! What were you trying to tell me?

Peter looked at his telephone. He stood there a moment, letting his thoughts come together. Then he picked it up and made two calls, to the Soviet desk and State Department Intelligence. Both requests were the same: send up anything you've had on the Soviet Six in the last few months. And check your files for any mention of the name Marco Polo. After that, he made one more call, to the Soviet section at Langley.

The requests were natural enough, given the scope of his work, and sufficient to alert official Washington. If the clues in Steve's message meant anything to the intelligence people, he would hear something back, if nothing more than reverse questions. Why are you asking? What do you already know?

Peter sat back and tried to relax, all he could think to do until he saw Nicole. He had called her first thing this morning and told her that Steve had been killed. But that was all he had told her. For the rest—how Steve died, and his message—he wanted to see her in person. And so they were having lunch.

But now, suddenly, he couldn't sit up any longer. He put out his cigarette, crossed over to the couch, stretched out, and closed his eyes. He could feel consciousness fading into exhaustion, his mind going numb, his brain ordering sleep. But there at the edge, he felt a sharp twist of pain. Once more he thought of Steve.

Steve, murdered by unknown assassins, in his own home, here in Washington, D.C. Three blocks from the Capitol building. Against that loomed the faces from the poster. The Soviet Six. If Steve was dead, if he could be murdered here, then they had no chance at all.

Maria Petrovskaya looked at her face in the mirror above the washstand. It was an old woman's face, colorless, with sunken cheeks and harsh lines around the eyes and mouth. Her hair, once black and lustrous, had turned a drab shade of gray. In less than a year the color had faded; the life, like her spirit, had gone.

The face in the mirror was an old woman's face, and yet Maria Petrovskaya was not yet fifty years old.

She tied a woolen scarf around her head and pulled on her coat—a shapeless garment, without style, without even much substance, but all she had to keep off the sharp river wind. The better to feign obscurity, she thought. Or the better to feign courage.

She was not feeling brave. She felt nothing. She had felt nothing for a long time. Her career was over, her medical license revoked, her records at the university destroyed, as if she never had studied so much as a chemistry course. She couldn't prove she ever was a physician. She would never practice medicine again, no matter what happened tonight. She had nothing left. Her husband and son were both dead, and her daughter had been banished to the Balkan Mountains. As good as dead.

Maria had not seen her daughter in more than two years, had despaired of ever seeing her again. And yet, here *she* was, a thousand miles from the camp that had been her prison, ready to begin the last leg of her journey to freedom.

Her own escape was a miracle. And if she could do it, perhaps . . .

She suppressed the thought, not wanting to let feelings stir themselves back to life, not wanting to let false hope make her vulnerable again.

She crossed the room, switched off the lights, pulled the curtains back from the window, and stood in silence, absorbing the last view of her homeland. A sandy beach stretched down to the water below. *Matushka*. Little Mother Volga, the greatest river in all Europe. After tonight, she would never see it again.

There was no moon, only the lights of a tourist steamer approaching the village from the Sokoli Gori, heading south to the Caspian Sea. Her signal. No moon, just those tiny lights and the surging blackness of water.

And silence. The house was completely quiet. Maria let the curtain fall back and made her way to the stairs. Of course it was quiet, she told herself. It was very late. The Peshkov children were staying with their aunt. Their father worked a night shift; he would not be home for hours. There would be only their mother, Nadia, a young woman of enormous courage, willing to risk her own freedom for a woman she had never seen before today.

Maria felt a rush of affection. Had it really been hours since she arrived on Nadia Peshkov's doorstep, trembling from exhaustion and hunger? Only hours? An instant of life! A meal, brief sleep, a sense of safety and comfort, basic needs Maria no longer assumed. A moment in time, void of fear.

But now she had to move on.

She reached the last stair and turned back toward the kitchen. Nadia was there, alone, sitting at the kitchen table, her back turned to the door.

"Nadia?"

The reply came from behind her. "Madame Peshkov cannot hear you."

Maria's heart stopped. Her mouth went dry. She swung around to the voice. A man, smiling obscenely, showed pleasure in this moment of triumph. He held a gun in his hand.

He said nothing as he crossed the room and stood over the unmoving Nadia. Then, cruelly, arrogantly, he placed a hand on her shoulder and pushed. She fell forward; her face hit the table hard.

A cry came from deep inside Maria's throat and strangled before it emerged. She stared at the man with an agony born of futility, with a mixture of fear and despair. Then slowly anger began to take hold. Pent-up emotion mushroomed into a fury, a final outburst of rage against injustice. She lunged at the man.

But her strength had gone.

The man grabbed her arm, threw her back against the wall, stared down at her, returning her anger with that gloating, obscene smile.

"The tape, Dr. Petrovskaya."

Maria did what Yuri had told her to do. She did not deny that she had the tape. She reached into her coat pocket and handed it to him.

"Thank you."

He stepped back, not taking his eyes off her. Then quickly he put his gun down on the table, removed a small recorder from his uniform pocket, inserted the tape, and let it start to play.

A click. A whirring of air. And then nothing.

The man's smile faded. He restarted the tape, listened again. Still, nothing. Not a sound. There had never been anything on it. This tape, like Danchenko's, was blank.

His voice erupted in rage. Maria clung to the wall; she felt only a sense of relief. He picked up the gun, came toward her slowly, menacingly. He crouched down on the floor beside her, grabbed her hair, pulled her close, pressed the gun barrel into her cheek.

"Who has it?" he demanded.

Maria stared back without fear. He could not hurt her now. They had done that before. They took all she had, left her nothing.

"I don't know."

His grip on her hair tightened. "You will tell me!"

She answered him calmly. "I can't, because I don't know."

Maria was telling the truth; she didn't know who had the tape. Within minutes, the man knew it too. He shoved her aside, stood up, and leveled the gun. Then he fired a single shot.

Maria welcomed the bullet. For her, it meant final release.

11

"STEVE'S DEATH WASN'T an accident," Peter said.

Nicole was sitting beside him, reading the menu, in a French café on M Street. She glanced up, at first startled, not sure she'd heard him correctly. Then she pushed the menu aside. "What did you say?"

"He was murdered."

Nicole's eyes widened with shock and disbelief. "But the newspaper said ten people were killed in that fire! And dozens of others were injured—"

"Which only tells you what kind of people killed him."

Peter signaled the waiter to bring them two more drinks. Then he reached for Nicole's hand across the blue-and-white tablecloth.

"I've read the papers," he said, "but I also know what I heard last night. I know what I saw and felt." He told her about the conversation he overheard just after Steve died. A bomb planted in Steve's building, the cause of the explosion and fire. And more than that, he told her about the *feeling* he'd had, the familiar smell of bombs and burning buildings, the nightmare come to life. "I'm not sure how to explain it, but I knew the fire was no accident even before I heard those two women talking. I knew before I saw Steve or heard what he had to say. There was an urgency in me, an instinct, and it's still there now. I know I'm right. That bomb had one target. Steve."

Nicole's eyes softened, and her hand tightened on his. "Oh, Peter, I know how you must have felt. No wonder it seemed so familiar! But it's hard to believe. Why would anyone want to kill Steve?"

"To prevent him from telling me or anyone else about something he knew."

"Worth killing that many people? What could be that important?"

"A major international disaster." Peter paused as the waiter appeared with their drinks. When they were alone again, he said, "I told you Steve called me yesterday and said he had to see me, but I didn't tell you why. He said he needed my help to prevent an international disaster. He wouldn't tell me what it was, but he said it was something bigger than I could imagine. It was that important, that urgent. And given what's happened, I don't think he was exaggerating."

"He wouldn't exaggerate anyway," Nicole said, and Peter felt relieved. Nicole hadn't known Steve the way he did, but she knew him well enough. She took what he said at face value, however hard to believe or understand. Peter didn't have to convince her that Steve was serious.

"When I got to him last night," he said, "he was still alive, but barely. He was in a lot of pain, but I think he knew what he was saying. I think he was trying to tell me what he wanted me to know."

"What *did* he say?"

Peter quoted Steve's last words: "Investigate the origins of Marco Polo. Avoid the obvious. And remember the Soviet Six." Then he leaned back and lit a cigarette, waiting for her reaction.

Nicole watched him in silence, her eyes thoughtful, her forehead creased in a frown. "That's what he said, exactly?" she asked.

Peter nodded.

"Then I agree with you. Those words aren't the ramblings of a delirious man. There's a pattern to them, a purposefulness, a message."

Peter drew on his cigarette, exhaled slowly. "A message,

yes, but what does it mean? What do you know about Marco Polo?"

Nicole shrugged. "Not much, I'm afraid. He's too far after my time. He was a Venetian explorer, of course. He traveled to China—"

"Was he born in Venice?"

"Probably. That's the obvious answer. Steve said to avoid the obvious."

"Then where in Venice? When? Who were his parents?"

Nicole shook her head. "I simply don't know, but it shouldn't be hard to find out. I'm going to the library this afternoon. I'll see what's there and call you." She picked up her drink. "In the meantime, I think you should talk to my father."

Peter was reluctant to go to Compton yet; he wanted to know more. "I intend to," he said, "but right now he has his hands full with the *Richmond*."

"Has it occurred to you that Steve's international disaster might *be* the seizure of the *Richmond*? Or at least that it might start there? Don't wait, Peter. I'm frightened. If what you say is true—if Steve knew something that important, and someone killed him to keep him from talking about it—then I'm frightened because he told you."

Peter's memory stirred. *They won't let you stop them. They got me, and they'll get you.*

He propped his cigarette against the edge of the ashtray, took Nicole's hand, and kissed it. "Don't worry," he said. "I'll be fine. No one knows what Steve told me."

Miloslavsky was waiting beside the monkey cage. His face was nearly hidden by the thick Persian lamb of his hat and coat collar. His hands were in his pockets, his feet in a pair of hand-tooled, fur-lined boots. A man on his lunch break, taking a walk through the small zoo on Durov Street, where few people came at this time of the year. He did not turn around as Levitsky came up beside him.

"You've heard from Dmitri?" he asked.

Levitsky nodded. "Katz is dead, and Lucas has taken the bait."

"Excellent."

Levitsky tossed a peanut to the monkeys and watched them scramble for it. There wasn't much time. He and Miloslavsky should not be seen here together.

"We had a close call, though," Levitsky said, and quickly explained. Lucas had been delayed. He didn't arrive until after the explosion, when it might have been too late. But Dmitri, as usual, had been completely thorough. He had posted an extra agent at the scene—a neighbor who was only too willing to cross police lines to help identify victims. The agent had found Katz alive before Lucas did and planted a microphone on him. Later, he retrieved it.

Katz had passed the message to Lucas—enigmatic, incomplete, but the more convincing for that. It contained the essential clues, Marco Polo and the Soviet Six, enough to get Lucas started.

"From now on, Dmitri will maintain close surveillance," Levitsky said. "He will leave nothing to chance."

"I should hope not! But tell me, how was Lucas delayed? Was it a failure in planning?"

Levitsky cleared his throat. "I'm sorry to say it happened because of a separate KGB operation, the assassination of Ambassador Jovan Kersnik. Lucas was there when it happened, but we couldn't have known that he would be."

Miloslavsky turned on him, glaring. His voice was coldly controlled. "And why was it necessary to take action against Kersnik?" he demanded. "Who made that decision?"

"I did," Levitsky said.

"You! *Why?*"

"Because we intercepted a top-secret memo from him to the Yugoslavian President. I believe he'd discovered the truth about Korcula and was on his way home to report it."

"And you had him killed?" Miloslavsky's blue eyes turned incredulous, and he struggled to keep his composure.

"The *whole* truth about Korcula," Levitsky said. "And I think I know how he found out. His military adjutant comes from Korcula and was recently home for a visit. He must have seen something there and told Kersnik. His name is Janovic, but he's a member of the Polo family."

Miloslavsky took in a sharp breath of air. "The house!"

"Precisely. If he knows that *we* have taken it over, then he may suspect what we're doing. Of course, he'll be taken care of, with an accident. But I consider Kersnik the higher priority."

"That's fine," Miloslavsky said, "but where is this going to stop? Will we have to kill the Yugoslavian President? Not that I care. It's just risky. Will we have to kill every member of the Polo family?"

"None of that will be necessary," Levitsky assured him. "I told you, we intercepted that memo. The President never saw it. He's not a problem. As for the Polos, I have another plan. We will clear everyone away from that end of the island, in the name of security, until our goal has been met."

Miloslavsky considered that. Slowly his face relaxed, and he turned back to the monkeys. "Peter Lucas is our last hope," he said. "Will he do what he must do now?"

"Dmitri will see that he does."

"At this stage, we can't afford a mistake."

"I'm aware of that," Levitsky said. "I promise you, there will be no mistakes with Lucas."

12

PETER LOOKED UP as Daniel Ravage appeared in the door of his office. "What can I do for you?" he asked.

"Do something for yourself. Go home. You look awful."

Peter managed a smile. "That bad?"

"Worse." Then Ravage's face changed. "Someone told me you were with Kersnik," he said. "I was sorry to hear what happened. It must have been a bad night."

"That's only the half of it," Peter said. "A friend of mine died last night, too."

"Oh, dear, I'm sorry. A good friend?"

"Yes." Peter didn't explain. He didn't feel like talking about Steve. "What have you got there?" he asked.

Ravage glanced down at the envelope in his hand. Then he handed it to Peter. "Your papers for the Korcula meeting. Travel schedule, hotel reservations, certification, special I.D., et cetera."

Peter chuckled. "What's the matter? Are the messengers tied up in conference?"

Ravage only shrugged. "I was coming this way. Check them over. Let me know if anything is missing."

"Thanks, I will." Peter put the envelope in a drawer and pushed it shut.

"Maybe you should take a look at them now," Ravage said.

But Peter shook his head. At the moment, travel information and hotel reservations were the last thing on his mind.

Still Ravage didn't leave. "To tell you the truth," he said, "I brought those by on purpose. I wondered if you'd seen the Secretary, if you'd had a chance to ask him about the *Richmond* and the other things we discussed."

The conversation came back to Peter in a quick succession of thoughts: Compton blinded to recent shifts in the balance of world power. Soviet retaliation in Norway and West Berlin. The Korcula conference, too good to be true. Ravage's doubts, his fears. Peter wondered now if he had dismissed them too lightly. Nicole was right. He had to talk to Compton.

But he didn't want to tell Ravage what he was thinking.

"You've got to stop worrying, Dan."

"I might, if I understood what was going on."

"Yes, well, I don't understand myself. We're negotiating for the ship; that's all I know. That's all I'm supposed to know. But I did talk to Compton briefly, and he assured me that the Syrian crisis will have no effect on Korcula."

Ravage said nothing, but he didn't look convinced.

"I'm sorry," Peter said. "You caught me at a bad time. I'm tired, and I've got other things on my mind."

"Something beside Korcula? It must be important."

Peter nodded but didn't explain.

"Anything I can help you with?" Ravage asked.

"It's a personal problem."

"All right, then I won't press." Ravage turned to go.

But Peter called him back. "Come to think of it," he said, "you might be able to help." Ravage had lived in New York for a long time. He still had friends there; he was well connected with the human-rights activist groups. "Have you heard anything lately about the Soviet Six?"

"The Soviet Six?" Ravage's eyes shifted to the poster on Peter's wall. He frowned, puzzled. "Nothing, not for a long time. Why do you ask?"

Peter tried to keep his voice casual. "It's just something someone told me," he said. "I wondered if anyone might be planning a new move to free them or to focus attention on them."

"*Now*? I sincerely hope not! Do you have reason to think so?"

"Not really," Peter said. "Just a remark I heard."

"Well, most of the people I know outside the department are reserving judgment on Korcula. They don't want to get their hopes up. But they're not planning anything that might disrupt the meeting."

"Could you ask around?" Peter said.

"Be glad to." Ravage started toward the door again, but once more he turned back. "I did hear one thing, about someone you know. Gena Danchenko."

Peter looked up with new interest. Gena Danchenko, Yuri's wife. A legend, however briefly, the widow of a living man. Peter remembered the first time he ever saw Gena, at an airport press conference when she first came to this country. She was a small woman, dark-eyed, with smooth olive-toned skin. An intensely private woman, thrust suddenly and harshly into the public glare, at the worst of times in her own life. Small and vulnerable, weary of public attention, and yet determined to have it. Determined that her husband would be free. He remembered the first time he saw her, and the last, at the airport again, on her way home to Tel Aviv. Determination wasn't always enough.

"What about Gena?" he asked.

"Did you know she was in New York?"

Peter did not. He was astonished.

"Now?"

Ravage nodded. "She's staying with an old friend of mine. Would you like to have the phone number?"

Peter wondered why Gena hadn't let him know she was coming back. And why she was here at all.

But, yes, he wanted to see her. He very much wanted to see her.

"I'll have to look it up," Ravage said. "Just a minute, I'll get it for you."

Ravage's old friend was Dr. Eleanor Benjamin, chairman of the International Relations Department at Columbia University. Ravage didn't have her home number. Peter called her at the office.

He explained who he was and how he knew Gena, that he was anxious to talk to her as soon as he could.

Dr. Benjamin gave him the number. "But I happen to know she's not there now," she said. "You might try in another hour."

Peter hesitated. The sense of urgency sharpened. He decided he didn't want to speak to Gena on the phone. "Can you reach her?" he asked. "Can you give her a message for me?"

"I can try."

"Tell her I'll be on the next shuttle flight, and I'll take a cab to the apartment. What's the address?"

It was just off Central Park West, at the corner of Ninety-sixth Street.

Peter hung up the phone and hurried out of his office.

Daylight was fading inside the apartment, but no one had turned on the lights. Bookshelves and big easy chairs were darkened by evening shadows. Only Gena's face was lit as she gazed through the window, like a piece of sculpture on temporary display, the only thing of importance in a darkened museum room.

"Gena?"

Dr. Benjamin was home by the time Peter arrived. She let him in and then left. Gena knew he was here, she had to, but she didn't turn around.

She was standing across the room, watching something in the park on the other side of the street below. Her back was straight, her arms folded, her hands gripping her arms. Peter sensed sadness in her silent posture, and a hint of tight self-control.

He wondered if he'd made a mistake arriving this way, so abruptly. He started to cross the room toward her, but then she spun around, and the look on her face brought him to a stop. Her eyes were dark, bright with anger. She glared at him with undisguised contempt.

"If you've come to bring me condolences from your government," she said, "then you might as well go. I don't want them. Or is it information you're after? Is that it? Don't tell me you've gone to work for the CIA?"

Peter couldn't have been more surprised if she'd pulled a

knife from her blouse and plunged it into his chest. "Condolences? CIA? What are you talking about?"

"You know what I'm talking about! I'm sorry you made the trip. I really don't want to see you." She turned back to the window.

Peter stayed where he was for a moment, studying the slope of her shoulders, the tight grip of her hands against her arms, still seeing eyes full of anger. He had not made a mistake. There was something seriously wrong. He had come to the right source.

He moved up beside her. "Gena . . . ?"

"Please go."

"I'm not going to go. I came here to talk to you, and the way you're acting only confirms that we need to talk. We were friends the last time I saw you. Now you're furious with me. There's got to be a reason for that, and I'm not going to leave until you tell me what it is."

Gena raised her eyes slowly to his. The anger began to fade, replaced by a look of despair. "*Please* go," she said. "I'd rather remember you as someone who tried to free Yuri."

Was that the problem? Did she think he had stopped trying? Did she think he would ever stop trying?

Of course, Gena couldn't know what was going to come out of Korcula. She couldn't know that the Soviets had agreed to release her husband and two hundred other political prisoners. Peter wanted to tell her, but he held back. He would make no promises until the pact was signed, until Yuri's freedom was guaranteed.

But he could offer reassurance. "I haven't forgotten Yuri," he said. "We're trying something different now, and I think—"

"Stop it!" she cried. The anger flared again in her eyes, anger mixed with pain. "Stop it! Go away! I didn't think I had any illusions left, but I never believed you could be so cruel!"

"Cruel! For wanting Yuri freed? What are you talking about?"

"*Peter*, Yuri is *dead*!"

"Oh, my God . . ."

Peter stared at her through the silence of the room. Utter

silence, as if the mention of death suspended life here, too.

"I can't believe it," he said finally. "If Yuri Danchenko were dead, the whole world would know."

"Not if it weren't reported," Gena replied coldly. "And of course it won't be. The Kremlin isn't anxious to have it known. If challenged, they'll deny it. I daresay they'll bring him forward for pictures. Why not? A few months in the Gulag, and everyone looks the same."

Peter stared at her, astonished. Disbelieving. Not wanting to believe. "How do you know?" he asked.

"I've kept up my contacts with the dissident underground. I have friends there. They told me."

Peter turned away. Her friends couldn't be wrong. They would be very sure before they told Gena her husband was dead. He'd been worked to death, or starved to death—that much was hardly shocking. Prisoners died in the camps every day. But the news still caught Peter unprepared. Whatever he was expecting, it wasn't this. An ache rose up in his throat, a new sense of loss, for a man he never met but considered a friend, for the goal that died with him.

And for Gena—what she must be feeling now! She had lost her husband a long time ago. Now she'd also lost purpose, all hope of getting him back. The same men who snatched him away and sent her into permanent exile had now denied her even the catharsis of official mourning. Yuri's death would not be reported. She could not share her grief.

"I'm so sorry," he said. "When did it happen?"

But Gena wasn't listening. She was studying his face, frowning—*puzzled*—as if she weren't sure whether she ought to believe him.

"Good God! You surely don't think I *knew* about this..."

Gena said nothing.

"You can't believe that!"

"Frankly, I don't know what to believe," she said. "I only know it's too late to be sorry. Yuri is dead. He was murdered, and your government—"

"Wait a minute. What do you mean, he was murdered?"

"*Murdered*. What else can it mean? He was shot to death by the *cheka*, three days ago, at Gagra."

"At Gagra! But he was at *Perm*."

Gena laughed wryly. "So you don't know about that, either."

"About what?"

"The escape."

"*What* escape?"

"The escape from Perm. Peter, your government *planned* it. The CIA? They *sent* Yuri to Gagra. They set him up and abandoned him to the *cheka*." Gena's eyes flashed. "Oh, yes, it was a KGB gun that killed him, but it couldn't have happened without the CIA. *Your government murdered my husband*!"

Oh, Christ! If that's what she thought, no wonder she was so angry! This was the widow lashing out, needing to place blame. Striking out at the Soviet system was a meaningless exercise. She needed to hurt someone who was capable of feeling. All right, if it helps, let her think what she likes, Peter thought. She deserved to release her feelings.

He reached for her arm, held it firm when she tried to pull away. "I don't blame you for thinking you hate me right now," he said. "But you've got to believe me. I knew nothing about this when I came here. I knew nothing about it until I heard it from you."

"Then why did you come?"

"Because a friend of mine died last night, and the last thing he said was about the Soviet Six. No, he didn't die; he was murdered. Like Yuri, murdered. What he said didn't make sense—ramblings about Marco Polo and the Soviet Six—but there was a message there, a warning. And that's why I came to see you, to try to find out what Steve meant."

"Steve?" Gena gasped. "Did you say *Steve*?"

"My friend. His name was Steve Katz."

"And he's dead? Oh, my God." Gena's hands flew to her face; tears welled up in her eyes.

Peter frowned. "Did you know him?"

Gena shook her head. "But Yuri was going to meet him here after he got out of Russia. If he's dead, then there's no one to help me find out why Yuri was killed."

Peter put his arms around her as the tears turned into sobbing. Anger and grief erupted, for a lost husband and the injustice of his death. Peter guessed that the tears had been pent up too long. He let her cry.

"I'm afraid you're stuck with me," he said finally. "I want to know why Yuri died, too. And why Steve died. I have a feeling there's one answer to both questions."

Gena looked up at him. "This man, Steve Katz, was a friend of yours?"

"A very good friend." Peter turned around and switched on a lamp. "Let's sit down," he said. "I'd like to tell you about him."

Limousines lined the circular drive on the south lawn of the White House, the drivers waiting idly for the party inside to end. Their passengers—governors from most of the fifty states—were dancing in the East Room, winding up their annual Washington conference with a formal White House ball.

Compton didn't care to stir up further speculation about the international situation by bursting in through the Diplomatic Entrance. He directed his driver to the Old Executive Office Building next door, then entered the White House underground by way of the West Wing tunnel.

A Viennese waltz was playing as he rode the elevator up to the second floor. Then the elevator retreated; a single soft buzz announced that the President was on his way up. Compton waited for him. They exchanged a few words and then made their way to the Treaty Room down the hall.

Three men at the table got up as the President entered the room. Compton closed the door, but the waltz remained faintly audible from the East Room downstairs.

The President, dressed in black tie, sat down at the head of the table and got straight to the point. "The deadline with Damascus was up thirty minutes ago. There's been no response to our diplomatic initiatives, though we've tried every available channel. It's now time to decide whether we proceed militarily, as planned, or seek another option." He turned to the Chairman of the Joint Chiefs of Staff. "General," he said, "tell us again, briefly, how your people plan to carry out the rescue."

The general produced a series of aerial reconnaissance photos and spread them out on the table. He pointed to one of the pictures. "We'll land a thousand Marines in an amphibious operation here," he said, "with air cover from the *Nimitz*. The Marines will take and hold the port, while we chopper in a rescue team of antiterrorist forces to evacuate the crew from the prison, here. The Navy will provide personnel to sail the *Richmond* out of the harbor once the Marines have secured her. Then, when the crew and the ship are safely away from the zone of the operation, the troops will withdraw."

The Secretary of Defense, who was sitting beside the general, nodded his approval of the summary. "We expect the operation to be entirely successful," he said. "With minimum casualties."

The third man leaned forward. He was the President's National Security Adviser, and his face reflected concern. "What are the worst possible case estimates?" he asked.

The Secretary of Defense deferred to the general. "At most, fifty casualties, and twice as many injuries. That's very low, since the operation involves more than a thousand people. And that's the worst possible. In reality, the figures are likely to be much lower."

The National Security Adviser wasn't satisfied. "Surely those figures can't include the possibility of Soviet intervention."

"No," the general replied.

"Why not?"

"Because the Soviets aren't going to intervene."

"Can we be so sure?"

Compton, who was sitting beside the President, spoke up for the first time. "Yes," he said, "we can count on it."

The National Security Adviser looked at him for a moment. Then his eyes shifted to the head of the table. "I'm sorry, Mr. President, but I can't just go along. I don't believe we should trust the Soviets in this matter. And I don't believe we've given enough time to the diplomatic process."

"I disagree," Compton said. "The Syrians have shown no interest in negotiating a solution, though they're fully aware of our deadline. They've rejected all efforts by us and the world community, including a strong protest from the Soviet Premier. We can't afford the luxury of waiting to see if they might eventually change their position and talk. This thing could go on for weeks, months, and we don't have that kind of time."

The President raised a hand to silence the discussion. He said nothing for a moment, as his gaze shifted from one face to another. Then finally he stood up. "I've made my decision," he said. "Notify the mission commander. The operation is on."

13

Investigate the origins of Marco Polo. Avoid the obvious. And remember the Soviet Six.

"Those were Steve's last words," Peter said. "There's an urgent message in them. I'm sure of it! I have to find out what it is."

Gena sighed wearily. "And that's why you came to see me. I'm sorry I didn't trust you before. I should have known I could believe you."

Peter dismissed the apology. "Will you help me?" he asked.

"If I can. Perhaps we can help each other. Where do you want me to start?"

Peter lit a cigarette and leaned back in his chair. "With Yuri's escape. Can you tell me about it?"

"There's so much you don't know," Gena said. "I'll tell you, but you're not going to be happy. It wasn't just Yuri. They all escaped, all six of them together."

"They *what*?"

Peter sat forward, astonished, but the look on Gena's face told him that it was true. For the briefest of moments his spirits rose, a purely instinctive response to something he had wished for so long. Then the feeling vanished as quickly as it began. Yuri escaped and was murdered. To escape was not to be free.

Gena confirmed the worst of what he was thinking: "They're

fugitives, on their own. They escaped from Perm, but they can't get out of the country. They can't survive. They're expecting help that won't come."

Peter turned away.

"That's not all," Gena said. "Maria Petrovskaya is dead. The KGB caught up with her at Khvalinsk, on the River Volga. She was going to escape by tourist steamer, traveling south to the Caspian Sea. But the KGB found her and shot her. There are only four of them now."

Peter felt as if he'd been hit. First Yuri, and now Maria! There was *no* cause for joy, only fury. The old story, the *same* story—people's lives arbitrarily shattered. As long as the six were at Perm, there was hope that their lives could be put back together. Now, even that hope was gone. Steve's words took on new meaning: *Save* the Soviet Six! Peter took a deep breath. The sense of urgency sharpened.

"What happened?" he asked.

"I told you what happened."

"I know. My government murdered your husband. And Maria too, I presume. I'm afraid I need more than that. Details. From the beginning."

"I don't know many details," Gena said. "I've learned what I know secondhand, through my contacts with the dissident underground."

"Whatever you tell me will be more than I know now."

Gena nodded and pulled her legs up into the chair, absently arranging her skirt around them. She began to tell him, softly: "The escape was a CIA operation. It began several months ago when a CIA agent in Moscow contacted the underground about a plan to free the Soviet Six, to bring them out of Perm and help them escape from the country. The CIA needed help, mostly manpower I think, and the underground agreed to cooperate."

"Do you know for a fact that it was the CIA?" Peter asked.

"The man was a known agent. He had worked with the underground on previous assignments. He was a friend. He was trusted."

"All right. Go on."

"I don't really know why the CIA wanted to do it," Gena said. "Perhaps their intentions were good. I only know they succeeded. They used a delivery truck, false papers, that sort of thing, and they brought them out at night, all six of them at once. The absence wasn't noticed until early the next morning, and by that time they were a long way from Perm. The operation had entered its second stage, final escape."

"From the Soviet Union."

"Yes, final escape, to freedom. They spent several days together at a safe house in Moscow, right under the Kremlin's nose. Then they separated, each to travel alone in a different direction, to six different destinations. Border towns. Gagra. Khvalinsk. Four others, thousands of miles apart. The CIA gave them money, papers, clothes; a date and destination. But no one determined how they would travel to those separate points of departure, so that no one would know where to find them. That was part of the CIA plan, to keep them apart until they were free, to make capture six times as unlikely. A good plan, I suspect. It might have worked."

"But something went wrong."

"Oh, yes. Something went wrong." Gena's mouth tightened. "Somewhere between the safe house in Moscow and those six separate destinations, the CIA *changed its mind*."

"I don't understand—"

"Nor do I!" Gena laughed; it was a thin, hollow sound. Then she looked down at her hands. "I don't know what happened to Maria beyond what I've already told you—she was shot just before she boarded the steamer—but I do know what happened at Gagra. I know just what happened there! The CIA was supposed to take control of a government villa in the mountains. It was Yuri's final rendezvous; from there they were going to take him by boat to Turkey, across the Black Sea. But first, the villa. He had to get there on his own...." Gena's voice faded to silence.

"Take your time," Peter said.

She shook her head. "Time won't make telling it easier." She paused for a moment to bring her feelings back under control. Then she went on: "Yuri walked across the Caucasus. He walked hundreds of miles, through the roughest terrain in the country. He *walked*, but he got there in time. There was a sign in the window, a signal for Yuri that meant the villa was safe. Others saw it—members of the underground who were waiting there in the mountains to warn him if there was trouble. But they didn't know there was need for a warning. They were fooled, as he was, because the sign was in place. Yuri walked into a trap."

Peter shook off a chill as the scene came to life in his mind. Yuri, exhausted after an arduous journey, reassured by a prearranged sign. Trusting, approaching the house. Expecting help. Meeting death. Peter shook off the chill, but he still didn't understand what Gena was trying to say.

She leaned forward and put her hands on his arm. "The CIA never was there! Don't you see? The plan was changed without warning. They canceled the operation, and the KGB moved in on it. Yuri and Maria were set up and abandoned, to the *cheka*. To the KGB!"

Peter stared at her as the words washed over him. Was it possible she was right? Was this more than the widow's need to place blame? Was the CIA guilty of murder, by neglect if not commission?

"How can you know that?" he asked.

"The agent in Moscow, the original agent—he as much as said so."

"He *admitted* that the CIA pulled out?"

"He wouldn't admit they were ever *in*. And he made it quite clear: the six were on their own. The underground would have to finish what *it* started. The CIA couldn't help."

"I can't believe it!"

"You can't? Or you can but don't want to?"

Peter sat back, smoking in silence. She was much too close to the truth of what he was thinking. "Why?" he asked finally. "Why abandon their own operation? Why set it up in the first place? Whatever you think of the CIA, they don't believe in murder just for the fun of watching it happen!"

"That's like asking me to explain why children have to suffer," Gena said. "You're looking for sense where reason has no answers. Our governments aren't really much different, it seems, not when they're protecting their own selfish interests or battling each other. They don't care about one man, or six men and women—"

"All right," Peter broke in. "Assume you're right—assume the coldest expedience. There still has to be a reason. On both sides. Is there any doubt about who killed Yuri and Maria?"

"None at all. There were witnesses."

"But why would the KGB *want* to kill them?"

"Why! Who do you think we're talking about? Your CIA might need its justifications, but the KGB doesn't need a reason for killing."

"In this case, I think they do. You said it yourself, Yuri's death won't be reported because the Kremlin doesn't want it known. He was too well known, too popular in the West. His death would be a public-relations problem, as cold as that sounds to us. Even if they tried to claim natural causes, that wouldn't say much for the conditions in the camps. He was a young man when they sent him to Perm. It wouldn't look good at all. So why kill him? Why kill Maria? Why *create* a problem? Why not just send them back to the camp?"

"Perhaps the Kremlin was afraid they would escape again."

Peter shook his head. "Once is highly unlikely, twice impossible. They'd have been guarded day and night. No, there's got to be more to it, something that made Yuri and Maria dangerous as long as they were alive."

Gena glanced away nervously.

"You know what it is, don't you?" Peter said.

"I think so." She turned slowly back to face him. "I think they may have been killed for the same reason you think Steve was, for something they knew or may have known. And it may be the *same* thing. Yuri was trying to smuggle a tape out of the country."

"A tape? What kind of tape?"

"A reel of recording tape. Don't ask me what was on it, I don't know. I only know that Yuri thought it was vital to bring it out—more important than his own escape, or the others'."

"Where did it come from?" Peter asked. "Was it something he brought with him from Perm?"

"No. Someone gave it to him after Perm."

"Who?"

"I don't know. But it wasn't anyone from the CIA. It was someone else, someone separate. The CIA people knew nothing about the tape."

"How do you know about it?"

"From the same friends who told me Yuri was dead. But

they don't know what was on the tape, either. Yuri didn't want them to know. He didn't want *me* to know. He thought it was that dangerous."

"The KGB must think so, too," Peter said. "No wonder Yuri didn't want you to know."

Steve's voice came back to him now, his words on the phone. The fate of the Soviet Six, however tragic, would not account for his language. A major international disaster. But this tape recording might. A tape to be smuggled out of the Soviet Union, so dangerous that Yuri Danchenko felt compelled to protect his wife from it. And Yuri was planning to come here as soon as he was free. He was going to come here to meet Steve.

"We may never know what it was," Peter said. "If Yuri had the tape, then the KGB surely must have taken it from him."

"Yuri didn't have it."

"But you said—"

"Someone gave the tape to him, and he was afraid the KGB would find out. He didn't want to carry the tape himself, so he gave it to one of the others."

"Which one?"

"I don't know. Yuri didn't know. He planned it that way, to protect them all—and, more, to protect the tape."

Gena explained: "While he was still in Moscow, Yuri bought five identical tapes with the money the CIA gave him. That's why he had to walk all the way to Gagra. The new tapes, of course, were all blank. Unused. He took one of them for himself, mixed the real tape in with the rest, and distributed them among the other five. No one knew which one of them drew the original tape."

"And so, if caught," Peter said, "none of them could reveal which one of them had it."

Gena nodded.

"Then there's still a chance the others might escape. There's still a chance one of them might get out with the tape."

"Unless Maria had it."

"Even so, there must be a way we can help them."

Gena's face turned bitter again. "No, Peter, the KGB won't permit it. They were there at Gagra. They were there at Khvalinsk. It's clear they've discovered the six destinations. They will be there each time. The tape won't leave the country. Within a week, all of the six will be dead."

They were trapped! Peter felt sick. *They won't let you stop them! They got me, and they'll get you*! He closed his eyes, passed a hand across them. But the urgency began to revive him again. Old feelings. New ones.

"I won't accept that," he said. "There has to be some way to help them. If only *we* knew where they were going to be!"

"I do know," Gena said quietly. "I know the escape schedule."

Peter looked up sharply. "All of it? Names? Places? Dates?"

"All of it," she said.

"Then for God's sake, give it to me."

"It doesn't exist in writing. I've memorized it. You'll have to memorize it, too."

Gena looked at him for a moment, saying nothing. Then she smiled, and the bitterness started to fade. For the first time tonight, Peter thought he saw hope in her eyes. Hope edged with sadness. She started to recite the information he wanted.

And the first name on the list was Yuri's.

Compton leaned back in his chair without taking his eyes off the data projected onto the screen in front of him. Policy had been decided. Now he was just an observer, sitting beside the Secretary of Defense in the semidarkened silence of what might have been a screening room at MGM or Twentieth Century-Fox. But the picture wasn't a Hollywood film, and the room wasn't a theater. It was the National Military Command Center—the War Room at the Pentagon—where multiple screens traced the movement of ships and aircraft in the Mediterranean and along the Syrian coast, as intelligence sources reported from the area.

Ships in the immediate vicinity showed up as dots on the main screen, each labeled for identification, with U.S. and Soviet forces shown in an overlay pattern. One side screen listed the Soviet capability to reinforce its Mediterranean Fleet; another, the American vessels standing by in the area; still another, extra strike forces available from the air.

A clock on the wall was adjusted to Syrian time. The troops were landing at dawn. The aircraft carrier *Nimitz* was in position, and the landing craft was closing in on their target. The operation was under way, in the hands of the action officers who manned the Command Center—representatives of all four services, an airlift man, intelligence people. All the human resources needed to handle a military crisis. There was also the gold telephone through which anyone here could reach the Commander-in-Chief.

Compton watched with the nervous, undirected energy of a man who was used to control but who no longer had a role in the action. His face was calm, but his stomach was a tight knot. So much was riding on the dots on that screen, now stationary; a soft click, now advancing.

Minutes passed. The dots shifted again. The operation proceeded. A click. Another shift of position.

The Soviet ships were moving!

An air of tension suddenly gripped the room. Compton sat forward, watching intently. Then a new alignment arranged itself across the main screen, and he began to relax.

The Soviet fleet had turned back, was moving away from the area, except for one ship that continued on a direct course toward the harbor at Latakia. Across the room, a young lieutenant ripped a piece of paper out of a telex machine and delivered it to the mission commander, who read the report and looked up.

"The vessel has been identified," he said. "It's the Soviet destroyer *Mukachevo*."

Compton smiled. "That's the ship to follow," he said, and sat back in his chair.

Premier Sukhov had kept his word. He had ordered his fleet to move clear of the area, to stay out of the way, all of it but the *Mukachevo*, which he ordered into the action—because the Syrians had *mined* the harbor at Latakia to prevent an American rescue operation. They had used a plan that was taught to them by Soviet military advisers. And now the Soviets were providing an escort service.

The *Mukachevo* was there to do what Sukhov had promised, to lead the American forces past the mines as they entered the harbor and then bring them—and the *Richmond*—out again. Compton picked up the gold telephone to call the President.

14

PETER WATCHED THE lights of New York fade into darkness as the plane banked to the south, toward Washington. His thoughts were on Steve Katz and Gena Danchenko. On a tape to be smuggled out of the Soviet Union. Murder. A widow's grief. And an international disaster.

Preventable. Steve said so. And now Peter was a step closer to it.

He was also thinking of something he hadn't mentioned to Gena. Korcula. She would know soon enough. If only the escape never happened! Yuri would be alive, and in another few days—maybe two weeks—he and the others would have been released.

Yuri's death was a terrible tragedy, all the more so because it didn't have to happen. And Peter was deeply worried. The Soviets had made a commitment to the Korcula meeting. Then they sent spy ships into Norwegian waters and beefed up their harassment in West Berlin. Their client state seized an American destroyer. And now they were killing dissidents they had promised to free.

Maybe Ravage was right. Maybe Korcula *was* too good to be true!

It was time to talk to Compton.

The four who were left—could they be saved? Was there

time left to save them? Peter's thoughts slipped back to the list he had memorized:

Yuri Danchenko, Gagra, October 1.

Maria Petrovskaya, Khvalinsk, October 2.

Maria's face appeared in his mind, smiling, as she was in the photograph in his files—a distinguished dark-haired woman with bright, intelligent eyes. Then the image changed: she was standing beside Danchenko, between two KGB guards. Her shoulders were straight, like Yuri's. Her back was erect, but her eyes were no longer smiling. They were full of pain. The verdict had been announced; they were on their way to Perm. The image changed once again, and Peter saw armed guards, barbed wire, the faces from the poster on his wall. Imprisonment for life. For nothing!

He pushed the images out of his mind and moved on to the next name on the list.

Nicolai Pinsky . . .

Pinsky was sixty-three, a widower, no children. A military hero who fought for his country at Leningrad and was decorated for his courage. A novelist whose work was highly regarded by objective critics around the world. Those were the things Pinsky had been. Now he was no one. His books had been banished at home, his medals retrieved, his heroism revoked. His name had been deleted from the pages of Soviet history. He was no one, just a name on a list.

Nicolai Pinsky, Tallin, October 3.

Tomorrow. So little time!

Then Peter figured the time change and closed his eyes. His shoulders sagged, and the ache rose again in his throat. *No* time. It was too late! Pinsky couldn't be saved.

In Tallin, October 3 was *today.*

Nicolai Pinsky stepped out of the shadows that surrounded the last house in Kohtu Street, on the hill of Dom Castle, overlooking the city of Tallin. The first daylight was his signal—the first hint of gray light as it touched the church spires rising up from the town below. The ruins of the castle were behind him here, where the hill dropped away to clusters of tiled roofs spreading north to the bay, to the Gulf of Finland and the Baltic Sea. To Stockholm. To freedom.

He paused there, looking out to sea through the dark mist that would dissipate with the rising sun. There wasn't much time. A fishing boat was waiting for him in the harbor, where sharp rocks lay submerged beneath the water's surface. A difficult port in the bright light of day, only more so now, before dawn.

But treacherous rocks hardly mattered. Pinsky had survived hidden dangers far more threatening. And he had no choice about the timing of his escape. The boat would sail before the sun broke into the sky. It was time to make contact now.

He stepped forward, toward the small platform that jutted out from the hill at the end of the street. His rendezvous. From here he would be seen, then guided down to the lower town, to the boat in the harbor, across the sea to Stockholm.

Suddenly he turned back. His name! He had heard his name called from the darkness behind him. A whisper, harsh against sleeping silence. He heard it. Or, in his exhaustion, did he only imagine he had?

"Nicolai!"

"Who's there?"

A figure appeared from the deep shadows on the far side of the street. A figure, a face. It was *Lev*—Lev Zhdanov, from the underground!

"Get back!" Lev called. "It's a trap!"

Pinsky stood where he was, confused by fatigue and conflicting directions. Then he stumbled forward—not back toward the house where he'd hidden himself through the night, but forward. Toward Lev.

"No, go back! Get out of—"

A sharp whining sound split the silence. Lev uttered a brief cry as the bullet struck the side of his head, sent him reeling back into darkness. Silence settled again on the hillside.

Pinsky froze where he was as the truth of the moment came clear. A trap! *Get back! It's a trap!* Lev had tried to warn him, but the warning had come too late. For Lev . . . and for him. Pinsky knew his life was over. He knew he would not escape.

But he could get rid of the tape. His hand found the reel in his pocket and heaved it away with the last strength he could summon. It wasn't enough.

The bullet struck from behind, caught him between the

shoulders. He stumbled, his eyes on the tape as it rose in the air—a few feet, no more. He saw it fall, heard it clatter against the concrete. He had tried and failed. He could do no more. He collapsed on the pavement beside it.

15

COMPTON WASN'T HOME when Peter got back from New York, and he hadn't answered Peter's urgent message to phone him. Now, the next morning, Peter knew why.

They'd sent *troops* into Latakia!

Peter stared at the TV set as the news story unfolded. Then he sat back on the bed, his feelings caught between shock and enormous relief. The captain and crew of the *Richmond* had been rescued in a daring military raid on the Syrian coast. The ship had been recovered and was en route now to another, friendlier port.

"A risky operation..." the newscaster was saying.

Risky! It was downright rash! A terrific gamble.

But it worked. The mission was over, successful. U.S. prestige was once again intact, with only minor casualties. One crew member and six Marines had been killed. It could have been worse. Far worse.

The President came on then, smiling broadly—as well he might. He had pulled off a dangerous coup. He had saved American lives and possibly averted new conflict in the Middle East. His personal popularity would rise precipitously in the polls; more importantly, so would his influence in the world.

Compton was nowhere to be seen, but Peter knew he was there one way or another. Masterminding. The President would never attempt this kind of maneuver without Compton's knowledge and blessing.

Then the scene shifted to a State Department briefing room where a spokesman Peter knew slightly was fielding reporters' questions with aplomb. Rumors and accusations, the meat of the Washington press corps. Stories had sprung up overnight from Damascus, that Soviet ships had been involved in the rescue. There were charges by opponents of the administration that the operation was ill-considered and might have escalated into a major confrontation. Peter smiled. You couldn't win! On the one side, collusion. On the other, defiance. It was all what you wanted to see.

There was no truth in any of this, the spokesman replied firmly. The seizure of the *Richmond* was incidental to the client relationship between Syria and the USSR.

"Is it true," someone asked, "that the Soviet government intervened with Damascus on our behalf, urging the release of the ship?"

The spokesman considered his answer. Then he said: "The Soviets weren't involved in any way, with the seizure of the ship or its rescue. To suggest the contrary is only political rhetoric and unhelpful at this time, given the sensitivity of negotiations preceding the most important Soviet-American summit conference since—"

Peter's smile faded as he shut off the TV. Korcula. Where did the Soviets stand? Cooperation or defiance? Why were they killing the dissidents they said they would free? One crisis was past, but another one loomed ahead. Steve's crisis. More threatening for its vague shape.

He was heading for the bathroom to shave when the telephone rang.

It was Compton. "I just got your message," he said. "What's so important?"

"I don't want to tell you on the phone. When can I see you?"

"Have you had breakfast?"

"Not yet."

"Then come over now."

* * *

Nicole was carrying her coat when she opened the front door for Peter. She smiled. "Daddy told me you were coming. I'm glad you got here before I had to leave."

"You can't stay?"

"No, I've got a class. Then I'm going back to the library to do some more research for you. I spent half the night in the reference room looking for the origins of Marco Polo."

"Did you find anything?"

"Not to speak of. I'm sorry. Not much is known about his early life. What we know comes from his own writing, and that began with his travels. But I haven't finished yet. Will you be in your office later if I have anything to tell you?"

Peter smiled. "Or even if you only want to say hello."

"Are things better today?" she asked.

"I don't know." Peter sighed. "I've got a lot to tell you. I saw Gena Danchenko last night."

"Is she here?"

"In New York. I flew up there so fast, I didn't take time to call you. But it was an important visit. I learned a lot. It's not good news."

"Can you tell me now?"

"Later. Right now I've got to see your father."

"He's in the dining room, waiting for you."

Peter took her coat and held it while she slipped her arms into the sleeves. He kissed her and then headed for the stairs.

Compton was sitting at the head of the dining-room table, backlit by the morning sun as it filtered through the curtains behind him. He said nothing as Peter walked into the room, merely nodded to the empty chair beside him.

An extra place was already set with Haviland china, with crystal and silverware. Peter smiled to himself as he thought of the breakfast he would have had without this invitation—instant coffee out of a mug that was the last of the set, cornflakes in a bowl that didn't match.

But Compton had Mrs. Ross, who could not only cook but also knew when to disappear. She was probably in the kitchen now, with the connecting door firmly closed, ready to appear if needed, but never in the way. Mrs. Ross had been with Compton for years. Her discretion was beyond doubt.

"You had a busy night," Peter said. "Congratulations."

Compton's expression dismissed the compliment as irrelevant. "It was a long, nervous night. But a good one."

Peter helped himself to coffee and a plate of eggs and bacon. "I heard on the news that the Soviets weren't involved."

"Officially, they weren't, but the truth is, we couldn't have done it without them." Compton chuckled softly, remembering. "They gave us an escort past the mines in the harbor—in and out, home again. No interference. That, by the way, is not for publication."

Nor even for repeating. Peter wasn't really surprised. Compton had already told him that the Soviets wanted to help. Now he understood the rumors out of Damascus, that Soviet ships were involved in the rescue. And he understood why the State Department denied them. The Soviet government couldn't afford to have it known publicly, at home, that it turned its back on a client. Cooperation could be easily misinterpreted as weakness, backing down to the threat of U.S. strength.

"But I don't think you came here to talk about the rescue," Compton said. "What's on your mind?"

Peter took a drink of his coffee and hesitated a moment before he looked up. "Do you really think Korcula is going to happen?" he asked.

Compton studied his face. "I take it that's not an idle question."

"No."

"Then maybe you'd better tell me why you have to ask."

Peter wasn't sure where to start. What to say. How to say it. Never in his life had he doubted Compton's judgment. And yet, isn't that what he was doing now? Questioning?

Doubting?

No, he was here to give information Compton didn't have. To give information and get some answers back. He shook the doubt off, along with his own feelings. Compton was his friend, but he was also the Secretary of State. And Peter was a professional. He was trained to report the gist of a problem rapidly and concisely. The problem and his source; then the details could unravel.

"I saw Gena Danchenko last night," he said, "and she gave me some extremely disturbing news about the Soviet Six.

They've escaped from Perm and are trying to get out of the country, but the KGB is heading them off. Gena's sources are certain that Danchenko and Maria Petrovskaya have been killed and that the others will be."

"Oh, Lord." Compton's eyes filled with pain. He turned away.

"She says they're being killed because CIA agents who set up the escape in the first place have abandoned them to the KGB."

Compton looked back sharply. "What the hell are you talking about?"

"A CIA operation to free the Soviet Six."

"You're kidding!"

"I wish I were."

Compton's jaw tightened. Anger flared in his eyes. "Christ almighty, I don't believe it! I have an agreement with the CIA—no moves against the Soviet Union without my direct approval."

"I'm not saying it's true," Peter said. "Gena could be wrong, though her sources have always been accurate in the past. And anyway, she's not the only person who seems to know about this. Do you remember Steve Katz?"

Compton frowned, as if the name were familiar but he couldn't quite place it.

Peter helped him: "He was director of Freedom International's Washington office. And a friend of mine. You met him once at my place."

"Oh, yes, I remember now." The frown deepened. "He was killed, wasn't he—in that explosion over on the hill?"

Peter nodded. "That's part of the story. I was there. And the last thing he said before he died was, '*Remember the Soviet Six.*'"

Compton's anger gave way to interest. He said nothing, but his silence invited more.

Peter told him about the phone call he'd had from Steve. "He said it was urgent, even told me to come after dark. He said he wanted me to help him prevent a major international disaster."

Peter glanced at Compton's face, expecting skepticism. Steve's words, alone, sounded melodramatic. It was hard to explain to someone who hardly knew him why they deserved to be listened to.

But Compton wasn't looking skeptical at all. His face was thoughtful, his eyes interested. "What, exactly, did he tell you?"

Peter repeated the phone conversation as well as he could remember it. And then Steve's last words. "He told me to investigate Marco Polo. And to remember the Soviet Six."

Compton raised an eyebrow. Doubt crept into his voice. "Marco Polo?"

"That's what he said."

"Do you know what he meant?"

"No."

"You're sure? You have no idea?"

Peter shook his head. "None at all. But obviously he knew something about the Soviet Six. Something he wanted me to know. Then, when I talked to Gena and heard what she had to say . . . well, you can see why I think it's all the same thing."

Compton nodded. He agreed.

"You're the only person who can find out what's true," Peter said.

"I intend to. I want you to tell me everything Gena Danchenko told you. Everything. Don't leave anything out."

Peter told him—about the CIA agent in Moscow, the escape from Perm, the six separate destinations. About Gagra and Khvalinsk. Then he recited the list he had memorized: names, places, dates.

"Wait a minute," Compton said. "Let me get this down." He took a small file card from his pocket and made notes as Peter repeated what Gena had told him.

"If the pattern runs true," Peter said, "it's too late now to save Pinsky. It may be too late to save Subolev."

Compton looked grim as he studied the notes he had made. "It may be too late to save any of them," he said.

"You can't mean that."

"Well, look at this—the last is five days from now! It may take me that long just to find out what has happened."

"Arthur, I *know* you."

"And you think I'm a miracle worker."

"What I think doesn't matter. I know about your priorities.

I have good reason to know. And I know you have influence—"

"Oh, sure!" Compton laughed dryly as he struck the card with the back of his hand. "Look at the influence I've got out at Langley! We're supposed to be in a period of mutual non-aggression. If the CIA was involved in this and the Soviets know about it, which it seems they do, then we have a very big problem."

Which brought Peter back to his original question: Korcula. "Is there any difference," he asked, "between this and what they're doing in Norway and Berlin? Is that mutual nonaggression?"

"There's a very big difference. I know what they're doing in Norway and Berlin. They're flexing muscle, just as I've said, for the benefit of their own people. The Soviets may not be allowed to speak out against their own leaders, but that doesn't mean the Kremlin can do what it pleases. They don't just have opposition over there. They've got enemies, on the inside. If you remember, Nikita Khrushchev got off an airplane in Moscow one day and was met by the chairman of the KGB."

"Are you sure that's all it is?" Peter asked. "Just muscle?"

"The Soviets have been absolutely candid. It's all been spelled out."

"What, Norway and Berlin? They're *part* of the preliminary agreements?"

"Not specifically, but Foreign Minister Miloslavsky talked to me even then about their need to deal from a show of strength. You're going to have to trust me. This is one area, Peter, where you're just going to have to trust me."

"I do trust you," Peter said. "God knows I trust you. But damn it, I'm worried. *Why* are they killing the dissidents? They promised to *free* them!"

"That, I don't know," Compton admitted.

"And it worries me, too. I'll talk to Voloshin. Hell, I'll go to Moscow if I have to. I'm going to find out what they're doing." He pushed his plate away; the eggs had turned as cold as his appetite. "Did Gena Danchenko tell you anything else?"

"Yes, she did." Peter took out his cigarettes and lit one. He hadn't mentioned the tape yet, on purpose. He had wanted to appeal to Compton's best motives, to make it clear that the dissidents were in danger. Now he would tell him the rest. "She said Yuri was trying to smuggle a tape out of the country."

Compton's face froze for an instant, and Peter knew why. It was possible that the dissidents were actually doing what they had been accused of at their trial—compromising state secrets. Espionage, however well justified. And if they were, that complicated Compton's position enormously.

Compton leaned forward. "What kind of tape?"

"I don't know much about it," Peter said. "Gena doesn't know what it is, only that someone gave it to Yuri and that he considered it more important than his own escape." He explained Yuri's ruse, the five blank tapes, the blind distribution of them.

"Then any of them could have it," Compton said.

"And all of them are in danger, at least until it's found."

Compton groaned. He sat still for a moment, then leaned back in his chair as his eyes scanned the room—the crown moldings, the French cupboards, the fall flowers arranged in a cut-glass bowl. "I'm glad you told me," he said finally. "I can't tell you what I'm going to do, because I don't know yet. But I want you to forget it."

Peter drew on his cigarette. "I can't do that," he said.

"If you can't forget it, then at least don't worry about it." Compton looked at Peter, and his face softened. "You look pretty worn out. Maybe you should take some time off."

"Now?" Peter was astonished.

"Why not now? Ravage seems to have things well under control. Go somewhere. Get some rest and meet us at Korcula."

It was an appealing idea. Peter could see himself on a beach, with Nicole, in a place where reality faded into a stretch of white sand running down to a blue sea. Then an image broke through unbidden. A white-sand beach like the one at Gagra, at the edge of the Soviet world.

"I don't think so," he said.

"Think about it. You've been through a lot these last two days, and you've got a lot just ahead. You'll want to be fresh for the conference."

"If there is a conference."

Compton smiled reassuringly. "There will be," he said. "You said you trusted me. Trust me to handle this."

Peter nodded without committing himself. "Will you let me know what you find out?" he asked.

Compton's face changed once again. A veil dropped over his eyes. The expression was all too familiar to Peter.

"I will if I can," Compton said. "It depends on what I find out."

16

COMPTON SAW PETER out at the front door and walked back to the library. A button worked the bookshelves; he made his way down the hidden stairs, through a narrow corridor, past the wine cellar and exercise room, into his private office.

He bypassed the CIA switchboard with a number that rang straight into the director's office.

"Yes?"

There was no need for caution. The phones at both ends of the line were as secure as any telephones in Washington. Nor was there a need for amenities. Compton was not in the mood.

"Is it true you people staged an operation to free the Soviet Six?" he demanded.

There was silence at the other end of the phone.

"*Well?*"

The CIA director cleared his throat. "It's possible—"

"And you didn't *tell* me about it?"

Compton's face turned red. He was outraged. "Don't give me possible! I want a complete report. Today. In writing. And don't leave anything out, including the fact that at least two of the six are dead."

"What did you say?"

"You heard me," Compton said. "If you don't know what I'm talking about, then I suggest you find out. And let me know. I want it all. So, by the way, will the President."

He hung up without another word. Christ, it *was* true! He dialed the phone again. This time, he called the White House.

Levitsky read the latest report from Dmitri:

Lucas' secretary had been to the State Department archives, asking for files on the Soviet Six. She had taken them back to her office, presumably for him.

And Lucas had had lunch with Compton's daughter. The agent who observed them in the restaurant had not been able to get close enough to hear what they said. But after she left, Compton's daughter went to the library at Georgetown University, where she put her own research aside to read about Marco Polo.

Another report would follow soon.

In the meantime, this was enough. Levitsky smiled and picked up the phone to arrange another meeting with Miloslavsky.

A steward in a blue blazer with a presidential patch on the pocket appeared to take Compton's coat. His manner was entirely gracious; he might have been working the White House, or Buckingham Palace, for thirty years or more. There was nothing military in his appearance, beyond the spit and polish of his black leather shoes, nothing to suggest that he was a junior Air Force officer with a prestigious assignment: the VIP compartments aboard the President's plane.

Compton settled himself into a beige armchair that made first-class seats on a normal plane seem cramped; he was facing the rear of the plane. The forward wall behind him adjoined the First Lady's compartment, beyond which lay the President's office. There were no warnings flashed to signal the plane's departure—no seat-belt signs, no smoking bans—only the feeling of movement as the jet roared down the runway, picking up speed for liftoff. Nor was there any waiting in line for position. In a moment, they were in the air.

The compartment where Compton was sitting was reserved for the President's special guests; staff and press were sitting aft in a separate section. One other guest shared the compartment and was already ensconced in his chair, reading from his briefcase, by the time Compton arrived. He was a Pennsylvania congressman whose district included wherever it was the President was appearing today. Compton spoke to him briefly but did not explain why he, too, was en route to Harrisburg, Philadelphia, wherever.

The reason was simple. Compton didn't care where the plane was going. He was here for one reason, because the President was here. And Compton had to see him.

He plucked a grape from the fruit bowl on the table at his elbow and absorbed himself in his own briefcase reading.

"Mr. Secretary . . . ?"

Compton looked up as a different steward appeared in the doorway. This one was wearing a gray suit, which signaled an even more prestigious assignment: he was a personal steward to the President.

"Will you come with me?" he said.

Compton followed him out into the corridor that ran along one side of the forward section, where two Air Force officers manned the computer console that was the plane's communications center. The First Lady's door was closed—Compton didn't know if she was even aboard—but the door to the President's compartment was standing open.

Compton entered and closed it behind him.

The President glanced up from his desk. His face was apprehensive. The Secretary of State was a frequent passenger aboard *Air Force One*, but he'd never before demanded a seat without regard for the plane's destination.

"We've got a problem," Compton said.

"So I gathered. What is it?"

Compton dropped into a chair. He leaned back, brought his hands together, pressed two fingers against pursed lips. His eyes never left the President. His voice was calm. "The Soviet half of the Korcula tape may be missing."

The President's face went pale. He stared at Compton across his desk.

"And that may not be the worst of it," Compton added. "Peter Lucas knows about Marco Polo. It can only be a matter of days until he finds out what it means."

17

THE CIA REPORT was lying on Compton's desk when Peter walked into his office. It was late in the day; the sky was dark on the other side of the windows. Lamplight glowed softly against the mahogany paneling and cast shadows across Compton's face, etching out lines Peter never noticed before.

Peter sat down. He knew Compton had been out of the office all day but didn't ask why. He was here because the report had arrived, because Compton had read it and called him. The envelope lay in a circle of light from the desk lamp, its seal broken, its contents closed inside.

"Can you tell me what it says?" Peter asked.

"Not everything," Compton told him. "This report is so classified, we don't have a category for it. But I'll tell you what I can, and I hope I can ease your mind."

Peter wasn't cheered. Compton's words didn't match his expression, the lines of worry, the anger that seemed to be lying beneath the appearance of self-control.

"The only thing that would ease my mind," Peter said, "would be if you told me that none of it ever happened."

"I'm sorry. It did happen. The Soviet Six have escaped from Perm. Danchenko and Maria Petrovskaya are dead, and so is Nicolai Pinsky. The report confirms it."

Peter sank back in the chair. "Then everything Gena told me is true."

"Not quite. There's one important difference between Gena's account and this one. The escape was conceived and controlled by others. The CIA was only giving assistance."

"And you believe that?"

"Yes."

"You're going to take the agency's word for it? For God's sake, Arthur, Gena would laugh if I told her that. She'd say it was perfectly obvious. Of course the CIA would minimize its involvement. And, frankly, I think I'd be with her."

Compton sighed. "I don't doubt Gena's sincerity," he said, "but that doesn't make her right. That doesn't make her sources right. God knows, there are politics in these underground organizations. Not all of these people are motivated by a good cause; some of them just don't fit anywhere else. That's something I know about." His hand came to rest on the envelope. "And anyway, it isn't a question of what I believe. It's all documented here."

"So what? The CIA manufactures documents every day."

"They didn't have time to manufacture these. Take my word for it. Trust me. The CIA did not initiate the escape operation, and to that extent is not responsible for it."

"To that extent!" Peter was shocked by the tone of Compton's voice. "Three people have been killed, and you're talking about the *extent* of our responsibility? What difference does it make? There are three more to be saved."

"It makes a very big difference." Compton picked up a paperweight from his desk, a small golden globe suspended in polished crystal. One world, a piece of infinity. The paperweight had been a gift from Voloshin. Compton looked at it without seeing, as he absently ran his fingers over its surface. "I have something to tell you in absolute confidence," he said. "I'm depending on you not to say anything about it, certainly not to Gena Danchenko."

Peter nodded, but he felt a new sense of apprehension. Never before had Compton stated the need for confidence; it had always been assumed between them. "Of course. What is it?"

Compton leaned back in his chair, briefly lost in his own thoughts. Then he turned back to Peter. "I believe I know what your friend Steve was trying to tell you. Obviously he knew about the escape. He was looking ahead to the position it would put me in, to the conflict I'm facing now—to something which, for him, would be nothing less than an international disaster. He wanted you to help him prevent the international failure of Korcula, by a choice forced on me from the Soviet side."

Then Ravage was right! Peter sat forward. "Are you saying that the Soviets never *meant* to let Korcula happen?"

"Not *the* Soviets, only some of them. I've suspected it for a long time." Compton's jaw tightened in anger; his hand closed around the paperweight as if to hide it from view. "I've told you Premier Sukhov has enemies inside his own government, people who disapprove of what we're trying to do, but I've never told you how strong they are, how committed they are. I think *they* planned this escape, involving both the CIA and the underground, playing them off against each other. That's what Steve Katz knew. He was trying to warn you that Korcula is in grave danger."

Too good to be true. Peter looked down at his hands; they were damp with perspiration, and yet he felt cold inside. "Who are they?" he asked.

"That's the trouble, I don't know."

Suddenly Peter realized what Compton meant by *conflict.* The conflict he was facing. An impossible choice! He looked up. "Arthur!"

"I don't know if I can save the dissidents."

"You *have* to!"

"Do I? Is it that simple? Then you tell me which is more important. Three human beings who have been denied every justice, who will probably be killed if I don't intervene? Or the thousands like them for whom Korcula means freedom? Which? You tell me."

Peter stared at him for a moment, then turned away. "I don't know."

"I don't either. I wish to God I did."

Compton put the paperweight down. A soft buzz sounded from the panel on his desk. He flipped the switch on his intercom, and his secretary's voice came through from the outer office. "It's the call you've been waiting for."

"Thank you." Compton picked up the phone. "Yes?" He listened a moment, then nodded. "Fine. I'll be there at eight o'clock." He hung up and looked back at Peter. "That's good news, anyway. Voloshin wants to talk."

"Good news? Can you trust him?"

"Absolutely. Andrei Voloshin is as committed to Korcula as I am. He and I will work something out."

"To save the conference."

"Yes." Compton leaned back and studied Peter's face. "I have one more thing to tell you," he said, "and this, too, must be kept in absolute confidence. I don't intend to make that choice. I intend to avoid it."

"How?"

"By handing the fate of the dissidents back to the CIA."

Peter sat where he was, not moving, but a smile began to spread across his face as he looked at the man on the other side of the desk, a man who had risked his own life countless times to save a few dozen children he didn't know. In those days, he had nothing more to risk. Now there was so much more.

But Compton hadn't changed. Three people still mattered. He would save them, as he'd saved the others before.

Compton smiled back. "Now, get out of here," he said. "This meeting never took place."

A fierce wind swept down off the hills surrounding the horseshoe harbor. The *nord* of Baku—it had plagued the town for centuries, blowing up without warning, forcing ships aground on the rocky shore of the bay. Fyodor Subolev had no protection against the wind, beyond his tan-colored coat, which he pulled closer around him as the wind pressed him back against the base of the tower. The Kiz-Kalasyi, where a maiden had long ago thrown herself into the sea, seeking death as release from a marriage to her own father.

Subolev turned his head so that he could look up at the hills. The wind buffeted his face with a stinging force, and tears welled up in his eyes. He was born here in the province of Azerbaidzhan; he had lived here in Baku. The *nord* was a memory of his own distant boyhood, a time that seemed as

long past as the plight of the tower maiden. It had been nearly
forty years since he left here to take up his studies in Moscow,
economics and history, to become Professor Subolev. Distinguished scholar. Economist. He stayed on.

Because Professor Subolev *believed* in the Soviet system.
Communism was the only way to end economic injustice. It
would spread throughout the world, as inevitably as the *nord*
struck—not by force, but by nature. Because it was fair. Because it was right. But Professor Subolev did not believe in
imperialism. Or tyranny.

Now he wondered how his life would have been changed
if he'd never left Baku. He'd have studied here, at one of the
branches of the Azerbaidzhan Academy. Or perhaps he'd have
gone to work in the oilfields. He might have married, had
children, settled into one of the tiny flat-roofed houses in the
castle district. He'd have been inside on a dark, windblown
night like this one, and not here, alone, with his back pressed
against the harsh stone of the tower, waiting to flee from the
country. But he still would have been a victim of the Soviet
communist system, where spiritual needs, like freedom, were
looked upon as irrelevant—or, worse, as a threat to the state.

Subolev had lost faith. He no longer believed that an economic system could have much effect on injustice. Only politics
mattered. Politics and power. He had no taste for these. He
had only wanted to leave. Quietly. To take up another life in
another part of the world. But the Soviet system had refused
to let him go.

And now he had come full circle. He was back in the town
of his boyhood, back in the curve of the hills that rose up from
Baku like a giant amphitheater. He had roamed those hills until
he knew every path, every crevice, every shrub and sapling.
The streets leading to them he knew like the lines of his face.
He knew *people* here, and he felt a rush of affection. A warm
feeling, gentle, like a breeze off the bay in summer.

But there was no breeze tonight. There was only the *nord*,
a savage, howling fury. There was sadness for a life long past.
Affection belonged to the years of his boyhood; it had vanished
with other illusions. He knew people here, but none that he
dared to trust.

The warm feeling passed, was replaced by something quite

different—a calm assurance that none of this mattered now. His journey was finished. He had come home. And he knew, somehow, that he wouldn't be leaving again.

A muezzin stepped onto the balcony of the Sinik Kala, the oldest minaret in the old town of Baku. He greeted the wind as a welcome accomplice, as he welcomed the cloud-covered darkness of night. He wouldn't need a silencer, with nature on his side.

The submachine gun was hidden among the folds of his sacred garment. The muezzin withdrew it now. He snapped the metal stock into place and raised it against his shoulder. Subolev, waiting below, came into focus. He might have been no more than five feet distant, an easy target. Motionless. Defenseless.

The muezzin didn't hesitate. He adjusted his aim, squeezed the trigger, and loosed a round of gunfire into the wind. Subolev stayed where he was, flattened against the tower, held in place by the *nord* of Baku, but a dark stain spread across the front of his tan-colored coat. He stayed upright for several seconds, until finally his knees gave way and his body began to slide down the wall. Slowly he sank to the ground.

A moment passed without movement. Then a uniformed man emerged from an alley below. The wind receded briefly, as if to his command. He strode across the open space to the tower, bent over the body. Then he shot a flashlight signal back toward the minaret.

The muezzin dismantled his weapon as he made his way down the steps and disappeared into the darkness.

The man from Department V searched through Subolev's pockets. Then he ran his hands over the body until he found a thickness at the hem of the bloodstained coat. He didn't bother to look for the place where Subolev had inserted the tape; he simply tore open the lining and retrieved it.

He stood up and flashed another signal into the night. An engine came to life, the noise of it barely audible over the wind. A moment later, a black Chaika pulled up beside him, and two men climbed out.

"Do you want us to wait for you?" one of them asked.

"You have only one job, to dispose of the traitor. I have my own transportation."

The two men lifted Subolev into the Chaika and drove away.

The man from Department V watched them go. Then he turned back to the tower and fitted a key into the padlock on the door. Inside, he removed the small tape recorder from the coat of his uniform. His face was tense, his eyes cold as he slipped the tape into place.

He waited. Then a smile spread slowly across his face. A shrill whistle emerged from the machine; it descended to a steady, low-pitched hum. The man smiled, though his eyes remained cold. It was a victory smile. Smug. And cruel for its high cost. Danchenko, Petrovskaya, and Pinsky—they mattered no more than the blank tapes they had died for. Subolev was no longer his concern. There was one thought in his mind. He had done it. He had succeeded.

The Korcula tape had been found.

But there wasn't time now for gloating. He pocketed the tape and quickly assembled the parts of his radio set. It took him no more than five minutes to send his brief message in code. He was finished here. He was ready to return to Moscow with the tape.

Then suddenly, from higher up in the tower came a flash of light—a spurt of blue flame and a soft rattling sound, a counterpoint to the wind. The man from Department V spun back with the force of impact as the bullets exploded inside him. He spun back and collapsed on the floor.

The smile was gone. In its place were shock and terror. He died as he lived, without pity. Without knowing who killed him. Or why.

_18_

IT WAS LATE afternoon in Washington by the time Nicole got home from the university. She dropped her coat on a chair in the entrance hall and walked back to the library, where she picked up the phone and called Peter's office.

Not that she had anything really to tell him. Marco Polo's birth, his early years, simply were never recorded; his origins were lost in the passing of time. Half a dozen biographers agreed he was born in Venice, in the middle of the thirteenth century—two bits of information that were both quite obvious to anyone with the slightest memory for history. Beyond that, nothing. Whatever it was Steve had meant was there or it didn't exist. Nicole had exhausted every resource she could think of. There couldn't be anything more.

And yet there had to be. Something less obvious, something Steve wanted Peter to know.

His secretary answered Peter's phone.

"Hi, Mary. It's Nicole. Is Peter there?"

"Sorry, he's in with your father."

"Oh."

"Do you want to leave a message?"

"It's nothing important. Just tell him I called and to call me when he can."

"I'll tell him."

Nicole hung up and glanced at the mail Mrs. Ross had left neatly stacked on the desk. Nothing of much interest. Most of it for her father. Two envelopes for her—a letter from a friend in Cairo and something official from the Department of State.

She read the letter first, felt a twinge of jealousy for her friend, just back from an expedition to the caves of Khirbat Qumran, and resolved to answer it soon. Then she picked up the other envelope and tore it open. Inside were her papers for the Korcula conference: departure information; a schedule of meetings, official dinners, receptions; a data sheet describing the local climate and customs; her hotel assignment; official identification. All routine and in order.

She started to put the papers back in the envelope, when suddenly something she'd passed over too quickly connected in her mind. What was *this*? Coincidence? Not likely.

She turned to the bookshelves, glanced through the titles, and chose one. A sense of excitement grew inside her as she scanned the table of contents. A familiar feeling, the excitement of discovery.

She found the correct page: the Dalmatian coast. Of course. Of *course*! It all fit. There was a picture of Korcula, medieval stone buildings with red-tiled roofs. An island inhabited since the fourth century B.C., a port city down through the ages. Korcula wasn't always a part of the communist world, though it had known domination.

Nicole snapped the book shut and called Mary back. This time she left a different message for Peter. Then she picked up her coat and hurried out again.

Eleanor Benjamin, Gena's hostess, had been head of the International Relations Department at Columbia University for more than a year, and she still viewed the job with ambiguous feelings. She was glad to have more control over curriculum and other academic issues, and she didn't object to this large corner office. But she regretted having less time for teaching, for her students, that her time was too much taken by minor administrative problems—like the one presented by the man sitting on the other side of her desk.

"I understand you're looking for information about someone who used to work here," she said.

The man was perhaps seventy and well dressed. He spoke excellent English but with a heavy accent.

"As a matter of fact, I'm looking for a relative," he said. "I've been trying to find her for nearly forty years."

Eleanor raised an eyebrow, inviting him to explain.

"My name is Ravitch, and I come from Warsaw. I won't waste your time explaining what conditions were like in Poland during the war. I'm sure you know."

"Yes, of course. Many families were separated."

"My own family was killed."

Eleanor did a quick mental calculation. He'd have been in his thirties then. A wife, perhaps, and children. "I'm sorry," she said.

Ravitch smiled. "I only mention it to help explain why I'm here. I had a young cousin who was never accounted for after the war was over, and I've never given up hope that she might have survived. If she did, I think she would be living here in America, and possibly in New York. She'd be grown now, of course, middle-aged. And if she ever married, then I don't even know her name."

"What makes you think she would be living here?"

"She was born here. Her father and mother immigrated to this country; they were only visiting Poland when the invasion came." Ravitch shrugged. "I have nothing but rumors to go on—some people think they saw her after the war. But I've searched every corner of Poland. If she lived, I think she must have come home."

Eleanor looked at him across the top of her desk, which was cluttered with paperwork waiting for her attention. She was fascinated by the story, fascinated and touched. But she didn't understand why he had come to her. "Is there some way you think I can help you?" she asked.

"I hope so. As I told your secretary, I'm looking for someone who used to work here. His name is the same as mine."

"Ravitch?" Eleanor frowned. "We had a Professor *Ravage* . . ."

"It's the same name anglicized. My cousins changed their name to Ravage when they came here. Others did the same thing; it wasn't uncommon. But I keep hoping I'll find someone someday who knows my cousin and can tell me where she is."

"I see."

"Did you know this Professor Ravage?"

Eleanor leaned forward, smiling. "I know him quite well," she said. "In fact, this is all rather remarkable. It's possible that you've come to the right place."

Eleanor poured herself a glass of sherry and sat down across from Gena. She kicked off her shoes, wiggled her toes to relax them. It had been a long day. She was glad to be home. "Have you heard anything from Peter Lucas?" she asked.

Gena took a drink from her own glass. "Not yet, but I'm sure I will."

"Well, I hope he can do something."

Gena shrugged. "I don't hope anymore. Then I'm not disappointed."

Eleanor nodded sympathetically. It was no wonder, given what Gena had been through. "Speaking of Peter," she said, "an odd thing happened today. Rather sad, actually."

"What was that?"

"A man named Ravitch came to see me. He's Polish. He had some American cousins who were visiting Warsaw when Hitler invaded and weren't able to get out again. They were killed, all of them except, perhaps, the daughter of the family— Sarah. A child of ten. She may have been killed too, but there was no record of it, and Ravitch is still looking for her."

Gena shrugged. So many stories, all alike, all with the same ending. Whole families killed, while others just disappeared. And yet hope remained.

"Why did he come to see you?" she asked.

"He wanted to know how to reach a man who used to teach in my department. Daniel Ravage. The name Ravage, he said, is a common anglicization of Ravitch; it was his cousins' name. When he told me that, I was sure that he'd finally traced someone who could help him. Because you see, *Dan's* parents immigrated here from Warsaw, and *they* were caught on a visit there with their children, Dan and a younger sister. They were all killed except Dan, but the stories were so much alike . . ."

Eleanor lowered her eyes as her words faded into unspoken disappointment.

"I gather he wasn't the right person," Gena said.

"No, though it turned out that Sarah did have a brother

named Daniel, and he would have been about the same age. But they're not the same. They can't be. The cousin, Daniel Ravage, was killed; Ravitch saw it happen. I felt so sorry for him. I was sure he'd finally stumbled into something, possibly even a relative he didn't know he had. I'm afraid I gave him a moment of false hope."

Gena finished her drink. "What does that have to do with Peter?" she asked.

"Well, nothing really. I was only reminded because it was Dan Ravage who told Peter you were staying here with me."

"Peter knows him?"

"Dan is at the State Department now. He's a specialist in Soviet affairs."

"I see." Gena shook off a chill, an aftereffect of the story. There was something wrong. She sensed it, but she didn't know what it was.

Eleanor noticed the change in Gena's face. "What's the matter?" she asked.

"I don't know. A feeling I had. It's nothing." She picked up her glass and started across the room. Then she suddenly stopped where she stood. A thought broke through from her past, a piece of knowledge filed away like so many others like it. Was it possible? Or was she starting to see things where they didn't exist?

She turned back to Eleanor. "What does Dan Ravage do at the State Department?"

"He was on the Soviet desk, but now he works in human rights. As a matter of fact, he's in charge of the arrangements for the Korcula conference."

Gena's face tightened. "Is Peter close to him?" she asked.

"I don't know. Does it matter?"

"It could matter, if I'm right about something. Did this man Ravitch tell you where he was staying?"

"Why, yes. I believe he said he's at the St. Moritz. Why, Gena? What's the matter?"

Gena didn't reply. She put down her glass and picked up the telephone book to look up the number.

Daniel Ravage looked at the auburn-haired beauty on the other side of the wooden booth. It was a professional appraisal, and he approved of what it told him. The tight clasp of her hands, the nervous look in her eyes, the firm set of her mouth. Sincerity. She was frightened by what she had told him, and yet she had the courage to see it through.

Beth Grant was a former student whom he had helped as an adviser in their university days. It was only natural she'd have come to him now. He'd encouraged her to do it; he'd been encouraging her for a long time. He had driven out to Manassas just to hear what she had to say, to this dark little bar full of pseudo-Tiffany lampshades and hanging philoden- dron, a place at the edge of the suburbs where it was unlikely either one of them would be recognized or known.

And now he knew that the trip had been worth his while.

The bar was nearly empty. They were here after the lunch crowd but ahead of the evening rush. Yet they kept their voices low. Certain names were suggested, not spoken.

"I'm as frightened by this as you are," Ravage said. "And you're right. Something has to be done about it."

Beth looked at him pleadingly. "But what? What *can* we do?"

"You can tell your story to the right person."

"Who?"

Ravage leaned forward a bit. "The man I work for."

"*Compton*?" Beth's voice was a whisper.

"No, of course not. Peter Lucas."

"Peter! But he's in Compton's hip pocket."

"I don't think so," Ravage said. "He may not want to believe you, but he will if you can show him documentation."

"Then you tell him," Beth replied. "I'm not sure I can get through this again."

"What kind of proof can I show him?"

Beth looked at him for a moment. Then she lowered her eyes.

"Believe me," he said, "it's far better coming from you, a direct source. And anyway, I've been raising too many doubts with Peter. He's beginning to think I'm a bit of a doomsayer and might not believe it from me. In fact, I don't think you should tell him you've even talked to me. He might think I've influenced your thinking."

"Well, you haven't," Beth said. "I'm perfectly capable of seeing the truth for myself. But it still took all my courage to talk to you about it. I don't know about Peter . . ."

"You know him, don't you?"

"Oh, yes. I've known him for a long time."

"Then talk to him," Ravage said. "Do it now, this evening. You can trust him to protect you."

Beth looked at him for a moment, her eyes full of reluctance—reluctance and anxiety.

"You have to," Ravage said. "What you've told me is serious enough by itself, but I think it fits into a larger, much darker picture. You must tell Peter. You must tell him tonight."

19

MILOSLAVSKY ENTERED THE conference room at precisely six A.M., the time for which Sukhov had called the meeting. He made it a point never to arrive ahead of a summons, just as he made it a point never to be even a moment late. A matter of simple courtesy, to be sure—but something more than that, too. Overeagerness, Miloslavsky believed, was the mark of a man who would never command respect.

He was, as always, immaculately dressed—his dark suit pressed, his tie knotted smoothly at the collar of his starched shirt—as if he had been waiting for the telephone call in the middle of the night and hadn't been roused out of bed like the other men gathered here at the conference-room table. In fact, Miloslavsky *was* up when the telephone rang. The summons from Sukhov came as no surprise. He was up and waiting for it.

He took the chair beside the one where Sukhov would sit— at the right hand of the Premier, his privilege by rank and age—and smiled a greeting to the men around the table. Their faces were somber but questioning. Each of them had received the same nighttime summons, direct from the Premier. Each of them wondered, but no one voiced the question. *Why* had Sukhov called them here so suddenly, and at this early hour? Only one man among them knew.

Miloslavsky averted his eyes and ran a hand along the carved edge of the table, a remnant of czarist times. They were here, the Council of Ministers, all but one—the KGB Chairman. Miloslavsky's face remained calm, but inside he was deeply worried. He was frightened. Levitsky should be here by now! He was two hours overdue.

Would Sukhov accept an excuse? *What* excuse?

Miloslavsky glanced up as an aide to the Premier entered and crossed the room. He pulled drapes across the windows overlooking Red Square. Heavy snow had fallen during the night and covered the rooftops of Moscow. Down in the street, snow was graying to slush.

The aide showed no interest in the men at the table, in a meeting which would never be recorded on the Premier's appointments schedule. He left as he came, quickly and quietly. Then the door opened once more, and Sukhov entered the room.

The Soviet Premier was a small man, but solid, with heavy eyebrows protruding over dark eyes that were set into a deeply lined, unsmiling face. He said nothing as he sat down, placed a folder on the table in front of him, absently squared up its corners and left it lying unopened. His eyes swept the faces around the table, then paused at the single unoccupied chair.

Miloslavsky cleared his throat. A *simple* excuse. Something pertinent. "Comrade Levitsky was called away unexpectedly," he said. "Something came up, a possible lead regarding the matter we are here to discuss. He was unable to reach you and so notified me."

Sukhov nodded, apparently satisfied, and Miloslavsky relaxed in his chair. Now he could only hope that Levitsky would *not* appear before the meeting was over, so that he wouldn't blunder into a different explanation for his absence and reveal to Sukhov that Miloslavsky had lied, as he'd been forced to lie so many times in these past few weeks.

"Comrades," Sukhov began, "we have a grave situation—a grave situation indeed. A Soviet agent was killed last night, quite unexpectedly, while carrying out a mission of immense importance. I was supervising his progress myself. I say he was killed unexpectedly, knowing our agents risk their lives every day. But this agent's mission was finished, accomplished. He had succeeded in recovering a stolen document and had only to return it to Moscow. We had no reason to suspect interference at this point, and yet the agent is dead. His death is regrettable. But our real concern is the document, which is once again missing. That document"—Sukhov paused to stress the importance of what he was going to say—"that document is the Korcula tape."

The reaction passed through the room like a small burst of energy. It was subtle but made itself felt by a quick intake of breath, a widening of eyes, a gesture frozen almost as it began.

Sukhov raised a hand to prevent the inevitable questions. "Comrade Levitsky has been in charge of the recovery operation," he said, and glanced at Miloslavsky, "reporting to the Foreign Minister and myself. Until now I've felt that their knowledge of the situation, and mine, was sufficient to protect the security interests of the nation. But now we have a new set of circumstances, and I believe it's imperative for the rest of you to understand fully what has happened. We must focus all our resources on this matter, to the exclusion, if necessary, of all other priorities."

Miloslavsky nodded to show his support for the Premier's decision. The potential danger of the situation could not be overstated.

"In the absence of the KGB Chairman," Sukhov added, "I will ask the Foreign Minister to brief you on the circumstances of the missing tape."

Miloslavsky felt a sudden sensation of panic. He'd been over this moment a dozen times with Boris, so that Boris could assume the pose that was needed here. But Boris was late, and now it was up to him to be convincing. Panic. No trace of it showed in his outward appearance. His eyes were calm. His expression revealed nothing but serious purpose, and that was not a pose.

"I will speak bluntly, because we have no time for the luxury of give-and-take," he said. "And I'll ask you to listen carefully, since I'll be mixing fact with conjecture, each as they came to us. As you know, the tape was in my possession, locked in my private safe under tightest security precautions, though apparently not tight enough. The tape was stolen from my safe several weeks ago. And that was a bit of work that could not have been accomplished by anyone but an insider.

"We know who it was, a secretary who had worked for me for nearly seven years. Unfortunately, she took her own life before we were able to interrogate her to find out why she had done it. Or, more to the point, for whom. In the absence of her testimony, we can only make a guess, an *educated* guess. We believe she was working for the CIA.

"You see, the tape was stolen shortly after another incident that bore all the earmarks of a CIA operation, the *escape*"— he spoke the word with derision—"of Yuri Danchenko and five other prisoners from the labor camp at Perm. For six people to walk out of Perm is impossible, of course. No one except the CIA has the capability of penetrating our security so effectively, and even they would be hard pressed to do it.

"The question is, why would the CIA take such a risk, one with so little chance for success, so great a chance for exposure? Why would they do it now, when the release of the dissidents was tentatively guaranteed by the preliminary Korcula agreements? We discovered a plausible answer when, shortly after the escape, we received an intelligence report that Danchenko was planning not only to leave the country but also to take something out with him. A document valued beyond any price, well worth any risk. What else but the Korcula tape?"

Miloslavsky took a deep breath. He suppressed the urge to express what he felt for Danchenko and his kind. Leniency and cooperation were official policy now. The death of the traitors was acceptable to the Premier for reasons of pure expedience, to protect the tape. Miloslavsky believed in expedience, but he deplored those who used it as an alternative to principle. The six should have died a long time ago! They were traitors, and that was enough.

And yet he was glad they had not.

Miloslavsky had negotiated the agreements with Compton. He did so because détente was official policy, because he had no choice. He negotiated the agreements and carried them home to Sukhov, assuming a pose of satisfaction with the work he had done. But he was not satisfied. To the contrary! He would never be satisfied until he had undone what he'd been forced to do. The Premier and the U.S. President. Compton himself. Korcula and all that it stood for. These were the things that Miloslavsky was plotting to destroy.

He suppressed the feelings, maintained the pose. "Washington seems to be saying one thing and doing something quite different," he went on. "But the Premier is convinced, and I concur, that the President and Secretary Compton are still committed to the Korcula pact. We can only draw one conclusion. We are up against a renegade faction within the CIA, an anti-Korcula faction—more elusive because it doesn't have the sanction of ranking U.S. officials, more dangerous because it operates without known control."

Miloslavsky quickly explained the developments leading up to the night before. "Chairman Levitsky assigned the job of tracing Danchenko to Department V, to a particular agent whose record for persistence and success were unmatched, even in that most effective department."

No one at the table needed to ask why Levitsky had chosen Department V—Mokrie Dela, the bureau of "wet affairs," so named for its bloody history of missions successfully finished. No one needed to ask about the fate of Yuri Danchenko.

"The agent succeeded," Miloslavsky said. "He recovered a tape from Danchenko—not *the* tape, but a blank. The agent then traced Petrovskaya; she, too, was carrying a tape—like Danchenko's, a blank. Of course, we knew what that meant. Danchenko had set up a ruse; there were six tapes, five of them blank. And none of the six escapees, apparently, knew who had the original.

"And so the agent proceeded to intercept the others, each one in turn. Danchenko, Petrovskaya, Pinsky. And then, last night, Fyodor Subolev. The agent reported by radio from Baku. The Subolev tape was not blank. It was, indeed, the one stolen from my office, and it was safe once again in the hands of the KGB.

"We don't know exactly what happened," Miloslavsky concluded. "The agent was shot shortly after he finished the radio transmission. He's dead, and the tape is once again missing. More importantly, we don't know who killed him. A renegade CIA faction? We might as well say a Russian with brown hair. We are no closer than that to knowing how to start a new search for the tape."

"What about the last two dissidents?" someone asked.

Miloslavsky nodded. "Nina Kovalyova and Vladislav Levitan. We can intercept them, of course, and we will, to prevent their escape. But the tapes they have are blank, like the first ones. Whoever took the Subolev tape certainly wouldn't use them to carry it out now, given what we know."

Sukhov leaned forward then, took over the meeting again. "Now you know why I've called you here at this hour," he said. "The theft of the tape is an outrageous act which, under other conditions, we would raise directly with the White House or Department of State. But Korcula stands on extremely shaky foundations, and the enemy's face is unknown. We dare not deal openly with Washington for fear of alerting the very people we seek to unmask. In the meantime, we are left to our own devices. We must recover the tape."

Sukhov's eyes swept the table, searching each face. Then he leaned back in his chair. "Now, comrades, I will entertain your suggestions."

Levitsky was back and waiting in Miloslavsky's office when the meeting in the conference room broke up. He was wearing the clothes he had put on the day before. His eyes were hooded, dulled by lack of sleep. He hadn't even taken the time to shave.

Miloslavsky was torn between lashing out and embracing the KGB Chairman. Instead, he crossed the room to his desk and sat down. "You missed an emergency meeting with the Premier and the Council of Ministers," he said calmly, as if this were routine information. "I explained that you had been called away on a matter related to the problem we were discussing. How was your trip?"

Levitsky smiled, and the smile brightened his face, erasing all signs of fatigue. He got the message. "Unproductive, I'm afraid. And I'm sorry I'm late getting back. My plane was delayed by the snow."

Snow. That much, at least, was the truth.

"It was a waste of time," Levitsky went on. "The report I had was a false lead. There was nothing to be learned from it."

The words were intended for unwanted listening ears, but the smile was meant for Miloslavsky alone. So, too the gesture—a hand pausing briefly at the side pocket of his coat.

"I see," Miloslavsky said. He nodded for Levitsky to close the door. "Are you certain you checked every angle?"

"Quite sure. I interviewed the agent who filed the report, and each of his sources. I also pursued a few of my own. The lead was false. Period."

"Unfortunate."

"Yes. Perhaps next time we'll have better luck. Is there anything new here?"

Miloslavsky described in detail the meeting he had missed. As he spoke, Levitsky reached into the pocket. He produced a paper-wrapped package and put it down on the desk. Miloslavsky only looked at it for a moment. The anxiety that had been pent up for so long began to find release. The weeks of planning, the meeting with Danchenko, more weeks of lying to Sukhov—of overseeing one operation to recover the tape while controlling another of his own making. That was Levitsky's job, to make sure Department V would *not* succeed, would *not* recover the tape—because it was Miloslavsky himself who had given it to Danchenko.

All of it washed over him now in a great rush of relief as he tore open the package. He was still in control; his goals would still be achieved.

He pulled off the wrapper and looked at the Korcula tape.

20

EVERYONE HAD GONE home by the time Peter got back to his office after his meeting with Compton, but there were several messages waiting on his desk. He glanced through them, tossed one into the wastebasket, and put the rest away for attention tomorrow morning. All but the last one. Nicole had called twice; the second message superseded the first. She was on her way out, but she wanted to see him tonight. Could he come by around nine o'clock?

That, thought Peter, would be no hardship at all. He had plenty of time to go home, change clothes, and get something to eat without having to hurry.

Leisure time. It felt good, even if it didn't last beyond this one evening. Or maybe Arthur was right; maybe he should get some rest before the Korcula meeting. A vacation now was out of the question, but he could take a day off. He and Nicole could drive out into the horse country for a look at the autumn leaves. They could have lunch at the Red Fox Inn—a long, unhurried lunch without the weekend crowds. They could drive back slowly, avoid the main highways, take their time. . . .

A sense of well-being passed through him. It wasn't just leisure he felt; it was enormous relief. Steve had put a terrible burden on him—the lives of six people, who might as well have been in another galaxy for the access he had to them. But now he had handed the burden over to Compton, who could do something to save them—could and would. Whatever it was Steve had wanted was no longer Peter's problem. It was Compton's—and that, no doubt, was what Steve had in mind all along. Peter couldn't forget it, but he could stop worrying now. The problem was in good hands.

He switched off his desk lamp and got up to leave. Then he noticed an envelope lying on the floor, where apparently it had fallen from his desk. An interdepartmental envelope, delivered by inside mail, sealed and marked for Peter's personal attention. *Confidential and urgent.* Peter frowned as he tore it open. A State Department cable, several pages, photocopied, and clearly marked "Top Secret." There was no covering memo, nothing to explain who had sent it to him or why. He felt vaguely uneasy as he started to read, as if he were listening in on a conversation he wasn't meant to hear.

> *Eyes only to Secretary Compton from Ambassador James Forrest, Belgrade. Subject: Jovan Kersnik. Date: October 3.*
>
> *In response to your instructions, I contacted the Foreign Ministry here for information about the postmortem examination performed today on the body of Ambassador Kersnik and have received a copy of the preliminary autopsy report, which is attached with an English translation.*
>
> *In summary, the autopsy surgeon concurs with the doctors who attended Ambassador Kersnik in Washington. The medical cause of death is not in question. He died of heart failure.*
>
> *However, as you suspected, there is more to it than that. The autopsy revealed that a foreign element had been introduced into Kersnik's body—a drug that causes a dramatic increase in blood pressure, and thus a sudden strain on the heart, while at the same time inhibiting the heart's ability to function in response to a crisis. Death is inevitable once the drug is introduced, and instantaneous once the symptoms appear.*

*   *   *

Peter dropped back into his chair, his attention riveted to the words on the page. A drug-induced heart attack? Impossible! Peter knew. He was *there*!

But the cable was clear.

> *Under the circumstances, it seems hard to escape the conclusion that Ambassador Kersnik was murdered.*
> *Furthermore, since the autopsy asserts that the drug had to be taken orally, and less than an hour prior to the onset of symptoms and death, it seems equally inescapable that he was murdered while he was a guest in the President's box.*

Miloslavsky was well aware of the risk he was taking. If his real intentions were unmasked before he could carry them out, neither he nor Levitsky had the slightest chance of surviving. He would be executed as a traitor or sent into exile, where his last years would be cheated of dignity and worth. He preferred the prospect of death.

But it wouldn't come to that now. He'd succeeded already where no one else had dared. He'd stolen a classified document and given it to an enemy of the state. He had given support to a CIA operation inside the Soviet Union. He had disobeyed orders, defied official policy, and lied to the Premier. He'd done all of these things without qualm, but he wasn't a traitor. He had acted from the most loyal motivation, for overriding reasons of national security, to preserve Lenin's great dream.

He glanced at Levitsky as they passed through security and into the cold air outside. Boris was—what?—nearing fifty now, far too young to have seen what Miloslavsky had seen. Boris saw czarist Russia as young Westerners saw the Depression or the barbarism of the Third Reich. He couldn't know the triumph of Lenin's victory, the oppression that Lenin had crushed. He couldn't know the new hope that swept across Russia when Marxism took control. There was no one else left who did know, who remembered, as Miloslavsky did.

And yet, the problems had started even then, under Lenin, with the temporary abandonment of international goals when the Revolution failed to take root worldwide. They had grown under Stalin, who was forced to ally with the West against

Hitler, a common foe. They had festered under Khrushchev. Khrushchev! A weak man, remembered for two great accomplishments—backing down to a brash young U.S. president and permitting the split with China. Miloslavsky's jaw tightened in anger even as he thought of it now.

But since that time, things had only grown worse. SALT treaties. Joint missions in space. Official visits exchanged between presidents and premiers, raising their glasses to toast the blurring of ideological boundaries, pledging cooperation. Pledging *trust*.

Well, why not? Why shouldn't they enjoy the comraderie of state visits while the whole world watched? They were so much alike!

Soviet leaders today were no kin to the great revolutionaries who had founded the nation, no better than their counterparts in the West. When they should have been building unity under the Soviet flag, they were losing control of communism in Italy and France. When they should have been building strength among existing communist nations, they were pandering to the satellite countries' demands for independence and national identity. Hungary and Czechoslovakia shouldn't have happened. Yugoslavia shouldn't exist. And China...

China!

Miloslavsky shoved his hands into his pockets and pushed the thought of past failures from his mind. All would be different, and soon. He turned to the right; Levitsky followed beside him. They walked at a normal pace, and would not talk until they were well past Red Square. Snowplows had passed this way, spewing up gray mountains on both sides of the street. Paths had been cleared through to shopfronts, much as they might have been in London or New York. Priorities. It was only too clear what they were: capitalism had crept into Moscow, and no one noticed. Or cared.

No one except Miloslavsky. The Americans were right, he thought. Their political rhetoric was, for once, frighteningly accurate. Détente locked the Soviet Union into trade agreements and more open communication. Contact with a world where profligate consumption was a way of life. Exposure to a world where political and social discipline had been banished in the name of free speech. The assurances that had once appeased idealists like himself—that there were good and tough reasons for holding back, a matter of buying time while world revolutionary forces grew and gathered strength—those assurances, once accepted, had dissolved as the pattern came clear. A pattern of abandonment, of original goals forgotten. Of Marxism *interpreted* and *brought up-to-date*!

Excuses! Justifications!

Miloslavsky no longer listened. He no longer believed. For years he had kept to his own job, biding his time, waiting for the pendulum to swing back. But now there was something more, far worse than SALT and state visits, the ultimate price for détente. Now there was Korcula, and Korcula had to be stopped.

But to do it, Miloslavsky needed the tapes. Both tapes, from opposite sides of the world, together—in the right hands, at the right time, in the right place. At the Korcula meeting.

With the Soviet tape, the problem had never been access. Miloslavsky had it in his own safe, as he had told the minister; he only had to remove it and then claim that it was stolen. But first he had to devise a plan for transporting it out of the country.

He could have done it himself, could have boarded a plane with the tape in his hands. No one would dare to question what he was doing. But what then? Who in the West would believe him against Compton? By the time they debriefed him and satisfied themselves that the tape was authentic, it would have been far too late. Furthermore, he had no intention of leaving the country for good. It was Russia he loved; he was needed here.

No, he couldn't do it himself, nor could Boris, for the same reasons. He needed a courier, someone whose intentions would not be suspect, someone whose credibility was assumed and would not have to be established. Then the CIA had come to his assistance.

The CIA, with its secret mission to free the Soviet Six! Of course the escape plan had worked! Miloslavsky knew about it long before it occurred, through Levitsky and his sources. He also knew he could count on Compton to call it off, whether or not Compton realized what he was doing. He knew and chose not to stop it. He wanted and permitted the escape to succeed. He needed Yuri Danchenko.

Once he was free, Danchenko's cooperation was easily acquired. Miloslavsky told him the truth; he needed to say nothing more. Then he "stole" the tape and gave it to Danchenko.

In the meantime, to protect himself, he reported the tape missing. He had stormed into Sukhov's office furious, outraged! The theft from his own safe was a serious breach of security, an immense threat. It was also a personal affront to him. He would be avenged. He would himself supervise Levitsky and the recovery operation. And when the thief—the *traitor*!—was captured, he would unleash the full fury of his wrath.

He regretted having to sacrifice a secretary who had served him loyally and well, but he had no choice. The woman had to be silenced. For Lenin's dream.

Levitsky had made a good show of his efforts to recover the tape. He had launched a massive search, fanning out over the country, making use of every resource at his disposal. He only had to avoid any link between the tape and the fugitive dissidents, at least until Danchenko was out of the country. And Danchenko would be the first of the six to escape.

But two things happened that Miloslavsky could not have foreseen. Danchenko didn't keep the tape; he passed it to one of the others. And Sukhov decided to oversee the recovery operation himself.

It was Sukhov who had seen the connection Miloslavsky described to the ministers, a clear link between the escape of the dissidents and the missing tape. Miloslavsky could no longer look the other way. He had no choice, short of confession, and that was not an alternative. He ordered Levitsky to assign an agent, the best man for the job, a man from Department V, as he would have done had he wanted Danchenko caught. He sent the agent to Gagra, to satisfy Sukhov and to protect himself. Then he also sent Levitsky, to make sure the agent didn't succeed.

But Danchenko didn't have the tape.

Miloslavsky sighed wearily. All of that was behind him now. The tape was his once again—his to direct, his to use. His hand closed around the package in his pocket. Then he took it out and handed it to Levitsky. "You know what to do with it," he said.

Levitsky nodded. "I'll have to leave today. I'll report to you when it's done."

"How is Lucas progressing?"

"Not as fast as I'd like. Dmitri is going to make sure he knows that Kersnik was murdered. He thinks that will frighten Lucas and spur him to press harder."

"Good, but not enough," Miloslavsky said. "There's too little time, only four days until the conference begins. It's time to take harsher measures."

Levitsky glanced up. "Do you have something in mind?"

"Yes." Miloslavsky sidestepped a patch of snow that had somehow missed being cleared. "I want you to contact Dmitri now, before you leave. Tell him I said it's time to use an assassin."

21

WHY WAS KERSNIK murdered? By *whom*? Was it something as simple, as predictable, as a terrorist act by one of the Yugoslavian anticommunist groups? Or a particularly fierce Croatian independence movement? Peter didn't think so. That would be a convenient explanation—a little too convenient. Too handy.

And yet it couldn't have been any of the people in the box that night, not unless it was Kersnik's own bodyguard or, God forbid, his wife. It certainly wasn't Nicole, or Compton, or Senator Harvey—not even her husband, the computer man, Michael Baker. Of course, if Kersnik had frozen to death for lack of adequate housing, that might have been another story.

Then who did it?

And *how*?

The only thing Kersnik had "taken orally" while he was in the President's box was champagne, and many of them had drunk from the same bottle.

A professional job? *In the President's box*?

And who had delivered the cable to Peter?

Compton?

No, Peter had just left Compton's office. Arthúr might have told him, and might have shown him the cable, but he would never permit this kind of information to be photocopied and sent through the interoffice mail.

But if not Arthur, then who? And, come to think of it, why *hadn't* Arthur told him?

Peter picked up the phone and called Mary at home. Yes, she had seen the envelope on his desk when she took his messages in just before she left the office. No, she didn't know how it got there.

"Was anyone in my office while I was gone?" Peter asked.

"Certainly not. At least not while I was there."

"All right. Don't worry about it. I'll see you tomorrow."

Peter hung up and looked at the cable again. At least the Yugoslavians didn't intend to make trouble. They expected an investigation (they hardly needed to say so), and they were dealing openly with both parties to the conference. A copy of the report sent to Compton had been sent to the Soviet Embassy as well. But the conference itself wasn't threatened. The Yugoslavians were anxious to cooperate with both sides. They would make no further judgments until the investigation was complete. They would not, at this time, make the nature of Kersnik's death public. Or an issue.

And that was a relief. This kind of thing could have destroyed the conference, or at least delayed it indefinitely. Depending on what the investigation turned up, it remained a threat. Peter should have been told.

But Compton didn't tell him. Why not? Had it slipped his mind? Unlikely.

And why did Compton *ask* the American ambassador in Belgrade to look into the autopsy in the first place? Did he have reason to think Kersnik had been murdered? What reason? Why was he suspicious?

The answer came to Peter. It was obvious, once he saw it. Kersnik's death could have destroyed the conference, and there were people in the Kremlin who were bent on doing just that.

Peter locked the cable in a desk drawer and left his office.

It was dark in the garage, though dim lights were burning overhead; the new government economies. Peter stepped off the elevator and headed for his car. He would see Nicole tonight—and, if he was home, Arthur. Otherwise, tomorrow.

Tomorrow, with all of its questions, and maybe a few answers. Peter wasn't sure he wanted to know what they were. Someone had killed Jovan Kersnik, as someone had killed

Steve. And Danchenko, Petrovskaya, and Pinsky. Daniel Ravage's words came back like a Delphic pronouncement: *It's all too good to be true*. Peter shoved them forcefully out of his mind and produced his keys. His car was just ahead.

Then suddenly he stopped. Someone was *in* the car! A woman, sitting on the passenger side, facing the other way. Nicole? No, the hair wasn't right, the posture, the incline of the head.

Peter approached the car slowly, not out of fear, only caution. Too much had happened lately, and this was one more surprise. The space next to his was vacant; he moved up beside the front window. Then the woman turned to face him, and smiled.

"Hi, Peter. Surprise!"

All very light, kind of cute—but she didn't quite pull it off. Peter hadn't known Beth Grant as well as he wanted to know her at another time in his life, but he knew her well enough to know that cute wasn't her style.

And besides that, she worked for the CIA.

He returned the smile. Lightly. "Beth! What are you doing here?"

"Waiting for you."

"Obviously. But why?"

She didn't answer the question; she parried with one of her own. "Could you give me a lift?"

"I guess so. Where are you going?"

"It doesn't matter."

Peter laughed. "What is this?"

"I want to talk, and a moving car's the best place."

"I see." Peter looked at her for a moment, then walked around to the other side of the car and got in behind the wheel. He knew, now, what was coming—some friendly probing about his timely interest in certain Soviet dissidents.

But why this kind of encounter? Why here? Why this way? Why hadn't she simply called him for an appointment—or a date, if she wanted to play it strictly undercover? And why was she here at all? Compton, no doubt, had raised hell with the top brass at Langley; the cause for Peter's interest must surely be obvious now.

But maybe the word hadn't filtered down yet to Beth. Or

maybe she was so used to cloak-and-dagger routines that she no longer knew there was another way.

He started the car and drove out of the garage, merging into the traffic. "Okay," he said, "what's this all about?"

"I was going to ask you the same question."

Peter glanced across the seat. "Would you care to be more specific?"

"Sure, I'll be specific. You've been asking around about the Soviet Six. They're a dead issue, or they should be from your point of view. What do you care what's happening to them now?"

"What do I *care*! Your people *are* damned pragmatic! In case you've forgotten, my job is human rights. Prisoners of conscience don't become a dead issue with me when they drop out of sight."

"I'm sorry, that was a poor choice of words. But you know what I mean. Why the new interest now?"

"Why do you want to know?"

Beth lit a cigarette, with a bit more concentration than the task required, Peter thought as he reached for one of his own. He'd also noticed her attention to the seat belt; she'd been running it through her fingers like a set of worry beads.

Obviously his interrogator was nervous.

"You're not making this easy," she said quietly.

"I didn't intend to." Peter glanced over his shoulder, then swung into the right lane and slowed to a stop at the curb. "Listen," he said, "I really don't like pretense between friends. You want to know something? Just ask me directly. Otherwise, you might as well get out here."

Beth looked away, but not before Peter saw something in her eyes. Was it *fear*?

She drew on her cigarette, looking out the side window, her face still averted from his. "Are we friends?" she asked.

"Of course we are."

"God, I hope so."

"Why?"

"Because I could get fired for what I'm about to do. I could be drawn and quartered, or shot at sunrise. Or I *could* be making a very big mistake."

"For Christ's sake, Beth, what are you talking about?"

The blast of a horn behind them prevented Beth's reply. Peter glanced back, annoyed. He was blocking the right-turn lane. He stepped down on the gas and made the turn, then pulled into a center lane and kept driving.

"I don't expect you to believe this," Beth said, "but no one sent me to see you. This isn't official. I'm here on my own."

Independence had never been a virtue in Beth's neck of the woods. Nor had candor. Peter reserved judgment.

"I'm here on my own," Beth insisted. "I swear it! I'm here because I damn well want to know what's going on."

"About the Soviet Six?"

She nodded.

"I daresay you know more than I do."

Beth sighed. "Of course I do. I'm still not being quite honest. I know exactly what's going on, and I don't like what I know. I guess I'm hoping you'll know something I don't— something to explain why it has to be this way. Either that, or you'll know how to stop it. Because I can't. Dear God, I'm breaking every oath I ever took just by talking to you."

Peter shrugged. "So far you've told me nothing."

Beth drew on her cigarette. Then she stubbed it out, unfinished. "Do *you* know what's happening to the Soviet Six?" she asked.

"That the CIA helped to spring them from Perm? Yes. That you helped set them up to escape from the Soviet Union? Yes. That they're being murdered one at a time? Yes, I know that too."

"Then you'll understand this is one operation I was glad to be involved with, until something went wrong. I don't pretend the agency's motives were all that pure—those dissidents, in the West, would have been an extraordinary propaganda weapon for us—but it was still a good thing to do. Any way you look at it, it was a—"

"Except it backfired," Peter broke in. "And now three of the six are dead."

Beth nodded. "Murdered by the KGB. But it's *our* fault. That's why I'm so upset. It's our *fault*!"

Peter turned to her sharply; then his eyes shifted back to the traffic. First Gena, now Beth. New words, from a different perspective, but the message was the same. He didn't want to hear it; he didn't want it to be true.

But he had to know.

"Take it easy," he said. "You can't control what the KGB—"

There was no humor in Beth's sudden burst of laughter. "Oh, we can't, can we? How do you think the KGB *knows where to find them*?"

Peter's hands gripped the steering wheel hard. His heart rejected the words he was hearing. Not true! Arthur *said* it wasn't true!

"There's a list," Beth said.

"I know about that."

"A top-secret memo listing dates and places for escape. *We* had that list. It was never put into writing by anyone but us."

"We? Us? Who?"

"The agency, damn it!"

"You mean someone at the CIA *leaked* the list?"

"No, Peter, that's what I'm trying to tell you. It wasn't a leak. It was deliberate policy. We *gave* that list to the KGB!"

The car swerved. Peter pulled on the wheel just in time to avoid hitting the taxi that was coming up on his right. He stepped down on the brake, slowing his speed until the first wave of shock had passed.

"You can't mean that," he said.

"I mean it, and I can prove it. There are documents, memos. I can show you."

"You're going to have to."

Beth stared at him for a moment. Then she said, "All right. Will you drive me out to Langley?"

22

PETER PORED OVER the documents Beth had placed in his hands. It was all there, proof of the worst kind of complicity. It was sickening; it was ruthless and cold-blooded. It was far worse than even Compton could know.

Because it all *started* with Compton.

Compton, fresh back from his meeting with Miloslavsky, the preliminary agreements for Korcula in his hands. With White House approval, he had sent out an interagency memo directing a moratorium on anything that might be interpreted as anti-Soviet activity on the part of the U.S. Indeed, he had ordered all government agencies to cooperate with the Soviets, as long as they didn't run contrary to the interests of the United States or its allies. Cooperation, in the spirit of Korcula. . . .

In the spirit of Korcula! The irony of it! The escape operation was already underway then, and the CIA, presumably acting on orders, washed its hands of it. It was *because* of Korcula that the CIA backed out!

Compton might know that much, that his memo had been misused, that the CIA had been caught mid-operation when Korcula was announced and had seized on the memo as a way out. But he couldn't know that the CIA had gone a step beyond that. He couldn't know that another decision had been made at Langley, that the CIA had deliberately *delivered* the Soviet Six to the KGB?

The documents Beth brought to Peter left no room for doubt. Internal agency memos—extraordinarily revealing, extraordinarily frightening. Action and counteraction. A new kind of foreign policy. Decisions based on contact—direct contact— between the KGB Chairman and the CIA Director. Contact. A request from Levitsky, unofficial and unreported. Deliberation. Responsive action, unauthorized by anyone outside the CIA.

Yes, Levitsky had discovered the CIA's role in the escape operation and saw it as a clear violation of the commitments established between Miloslavsky and Compton. He wondered about the sincerity of the American commitment. Of course, if the CIA were now to act in good faith, then the incident could be forgotten. And what would constitute good faith? The revelation to Levitsky of the places where the dissidents could be found.

There followed a series of interagency memos—conflicting opinion, dissension among the CIA hierarchy. But one line of thinking emerged: CIA sensitivity to hostility in Congress. The agency's rope had been shortened already; there was little they could do without first airing it out in six different subcommittees. Now, if Korcula were to fall apart, and the fault were laid on the doorstep at Langley . . .

That couldn't happen! It must not be allowed to happen. The damage had to be undone, the request granted, the list turned over to Levitsky.

There, at last, was approval, yet another memo—initialed by the Director himself.

Peter looked up at Beth, who was sitting on the other side of the car, watching in silence as he read the damning details. She had gone back to her office alone. Peter dropped her off and then picked her up on Route 123, near the CIA turnoff. They had pulled in at an Exxon station that was closed for the night. Closed and dark. There were no other buildings nearby.

Peter tried to speak, tried to express his outrage, but nothing came out. There weren't words to describe what he felt.

"Do you understand now," Beth asked," why I had to take this risk? And why I'm so frightened by it?"

"Oh, yes, I understand."

"Someone has to do something, Peter. This has to be stopped before all of them are killed."

Someone was doing something, Peter thought. But someone had been lied to by the CIA. If Compton knew what Peter knew now, there wouldn't be chains strong enough to lash down his anger.

And of course, he had to know. Peter would have to tell him.

He put the documents back in their envelope and started the car.

Beth sat forward, alarmed. "Where are we going?"

"To show these to someone."

"No! They've got to go back to the safe. I've kept them too long already. My God, if anyone finds these missing—"

"Damn it, Beth, what do you want me to do?" Peter kept the motor running as he turned to face her across the front seat. "You've taken one risk by talking to me. Now you've got to take one more. We have to show these to someone who can do something about it. We have to do it together. We have to see Arthur Compton."

Beth laughed, a harsh sound in the small space of the car. "You think *Compton* will care about this?"

Peter studied her face, surprised by her reaction. "Of course he'll care. If he knew, he would—"

"He *does* know."

"Part of it, maybe, but he can't know about the list. He can't know they turned over the list."

"Peter, we sent him a full report."

"I know, but it didn't include this. It couldn't have. He told me—"

"I don't care what he told you. He got a report with copies of everything you've seen here, and a lot more besides. He knows everything."

Peter didn't believe it. "How can you know what he knows?"

"Because *I* prepared the report."

Peter opened the window. It was warm in the car. His face was hot, from anger and something more. A defensive feeling, like a knot in his chest. Because he wasn't sure.

Damn it, no! Compton couldn't have lied. He had *never* lied to Peter.

Beth touched his arm. "I'm sorry," she said. "I know you and Compton are friends. And anyway, I was wrong when I said he wouldn't care. He's *furious* about the box this puts him in, because there's no good way out of it now. It's funny. Compton would have applauded the escape operation if he'd been there when we planned it. He'd have approved more than anyone. He would have welcomed a move to free the Soviet Six. But he wasn't there, and we didn't know what he was negotiating with the Russians, until it was too late. Now we're all in a box...."

Beth's words washed over Peter, making little impression, taken in without being heard. His mind was jumping from one thought to another, seeking justification. Compton *said* he couldn't reveal everything in the report. He made it clear from the start. He *said* he couldn't share all of it, and he must have a good reason for not wanting Peter to know.

Then something broke through his thoughts and he turned sharply back to Beth. "*What* did you say?"

"I said we're in a box over this—"

"No, no, before that—something about *planning* this operation."

Beth frowned. "I don't know what you mean."

"You said *you* planned it. The CIA. But you didn't. You were only giving assistance—"

Beth laughed again. "Where did you get that idea?"

"Someone else planned it. Maybe the underground. Maybe even the KGB. The CIA was only giving support."

"Is that what Compton told you?"

Peter didn't reply, didn't have to.

Beth sighed, a sigh of sympathy and frustration. "It wasn't that way at all," she said. "The underground was involved, but only supporting us. It was our mission from the start. That's what makes it so bad—because we set them up, and then we pulled out. It's our fault because it was our operation."

Peter's face went pale in the darkness. He grabbed the steering wheel hard with both hands as he fought to control his feelings. *Everything* Gena had told him was true! But Arthur had denied it! What about what he'd said? Was it *all* false?

Was *any* of it true?

He turned back to Beth. "What is the CIA doing now?"

"About the Soviet Six? My God, *nothing*! We've been told to keep our hands off, not to touch it."

"*Who* told you?"

Beth looked back at him sadly. "You know the answer to that."

Compton! Who never lied. Who made promises, and kept them.

Peter sank back against the seat. A few cars streamed by on Route 123, late-working commuters on their way home to the suburbs. But Peter didn't see them. He saw only the face of the boy who had saved his life, the man who had been his friend. Beth's words cut through years of trust. Special trust, built layer by layer, the only lasting foundation in Peter's life. Now, in the fraction of time it took to absorb Beth's meaning, that foundation lay in a rubble.

Peter sat a moment, not moving. Then, without looking at Beth, he handed the envelope back.

"What are you going to do?" she asked.

"Something. I'll let you know."

He had no idea what, and right now he didn't care. He only knew that Beth wasn't lying. And the CIA hadn't lied to Compton, either. The truth was there in the report lying on Compton's desk. The truth was here now; Peter had to face it.

It was Compton who lied, and more than once. It was Compton who lied. To him.

Compton swung into the parking lot, and his headlights caught the DPL license plate on the back of a small dark car. He glanced at his watch. It wasn't quite eight o'clock; Voloshin had come early. Like Compton, he had dismissed his regular driver and come here tonight alone.

The lot was empty except for the two cars—empty and dark, which was why they had chosen to meet here, at Glen Echo, the abandoned amusement park overlooking the old C&O Canal and the Potomac River. Compton cut the engine, got out, walked around the car.

Voloshin rolled down his window. "Shall we talk in your car or mine?" he asked.

"Neither. Let's go for a walk."

"As you wish."

Compton led the way up the walk to the darkened midway. Glen Echo was an art colony now; summer weekends brought crowds once again. But tonight moonlight threw deep shadows across the facades of old buildings. The Cuddle-Up and the Penny Arcade. Crystal Pool. And the old Spanish Ballroom, where people once danced to the music of the big bands. Now there was a no-trespassing sign posted on a crumbling balcony under the tiled roof. One wall was boarded up as a gesture to damage by fire. A popcorn sign had been stripped of its neon trappings. The events board was a blank. Glen Echo, the shadow of an era out of the past—mocking in its silence, foreboding in its moonlit isolation.

Compton turned to Voloshin. "I've just learned about the escape of the Soviet Six," he said.

Voloshin grunted. "How much do you know?"

"As much as there is to know. How it started and how it finished. That our separate intelligence agencies dealt with it on their own."

"I see."

Voloshin didn't press him to admit the CIA's role in the escape; no admission would be forthcoming. Nor did Compton press him to acknowledge what the KGB had done. The truth lay between them, understood and unspoken. But Voloshin looked relieved.

"I'm glad to know you've just found out," he said. "I'd wondered."

"If I knew all along?"

"Yes."

"I can see how you would. Rest assured, I did not. If I had, I would not have permitted the escape to occur. At another time, yes, I might have. But not now. It's not helpful to either of us."

"Nor to the spirit of Korcula."

"After all," Compton said, "three people are dead, three people who would have been not only alive, but free, if we'd had our way."

"Four people," Voloshin said quietly. "Fyodor Subolev tried to escape and was killed."

Compton closed his eyes against a swelling sadness. He had known that Subolev's name was next on the list, but he hoped there might still be time to save him. "Who's responsible for the order to kill them?" he asked.

"Miloslavsky."

"Yes, I would have thought so."

"He's a hard man," Voloshin said. "He believes that dissidents are the worst kind of traitors, worthy of no compassion."

"And you?" Compton asked. "How do you see them?"

Voloshin chuckled. "I'm afraid I've been away from home too long. I've gone soft about the belly in more ways than one. I have no stomach for killing a man because he disagrees with me."

Compton looked at the man walking along beside him. Moonlight brightened Voloshin's face but left his eyes in shadow; it was hard to know what was going on in his mind. Compton wondered, as he'd wondered before, if Voloshin would ever return to Russia—if, when the Kremlin recalled him, he might simply say no. Then he recognized the thought for what it was, a selfish wish of his own. He had worked with Voloshin for so many years, it was painful to think of him gone.

Once again Compton chose not to voice the thought. He knew there was value in having a man like Voloshin on the other side, a man for whom ideological differences had become secondary to the nobler cause of maintaining sanity in an increasingly troubled and precarious world. And if, together, they could stave off the ultimate confrontation, there was hope that the world might someday be ruled by such men.

In the meantime, there was Korcula, and Korcula had to be saved.

"Unfortunately," Compton said, "we have to deal with circumstances as they are, and not as we wish they would be. I've discussed this situation with the President, and we're in complete agreement. The escape of the dissidents must not interfere with the Korcula conference. Our intelligence agencies may have acted unwisely, but they have come to terms. We are willing to leave it at that."

Voloshin said nothing.

"However," Compton added, "a point of conflict remains. The Soviet Six, as you know, were a part of our preliminary agreements; they were to have been released after the pact was signed. We are concerned about the three . . . the *two* who remain. We understand, of course, that the situation has changed, and we're willing to renegotiate their freedom. In fact, we would dislike having that option denied us. We can't renegotiate if none of them are alive."

"A reasonable position," Voloshin said, "but I'm not sure I can promise you that."

"We would regard leniency as a sure sign of good faith."

"Are you stating this as an official request?"

Compton hesitated a moment. Then he said, "Under the circumstances, we don't feel we can be that assertive. This is not an official request. It's merely a strong statement of our position."

Voloshin smiled. "I'll report your feelings to Moscow. And if I may say so, you're taking the right approach. My government is still committed to Korcula. Your feelings will be considered."

They walked along for another moment in silence. In the distance lay the lights of the city, but here they were quite alone. Nonetheless, Compton lowered his voice. "And now," he said, "are you going to tell me about the missing tape?"

"Ah, so you know that, too."

"It is missing, then?"

"Unfortunately, it is."

"For God's sake, what happened?"

"It was stolen from the safe in Miloslavsky's office."

Compton stopped abruptly. His mouth dropped open. "You're joking!"

"I wish I were."

Under other circumstances, Compton might have been happy to hear that the Kremlin's own internal security was vulnerable to theft. In this case, it was anything but good news.

"How could such a thing happen?" he asked. "And why wasn't I informed?"

Voloshin raised his hands. "How do these things happen? A woman who worked for Miloslavsky for years wasn't as loyal as he thought she was. Exactly why she did it, we'll never know. She's dead."

"More of Miloslavsky's handiwork?"

"Her own. As for our not telling you, I understand how you feel. If it were up to me, I'd have told you as soon as I knew myself. But the view from Moscow is different. For one thing,

Premier Sukhov anticipated that the tape would be quickly recovered. For another, there has been speculation at home that the tape was stolen by the CIA."

"By the CIA? That's nonsense!"

"Is it?" Voloshin asked. "Can you be so sure? Obviously we've had a security break on our side. The same thing might well have happened here."

"Not through the CIA," Compton assured him. "We never did take the agency into our confidence about the Korcula meeting. As you know, our security team for the preliminary meeting came from the State Department's own intelligence section. Each man was handpicked by me."

"As the woman who worked for Miloslavsky was handpicked by him?"

Compton conceded the point without argument. "But," he said, "I have reason to believe the CIA is still unaware that the tapes even exist."

"Then I ask you, how else could the tape have fallen into the hands of the very dissidents the CIA set free?"

"Do we know that?" Compton asked. "Are you sure the tape the dissidents are trying to smuggle out of the country *is* the Korcula tape?"

"There can be no doubt. Subolev had it."

Compton sighed. That, at least, was a relief.

"It was given to him by Danchenko," Voloshin went on. "The question is, how did Danchenko get it?"

"I have no idea. But the tape is what matters. Thank God it's been recovered."

Voloshin cleared his throat. "I'm afraid it's not quite that simple. The tape was recovered—as I said, Subolev had it— but then it was stolen again."

"*Again*? By whom?"

"My government believes it was taken by the CIA."

Compton spun around, his eyes blazing with anger, his impatience erupting as rage. "Then damn it, you tell your government to get off that track and start looking somewhere else. I'll take care of the CIA, and if there's anything wrong there, I'll stop it. If I have to have everyone who ever worked there locked up, I'll do it. I'll do it as a precaution alone! But the CIA *isn't* the problem. I'm as sure of that as I am of myself and you. In the meantime, you tell your government to start looking closer to home. For God's sake, we've *talked* about adversaries inside the Kremlin! Why don't you start looking there?"

"We are," Voloshin said. "Be assured that we are. In fact the Premier has someone in mind. But first we had to be sure of you."

Compton released his arm. "You have someone in mind? Who is it?"

"I'm afraid you're going to be shocked. The Premier and those of us who are loyal to him suspect Miloslavsky."

"*Miloslavsky*!" Compton wasn't just shocked; he was horrified.

He knew Korcula had enemies inside the Kremlin, and lately, as he told Peter, he'd begun to suspect a plot to destroy the conference and everything that lay behind it. But he never dreamed it might be led by anyone as powerful, as high-ranking, as formidable as Yevgeni Miloslavsky. The Soviet Foreign Minister! What the devil! It was Miloslavsky who sat down with Compton to *create* the Korcula pact!

And yet he knew that Miloslavsky had always leaned toward a hard line, especially where issues of human rights were concerned.

"What makes you suspect him?" he asked.

"Many things. Among others, the CIA theory was his—a 'renegade faction' inside the CIA, out to undo Korcula in defiance of U.S. policy. A small twist on reality, perhaps. Part truth, part lie."

Compton took a moment to regain his composure. Part truth, part lie. A familiar stance, too recently familiar.

"Premier Sukhov never believed that," Voloshin said, "especially after the CIA withdrew from the escape operation. Like you, he suspected someone closer to him. Of course, he hasn't mentioned this to Miloslavsky."

"What do you think he has in mind?"

Voloshin shrugged. "Maybe nothing. We may be doing him an injustice. But the Premier gave me permission to use my own judgment, to tell you if I thought you should know."

"I'm glad you did. This answers a great many questions. And raises others. What are you doing about him?"

"At this point, we are keeping him under surveillance. He's being watched—given rope, as you say. We don't want to make a mistake. We have to be sure before we take action against him."

"I should think so!"

"We will take care of Miloslavsky," Voloshin said. "It's our prerogative, as the CIA is yours."

"All right, but tell me one thing. Who is responsible for keeping him under surveillance?"

"He's in good hands." Voloshin smiled as he started walking back toward the parking lot. "He is being watched by no less than the KGB Chairman, Boris Levitsky."

23

"What's wrong?" Nicole asked.

Peter looked up from the couch. Nicole was standing above him, a brandy glass in each hand, her face unsmiling but incredibly soft.

He hadn't told her about her father's lies. He couldn't tell her. It would hurt her far too much to know what he was thinking. And besides that, there were new doubts in his mind, questions of national security. It was Compton he had to see.

"It's only an office problem," he said as he took the two glasses and set them on the table. Then he pulled Nicole down beside him and let his fingers trace the lines of her face, her smooth skin.

"I don't believe you," she said.

Peter smiled. "You're too damn smart."

"Not smart, just intuitive. Or maybe I know you too well. That look in your eyes is not an office problem. Don't deny it. I can tell."

Peter hesitated a moment. Then his smile faded. "You're right, it is more than that, but I can't talk about it to anyone but your father."

"And I thought you came here to see me!"

"That, too." Peter kissed her. The comment was Nicole's way of changing the subject, of saying she understood. He pulled her to him and held her, saying nothing. It had been a long night.

He had dropped Beth at her house and then driven aimlessly through Washington, reviewing it all in his mind. Compton had lied. The truth of that struck him again with a sharp new stab of pain. Oh, sure, he had hedged in his office this afternoon; he hadn't pretended to reveal everything he knew. In fact, he made sure Peter knew that. But on one point he was absolutely clear: the CIA did not initiate the escape operation and to that extent was blameless in the deaths of the Soviet Six. Gena Danchenko knew better. So did Beth Grant. Now Peter did, too.

But Compton wasn't content to leave it at that. He went on to imply—he practically said it!—that the CIA wasn't finished with the job, that we were planning to send them back to undo the mess they had made. Another lie! The truth was quite the opposite.

Did he have something *else* in mind? Something he couldn't tell Peter?

Still, why did he *lie*? If there were more to it than he wanted Peter to know, why didn't he simply duck under his own hedge?

The answer had come to Peter with the shock of revelation, and it turned him cold inside. It hit him while he was driving through the city on his way, inevitably, here. Compton wanted him to believe something else, to stop asking difficult questions. Compton wanted him out of the way. My God, he'd even suggested a vacation!

Had he stopped trusting Peter?

Why?

There was only one way to find out, and that was to ask him.

Peter didn't remember making the right turns. He had come here as if by instinct. To Nicole. To Compton. But now that he was here, he wondered if he could face Compton with the truth of what he had learned. Or if it would do any good. The bond between them had suffered a harsh blow. When Compton explained, Peter didn't know whether he could believe him.

And that was something he couldn't share with Nicole.

"I've got something to tell you," she said, leaning forward

to pick up her brandy. "Or had you forgotten you gave me an urgent assignment?"

Marco Polo! He had forgotten. Too much had happened since then.

"I'm sorry," he said.

"I've learned several things, and they could be important."

Peter sat back and loosened his tie, waiting for her to tell him.

"Well," she said, "historically we know very little about Marco Polo before his travels began. He was born in Venice about 1254. His father was Niccolo Polo, a wealthy Venetian merchant. Apparently his mother's name isn't known; she died when he was a child." Nicole raised her hands in a silent apology. "Those are the facts, and that's all there is, but I've done some detective work beyond that. Are you interested in conjecture?"

"Of course. That's why I asked you. I can read an encyclopedia by myself."

Nicole nodded and tasted her brandy. "He *was* born in Venice," she said. "All accounts of his life agree there. But I think you asked the right question at lunch yesterday—*where* in Venice—because in the thirteenth century the city as we know it wasn't there. Venice was a large republic then, with territory stretching south to the Mediterranean Sea and even to some ports in the Aegean."

Peter fished out his cigarettes, frowning with new interest. "So while he was born in Venice, he may not have been born in the *city* of Venice."

"Exactly. Picture the area I'm talking about—south from Venice, past Italy and Greece, at least as far as the Mediterranean, including—"

Peter was way ahead of her. "Yugoslavia," he said.

"And possibly Korcula."

Peter's eyes locked on hers. Neither one of them spoke. Both of them were remembering. *Avoid the obvious*. Avoid *Venice*. Look to Korcula for the fate of the Soviet Six.

"There's more," Nicole said quietly. "Let me show you something." She picked up an envelope that was lying on the table. "Remember what I told you. Marco Polo was born in

Venice, period. Beyond that we have only myth and legend. Lots of places claim to be the birthplace of someone famous. Usually there's nothing more than slim evidence to support such claims, but frequently when new evidence is unearthed, this kind of local folklore turns out to have basis in fact."

"Which means?"

"You've just heard my official disclaimer. Now, look at this."

She took a piece of paper from the envelope in her hand, unfolded it, and handed it to him. It was her room assignment for the Korcula meeting: one room with a private bath in the Marko Polo Hotel. Peter read it, frowning. Then suddenly he laughed.

"Is it funny?" she asked, puzzled by his reaction.

"Yes, in a way. Does this mean what I think it does?"

She nodded. "Local folklore. The Korculani believe Marco Polo was born on their island. There are still Polos living there. There's even a house that's passed off as his birthplace, with a modest admission fee, but it dates to a later time and means nothing. In fact, there's no evidence except for the persistent belief of the people, but I didn't think that would matter."

No, it wouldn't matter. And didn't. Peter drew on his cigarette, strangely calm. The connection was clear. Steve's message took on precise meaning: Investigate the origins of Marco Polo. Avoid the obvious. Avoid Venice. Investigate *Korcula*— because Korcula meant death for the Soviet Six. It fit what he had discovered on his own.

He pulled Nicole to him again, half-smiling, seeking comfort in having her close. "You're wonderful," he said. "You've confirmed something for me unmistakably."

Nicole was startled. "You knew this?"

"Not what you just told me. But I knew Steve was talking about Korcula one way or another."

She looked into his eyes, her own worried. "Peter, what does it mean? What does Steve's death have to do with the Korcula conference?"

"With the conference itself, nothing. It's something that's already happened, something that's happening now. It's what Gena Danchenko told me when I saw her in New York." Peter paused for a moment, collecting his thoughts. He couldn't tell her what Compton had said, true or false; he had promised he wouldn't. He didn't want to mention Beth, either. But he couldn't lie about it. Part of the truth would have to do.

Part of the truth, which was almost the same as a lie. Was that how Compton's thinking had gone? he wondered briefly, bitterly.

"It's a long story," he said, "but the gist of it is that the CIA had an operation to free the Soviet Six, an escape plan that was already in progress when your father went to meet with Miloslavsky. When your father came back, he made the first public announcement that Korcula would take place. Then he sent out a memo to all government agencies ordering a halt to any anti-Soviet activity on the part of the United States. The CIA got the memo and aborted the operation. But the dissidents were already out of Perm and on their way out of the country. The CIA left them stranded there, expecting help that they didn't know had been canceled."

"Oh, Peter . . ."

"It's worse than that," he said, and went on quickly. "The KGB is onto them now. At least three of the six have been killed."

"*Peter*!" Nicole's body stiffened, and the worry in her eyes gave way to a look of horror. "Then they died *because* of Korcula!"

"That's what Steve was trying to tell me when he died."

Nicole sat forward and took a drink of her brandy, letting Peter's words sink in. "So that's why you had to see Daddy when you came here for breakfast," she said.

"Yes." Peter wanted to steer the conversation away from Arthur Compton. "And it's funny," he said, "because I could have saved you the trouble of all this research. Dan Ravage gave me *my* papers for the conference yesterday, but I didn't look at them."

He remembered the envelope Ravage had dropped on his desk. He had put it into a drawer, unopened, not caring about the details of the conference, thinking only of Steve. Yes, it was funny. The answer to the mystery of Marco Polo had been there for him to see, if he'd only bothered to look.

"But if you had," Nicole said, "then I wouldn't have looked into the rest. Now I think I'd better tell you."

"The rest?"

"Do you remember what Ambassador Kersnik said to me just before he died?"

Peter sat rigid at the mention of Kersnik's name. "Not exactly. Why?"

"I'd forgotten myself. But once I learned that Steve's message had something to do with Korcula, I decided I'd better find out. I went to see a professor I know who's an expert in Slavic dialects. The ambassador, he told me, was speaking Serbo-Croatian. I thought there were three separate words— they sounded like 'spray,' 'key' and 'Korcula'—but there were only two. *Sprechi Korculu. Spreche* means '*stop*,' or really something more forceful. Something more like '*destroy*.'"

Destroy? Destroy *Korcula*?

Suddenly Peter felt intensely cold. A new line of truth exploded into his thoughts. Korcula—spoken of twice in one night by two murdered men in their last moments of life. *Investigate* Korcula. *Destroy* Korcula.

He set his drink down hard on the table and pushed himself up off the couch. "I've got to go," he said.

Nicole jumped up after him. "What's wrong? What does it mean?"

"I can't tell you now."

"My God, Peter, this is twice this has happened. You come here, sit down, have a drink, then something happens and you have to leave immediately. Five minutes ago you had to see Daddy . . ."

Peter's thoughts blurred. He had no idea where he wanted to go or what he wanted to do. But he knew he could not see Compton. "I've changed my mind," he said.

"Why? What is it? What's wrong?"

"Trust me."

"*Trust* you! Trust isn't the point. Last time you had to see Steve, and Steve died that night. What is it this time? Is it Kersnik?"

"No!" Peter stopped and took a deep breath. Then he turned back to Nicole, put his hands on her shoulders, looked down into her eyes. "Yes, it's Kersnik," he said. "I can't tell you more than that. You're just going to have to trust me. And promise me something. Promise you won't tell your father."

Nicole looked back at him, frightened and confused. "That I won't tell him what?"

"Don't tell him anything. Don't tell him I was here to see him tonight. Don't tell him there's anything wrong. And for God's sake don't tell him what Kersnik said."

"But *why?*"

"I can't tell you now."

"You can't? Or you won't?"

"At the moment, I really can't. I've got to go. I've got to go *now*, before—"

But it was already too late.

Peter heard a key in the lock, the sound of the front door. Compton was home.

He came into the room, and a smile broke over his face. "Good evening, you two."

The same confident face. The same bantamweight stride. Peter felt numb as he looked at the man to whom he owed more than he could ever repay. Who had been so much more than his closest friend, who was now a stranger. Peter felt numb, and something more—he was frightened.

"Are you leaving, Peter, or can you stay for a drink?"

Peter didn't have time to answer Compton's question. It was Nicole's voice that filled the silence. Nicole talking, explaining that Peter had to leave. A hard day. He was tired.

And he loved her more in that moment than he had ever loved her before.

"Thanks anyway," he said to Compton. He bent down to kiss Nicole. "Call you tomorrow."

"Please do."

Peter squeezed her arm gently. Then he left as fast as he could.

Because one thing was clear in the jumble of thoughts that left him numb and frightened. There was much more to this—more, even, than the lives of six human beings. He had made one mistake, one assumption he knew now was false. Up to now he'd believed that the conference itself was tangential to everything else—ill-used by the CIA and perhaps under threat from the Soviet Union. He had believed that Korcula, at most, had set off conflicting factions, and that it needed to be protected from them. Now he knew more—not much, but enough.

Two men had been murdered, and though they had never met, each one had used his last strength to utter a message. A warning. The *same* warning.

And now, finally, Peter understood. The problem wasn't only related to Korcula. It *was* Korcula.

Investigate and destroy.

24

PETER SAT ON the stone embankment at the edge of Rock Creek, where water rushed over a dam to a deep rain-swollen channel that ran past Pierce Mill and on under the narrow Tilden Street bridge. The mill was off to his right, old stone walls brightened by moonlight. But otherwise there was darkness, hemmed in by trees that cut off the lights of the city. Darkness and silence. Cars passing over the bridge came at long intervals now, and no one was strolling the path that skirted the water. It was past midnight; sane people did not come to the park at this hour. But Peter hadn't noticed the time. He didn't even know how long he'd been sitting there.

He didn't know, and he didn't care. He felt only the ache, like a bruise swelling inside. For Steve, who had died trying to tell him that Korcula was contaminated. For the murdered dissidents he had wanted so much to free. For Arthur Compton and the trust that had turned to deception. For lost hope. For caring. For himself.

He didn't care, damn it! Korcula *was* Steve's international disaster. Somehow, some way, Peter's goals had been perverted, had taken on a new, unwanted shape. So what? Let it happen! He was powerless to prevent it. What could he do that he hadn't done already? Go to Compton?

Sure! Compton was no better than saints and guardian

angels. His promises vanished like theirs, as useless as rosary beads, as useless as strings of popcorn. Injustice was simply the way of the world. It was arrogance to think that he might have changed it.

And yet something inside him would not let him leave it at that. Somewhere beneath the ache, beneath the despair and futility, he was angry. Coldly outraged. He'd been lied to, he'd been used. Somewhere between conception and reality, Korcula had been perverted.

But for what purpose? And by whom? By Compton?

Peter reached for a stone and heaved it into the water; one stone, then another. Something brushed his hand in the darkness—a movement of air, some kind of flying insect. He pulled back instinctively, flicked his hand to brush it away. Maybe Ravage was right all along. Maybe the Russians had seen Korcula as a chance to create a false atmosphere of confidence and trust as a cover for hostile action somewhere else in the world. In Norway. In Berlin. But was Ravage right about Compton? Had he been fooled? Was he blinded?

Peter picked up another stone. Then he heard a sharp sound and turned to the trees behind him. The snapping of a twig, a falling rock. A raccoon perhaps. A stray dog or cat.

But as he turned, something glanced off the rocks beside him and careened off into the water. Peter stared into the darkness, his suspicions aroused. This was Rock Creek Park after midnight, not a safe place to be. He might have thought of that sooner!

Another sharp sound. Something pinged off the rocks, closer this time. And suddenly Peter knew what was happening. Good God! Someone had a gun. Someone was *shooting* at him!

He pushed himself up off the rocks and over the edge of the dam, out of the line of fire. A six-foot drop, maybe less, but he landed hard against the rocks at the bottom, where the water surged up in a spray of white foam. Jarring pain jolted through him. Then he slid down into the numbing cold of the water.

He wasn't hurt, only shaken—but Christ, it was cold! And dark. The water coming over the dam churned up the soft mud of the creek bed. Peter couldn't see anything. He tried to stand up, but his feet sank in to the ankles. He had to swim—away from the dam and the trees where the sniper was hiding, to the opposite side of the creek.

His face broke through the surface, a pale blur against the darkness of water—a target, waiting. But there was nothing, no movement, no sound. He stayed where he was, treading water. Then another bullet struck the rocky bank behind him. He took a deep breath of air and dived under again.

What the hell! If he'd wondered before, now he knew. Someone was trying to *kill* him. And he couldn't see a way out.

No way out, except the exposed banks rising up on both sides of the creek. He couldn't swim downstream, where after a few hundred feet the creek bed ascended sharply and the water depth ran on in inches. There was only this deep channel, carved out of soft mud by the water rushing over the dam. He was safer staying here, but he couldn't do that for long.

The cold was getting to him, stiffening muscles, making it hard to move. His coat weighed him down, too. He slipped it off and swam several yards under water, back toward the place where the shots had come from. When he surfaced again, he was at the edge of the water, where the slope of the bank and a low-hanging tree gave him a little cover. A little, but not much. He waited a moment, listening. Then his feet found a firm foundation and his hands dug into the slippery, stone-covered bank. He pulled himself partway up, breathing silently, trembling as the air touched his wet skin and clothes.

But his mind was clear, as clear as the moonlit night, as clear as the whisper of sound that came from the trees where the killer was hiding. A whispering voice, and then movement. A shadow emerged from the darkness into the moonlight, one shadow and then another—not one man, but two! Peter took in a sharp breath of air. What kind of killers worked in pairs? Pros.

Two professional killers. He could tell by the way they moved—slowly stalking him, making their way inevitably toward the bank of the creek. They had to know he was there, if only because they didn't know where else he could be. If he'd tried to escape, they'd have seen him. And they certainly weren't in a hurry. There was no urgency in the even pace of their steps; they knew he was trapped there.

Peter was shaking violently now inside his wet clothes. He clung to the rocks with hands that were stiff from the cold. He'd rather have done almost anything than get back into that water, but danger revived old feelings, an instinct for survival. He had no choice. He released his grip and let himself slide back into the creek.

For a moment he felt a false sensation of warmth, a contrast to the night air. Then the water closed around him, paralyzingly cold. He couldn't move, couldn't *move*. Still, he had to. He ignored the cold and paralysis, listened only to the urging of his mind. *Swim*. His face broke through the surface again.

The two killers reached the edge of the dam, where minutes before Peter had been sitting. They stood there a moment, talking, not loud enough for Peter to distinguish words or intentions. Then he realized that volume wasn't the problem. It was language itself. They were speaking Russian!

Russian? Were they from the KGB?

An icy fear gripped Peter that had nothing to do with the water or the night air. He didn't know how, but he would escape. He wasn't ready to die.

There was too much to do, too much to prevent. The Russians. Compton. Korcula.

Peter stayed where he was, treading water. Watching. Waiting. One of the killers had a flashlight out now, was shining it over the surface of the water, moving it steadily back and forth in a sweeping motion, from the dam to the opposite bank and back, then farther the next time. Peter prepared to dive again. The sweeping light closed in, swung away.

The other man spoke up clearly, in Russian. "What's that?"

"Where?"

"Over there."

The light swept across the creek to a shapeless light-colored mass clinging to a low-hanging branch on the other side. Peter's gaze followed the beam of light. His coat! It had come to the surface on the other side. The man with the flashlight raised his gun, took aim.

A chance. Not much, but all he would get.

A flash of blue flame spit out of the gun. For a moment, both men were distracted. Peter burst up out of the water and onto the bank. Loose rocks gave way underfoot. He slipped back, almost fell. But then he was up and running without looking back, his legs stiff with cold, his body heavy with the weight of his waterlogged clothes. He didn't think about the killers behind or the darkness ahead. He ran, his mind on one goal. Escape.

A voice erupted from the trees near the mill. "Police! Stop where you are or I'll fire."

Peter couldn't stop. His legs kept moving from their own momentum. A gunshot rang out. A shout, running footsteps. Peter stumbled, fell forward, caught himself, tried to run on. But momentum was gone. Paralysis took over. He fell forward onto the ground.

It was two A.M. when Gena Danchenko tried to reach Peter once more. She dialed his number from the card where he'd written it down, let it ring for a full minute. Then reluctantly she dropped the phone back into place.

Two A.M., and he still wasn't home. Where was he? Why wasn't he there?

That, she suspected, was none of her business. She leaned back on the bed, closed her eyes. There wasn't much point in trying again; she would have to wait until morning.

And anyway, Eleanor might be right. She had probably jumped to conclusions, found trouble where there was none. She had become too suspicious, too quick to accept the darkest view, too easily persuaded that things were not as they seemed. Daniel Ravage was, no doubt, a perfectly nice man, no more and no less than he seemed to be. Eleanor thought so.

But what did Eleanor know of intrigue and deception? Gena didn't agree. Ravage fit the pattern too neatly. Right or wrong, she had to tell Peter.

But not now, not tonight. Gena's eyes felt heavy as her mind drifted toward sleep. Thoughts came less clearly. Only one remained: she would call Peter first thing in the morning. She had to reach him, to warn him. But now she had to sleep.

Peter opened his eyes slowly. A man was leaning over him in the moonlight, a strange figure, unreal, all in black, from his clothes to the full beard that covered the lower part of his face. Peter shook his head to clear away confusion, to stir memory reluctant to return.

"Are you all right?" the man asked.

All right? Peter was freezing, trembling inside his wet clothes. "I think so," he said.

"Then we'd better get moving. There are no police here. I did that to scare them away. I figured it was better than taking them on."

Memory came back. Peter pushed himself up, ignoring the resistance of muscles still stiffened by cold. He stared into the darkness of the trees around him, his senses alert to danger, his body poised to run.

But nothing was moving there.

"Take it easy," the man said. "They're gone. You're safe now."

Memory and relief. Peter nodded numbly. "Thank God you happened to be here."

The man smiled gently, a crooked smile, distorted by shadows of moonlight. "You're no more glad than I am," he said. "I might as well tell you the truth straight out. I didn't just happen to be here. I've been following you for three days."

Peter didn't think there could be any more surprises. "You've been *following* me?"

"Since Steve Katz died."

"Why, for God's sake? Who are you?"

"It's a long story, too long to go into here. For now it's enough to tell you that my name is Eric Levin and I was working for Steve. Since he's gone, I'm on my own, and I need your help."

Peter closed his eyes against a wave of enormous relief. Someone who worked for Steve. Someone to *help* him!

"Steve told me I could trust you if anything happened to him," Levin said. "But I had to be sure. That's why I was following you. Now, tonight, those assassins convinced me."

"*Assassins*? You know who they were?"

"I know how they work. KGB."

Then it was true! Peter's face turned hot, even as his body was trembling with cold. Fear rose inside with a physical force. Old feelings, old terror. Assassins. Professional killers.

The *nightmare*. . . .

Levin reached out a hand to steady him. "It's all right," he said. "I told you, they're gone. You're safe."

Safe now, but for how long?

Peter's gaze shifted to the glow of light on the other side of the trees, which rose up around him like the iron gates of the orphanage, cutting him off, isolating him from the world outside. City lights, pale yellow against the dark sky, not the burning fire of Europe under siege. This wasn't Amsterdam. This wasn't Paris or wartime. This was his world. Safe. Routine and familiar. This was Washington, with its white marble monuments to men of freedom and peace. Men like Compton. . . .

But Compton had lied.

The nightmare was real, in a city that was no longer safe for Peter. It was real here, inside him, in the certain knowledge that KGB killers don't fail. They would come back again, like the soldiers. And this time they knew exactly who he was.

Peter took a deep breath. All right, the killers had failed. Because of Levin, whoever he was, they had failed. A stroke of luck, a twist of timing. Once again, he was a survivor. But he knew he couldn't count on luck to save him the next time. If the KGB wanted him out of the way, he had no more chance than the dissidents. Or Steve.

He turned slowly back to Levin. "Why me?" he asked. "Why would the KGB want to *kill* me? How could I be a threat to them?"

"It's probably something Steve told you before he died."

Peter wasn't ready to reveal how much he knew. "Steve was delirious by the time I got to him. Nothing he said made sense."

"But the Russians don't know that." Levin paused a moment. "And anyway, if that's true, then why did you go to see Gena Danchenko the day after Steve died?"

"Gena's a friend of mine. I don't need a reason to see her."

"Sure. She's also the widow of a man who died because he knew what was on the Korcula tape."

"The *Korcula* tape!" Peter trembled against a new chill. His last shred of hope fell away. The tape—even *that* was a part of Korcula. And yet, oddly, relief rose again inside him. At last, he thought, he was going to learn the truth.

Levin got to his feet and held out his hand to Peter. "Let's go to my place. We'll be safe there, and we need time to talk."

Peter pulled himself up, shivering, bitterly cold. "You said you needed my help. For what? Tell me now."

Levin stood where he was, his expression still hidden by the darkness that covered his eyes. "You want to know?" he said quietly. "All right, I'll tell you. Quickly. I need your help to prevent an assassination. As a matter of fact, a double assassination. And we don't have much time. Nine days. It's going to happen on October 12."

Peter's mouth fell open, but no sound emerged. The shivering stopped, was replaced by a chill far more numbing than night air against wet skin. He stared at Levin through silence and moonlight shadow. The truth, at last; no names, just a date. October 12. The same day two men were scheduled to come to Korcula.

A *double* assassination.

The American President and the Soviet Premier.

25

Levin had a basement apartment in an old town house near DuPont Circle, three rooms end-to-end like railroad cars on a siding. The front room was cluttered with books and papers, some clothes thrown down, a few dishes with the crusted remains of last week's dinner. Obviously he didn't spend much time here, or when he did, he had other things on his mind.

He cleared one end of the couch and gestured for Peter to sit. "Would you like a beer?" he asked. "I don't have anything stronger."

Peter had stopped at home to shower and change. He was dry now, but the chill stayed with him. "I could use something hot."

"Coffee?"

"Fine."

Peter watched as Levin disappeared into the kitchen. He heard the sound of tap water running, the refrigerator door pulled open and then shut, the soft hiss of a pop-top can. It was dark outside, but another couple of hours would bring the first hint of dawn. It had been a long night, and it was going to get longer, because Levin had a lot to explain.

To start with, himself.

Peter leaned back and lit a cigarette, taking advantage of these few minutes to think. At least the killers weren't waiting for him at home. Or had they been there, seeing but unseen? Levin said Peter's building was sure to be under surveillance; he insisted on going along and waiting while Peter changed. Then he drove them here by a roundabout route, increasing his speed to shoot ahead, dropping back without warning, even cutting his lights as he ducked through an alley—all the while not talking, his eyes constantly shifting from the road ahead to the rearview mirror and back.

Yes, Levin knew Washington's side streets the way Peter knew the broad avenues that ran through the city like the spokes of a wheel. More than that, it was clear that he knew exactly what he was doing.

All of which made Peter wonder: who was Eric Levin? Where had he learned how to recognize KGB tactics and how to escape from them? Certainly not as a press aide or research assistant in Steve Katz's office. Where did he come from, then? What did he do before? And why had Steve never mentioned him to Peter?

Why, indeed. There was quite a lot Steve never mentioned to Peter, until it was nearly too late, and even then he had raised more questions than answers.

Peter drew on his cigarette, exhaled slowly, watched the smoke as it rose and disappeared into the air. Something else was bothering him, too, something about the two men in the park. KGB agents—Levin said so, and confirmed Peter's instincts. They fired at him three times.

Then why wasn't he dead?

Were they such poor shots? He didn't think that was likely.

But could they have missed him on purpose? *Why*? A setup? For what reason? And was Levin part of it?

Did Levin really work for Steve?

Peter looked up as a teakettle whistled sharply from the kitchen. A moment later, Levin was back with a beer for himself and a cup of coffee for Peter. "I hope you like it black," he said. "I'm all out of milk. I'm afraid I don't do much entertaining."

"So I gathered." Black was fine. The coffee was hot, and that was all that mattered. Peter took a drink and looked up again. Whatever his doubts, he knew one thing. He wanted to hear what Levin had to say.

Levin sat down in a chair, propped his feet on the coffee table, and took a drink of his beer. It left a line of white foam across his mustache; he wiped it away with the back of his hand. "Feeling better?" he asked.

"Physically, yes. I'm beginning to think I might get through this with nothing worse than pneumonia."

Levin smiled, the crooked smile of the park. Now Peter could see that it wasn't a moonlight distortion but part of Levin's face, which was oddly out of balance, as if modeled roughly in clay with the sculptor's thumbprints still showing. His hair was thick and curly, dark like his eyes and beard, a harsh contrast to the pale, almost pasty color of his skin. Peter had the same feeling now he had when he first saw Levin: a strange figure, unreal, at home in the night, as intangible as a shadow. But on his face was a look of genuine sympathy.

"You're taking this rather well," he said. "But then, it isn't the first time your life has been in danger."

"So you know about that, too."

"Steve told me."

"I see."

"Even so, I'm impressed. Most people couldn't handle a threat from the KGB."

Peter looked at him through the smoke that rose from his cigarette. "I'm not sure I deserve so much credit."

"No? Why not?"

"Because I'm not sure I was really in that kind of danger."

Levin looked startled, as if he thought Peter had gone slightly daft.

"If the KGB wants me dead," Peter said, "then why am I still breathing? They shot at me three times. Are they that hard up for marksmen?"

"It was dark out there."

"Not that dark. And anyway, if they're after me because they saw me with Steve, why did they wait until now? I could have told half the world what he said in the meantime."

Levin's gaze turned thoughtful. "You may have a point."

Peter picked up his coffee and leaned back against the couch. "Maybe they were only a couple of psychopaths on the loose in the park."

"And they happened to choose you? At this precise time in

your life, just when you've managed to get yourself in the way of an assassination?" Levin shook his head. "I'd like to believe that, but I don't, and you don't either. Still, you're right to wonder about it. It's possible they were only trying to scare you."

"But why? Why tonight? Why not the night I saw Steve?"

"Obviously, something you've done since then. Maybe it was your visit to Gena Danchenko." But then Levin shook his head, rejecting the idea. "Have you done anything I wouldn't know about?" he asked. "Have you talked to anyone privately?"

Peter was purposefully vague. "Some people at the State Department. I've been asking questions about the Soviet Six. That's hardly unusual for someone in my job."

"No, but your timing is lousy. It could be a cumulative thing—the fact that you were there with Steve when he died, your trip to see Gena, and your questions on top of that. Maybe you've been too persistent."

"But how could they know? You've been following me, but you don't even know everything I've done."

Levin shrugged. "They're more effective than I am. It's good news if they only wanted to scare you. If you're careful now, they probably won't try it again. But if that's the case, then they must have an inside line on what you're doing, more than simple surveillance. Someone reporting to them, someone close. Quite possibly someone you work with."

Peter's eyes turned cold. "I don't believe that."

"Why not? Do you think the State Department is immune to Soviet infiltration?"

"I'm sure it's not. It's just..."

"The shock of knowing that someone *you* work with might be a Soviet agent."

Peter looked at him for a moment, then turned away. The past rose up again: Paris, the orphanage, a boy named François with red hair and freckles who slept in the bunk above his. Peter could see his face as clearly now as he had seen it then, and it still evoked hatred and fear. A boy who became a pariah, who squealed on his friends, who identified other children to the Nazis.

Peter shuddered against the memory. He wondered what had become of François. Had he grown up to regret what he'd done? Or did he even remember?

And was there a new François in his life? Someone in his own office?

Whom did he talk to? Mary, his assistant, but she was out of the question. Anyway, he'd only asked Mary to get him the files on the Soviet Six; beyond that, she knew nothing. He'd talked to Dan Ravage, but that was impossible too. Of all the people Peter knew, Dan was the *least* likely to switch to the Soviet side; he had lived behind the Iron Curtain and escaped with good cause as soon as he got the chance.

Who else? He'd talked to people on the Soviet desks at State and the CIA, but they were hardly in a position to tell anyone what he was doing. There was Beth Grant, but she approached him, not vice versa. There was Gena. Nicole. And Compton.

Compton! A chilling new thought came to Peter: how far was Compton willing to go in the name of cooperation? Would he risk Peter's life? No! That was inconceivable. Absolutely out of the question.

"For our purposes now, it doesn't make any difference," Levin was saying. "We can't assume that it was an attempt to scare you. We have to treat it as a serious threat. You're going to have to be extremely careful from here on."

Peter took a drink of his coffee. It was not only black, but strong. Bracing. "I won't argue with that," he said.

"That's not just a friendly warning," Levin added. "I'd like to see you get out of this on principle, because you've paid your dues and don't deserve this kind of trouble. But there's more to it than that. I can't *let* anything happen to you now. There's a job to be done, and you have to do it."

Peter raised a hand. "Just a minute, you're getting ahead of me now. I don't want to sound ungrateful—I don't know what would have happened if you hadn't shown up when you did—but I'm not ready to start taking orders, either. You know a lot about me, but two hours ago I didn't know you existed. Frankly, I wonder why I should believe anything you tell me."

"Because you want the truth," Levin replied calmly. "And unless Steve told you more than I think he could have, you're going to have to get it from me. I know because Steve confided in me, because I was working with him."

"So you said." Peter leaned forward. "But how do I know that? You're hardly the sort of person Steve was likely to hire. I mean, what the hell, you tell me those men in the park were

KGB agents; you don't know them, but you recognize their techniques. You take me home, my own personal bodyguard, as if your presence alone guarantees my safety. Then you drive me here like someone who learned how to get rid of a tail about the time I was learning to read."

Levin chuckled. "You flatter me."

"Maybe so. But you told me yourself, you've been following me for three days. Yet I had no idea. That suggests a level of professionalism to me. You talk about surveillance and infiltration as if they were commonplace. And"—Peter leaned back—"unless I'm mistaken, you're carrying a gun."

Levin didn't move for a moment. He looked at Peter with a mixture of amusement and admiration. Then he got up and took off his jacket. The black metal grip of a large pistol protruded from a holster strapped to his left shoulder.

"Standard issue at Freedom International?" Peter asked.

"You know it's not, but my job wasn't standard, either. I didn't tell you I was armed precisely because I didn't know how you'd react. But I see your problem. You want to know more about me. I don't blame you."

Levin took off the holster and hung it over the back of a chair. Then he sat down again. "You're right, I have had professional experience. I spent fourteen years in military intelligence. DIA. Vietnam, Berlin, Lebanon. Then I was transferred to Tehran, and that's where I met Steve."

Peter frowned slightly. "You met Steve in Iran?"

"He was there on a fact-finding mission. I met him through a friend of mine who used to be in the Peace Corps but was, by that time, involved with the anti-Shah forces. Tehran was a kind of turning point in my life. I didn't like what I saw there. Mostly, the U.S. turned its back on what SAVAK was doing. For a while, I did too. It wasn't up to me to question policy. I didn't wear a uniform, but I was a good soldier. I followed orders—right?—even when it meant ignoring what I believed in."

Levin paused and took a drink of his beer. "But you can't get by with that. The more I saw, the more I was sickened by it—the worst kinds of atrocities. Torture. Murder. For purely political reasons. I don't have to tell you about it. It was barbarism, no less, done in the name of self-defense, to keep the

Soviets at bay on the other side of the border. Okay, that was partly true, but it wasn't the whole truth—because anyone who criticized the Shah or the people who worked for him could be accused of treason and dragged off to one of SAVAK's torture chambers. Some were released later, only slightly worse for the wear—missing a leg or arm, maybe an eye, maybe blinded. Others weren't so lucky. They died there, though their families were rarely informed. And the U.S. turned its back on that. It was *policy*."

Levin's jaw tightened as he thought of it now. Anger flared in his eyes. "The more I saw," he said, "the more I was convinced that our policy was wrong—not only because it was alien to everything this country stands for, but because I believed it was going to be fatal to our own selfish interests there. I won't press the point; recent history has proved it for me. I'm only telling you this because it explains where I was when I met Steve."

Peter put his cigarette out in the ashtray. He'd heard the story a hundred times before, with a hundred different settings, but this time it was more painful—because it led inevitably to thoughts of a dream in ashes. To Korcula. He picked up his coffee and waited for Levin to continue.

"Steve was trying to document the things I had seen," Levin said, "but he was getting nowhere. Oh, sure, lots of people talked to him—he knew what was going on—but he needed evidence that he could take back home. His object, of course, was to bring public pressure to bear in the U.S. and other Western democracies, in Congress and European parliaments, to force policy change. I agreed to help him." He shrugged. "Maybe that makes me a traitor, but I don't think so. If I was a traitor, then Steve was too, and you know he wasn't. We were hoping to help prevent exactly what has happened between the U.S. and Iran, and to save a few lives in the process. Obviously, we didn't succeed. The evidence I had access to wasn't enough. The government there changed hands, but the slaughter continues. It's all too familiar, isn't it?"

Peter glanced down at his hands. All too familiar, yes. It took five years of work to produce a day of progress. Much of his own work was only a futile attempt. He raised his eyes to Levin again. "I understand what you're talking about," he said. "God knows, I understand. But that still doesn't explain how you got from there to here."

"Well..." Levin's face changed, as if he had erased the past by sheer force of will. "The experience soured me on the work I was doing, and when my tour was up, I didn't reenlist. Steve said he could use me here, and I took him up on it. He was an idealist—that's not news to you—but he was also a realist. He understood that overt tactics only go so far when you're fighting oppression. He put me on the payroll as a consultant. I became what I was before—a spy and a thief, an infiltrator, an interrogator, a second-story man. The same job, but with one big difference. I no longer had to work against my own conscience."

Levin laughed dryly. "Maybe that sounds like a contradiction to you. I daresay you wouldn't approve of my methods. But I'm not here to argue the gray shades of morality. I had a job—I supplied information that couldn't be had through orthodox channels—and as far as I'm concerned, I still have a job to do. I have to prevent an international disaster, and I need your help to do it."

Steve's own words.

Peter felt his doubts easing. Levin's story made sense. His picture of Steve—the pragmatic idealist pushed into taking measures his gentler side disapproved—was completely consistent with what Peter knew. He knew now how Steve must have felt.

But there was still so much he didn't understand.

"I'm not asking for promises now," Levin said. "Just hear me out. When you have, I think you'll agree, neither one of us has a choice."

Peter nodded. "All right. I'm listening."

A look of relief passed briefly across Levin's face. Then he was all business again. "How much did Steve tell you?"

Peter hesitated, not sure yet how much he was willing to confide. "He told me a lot and a little. He was delirious, talking nonsense, but two words were clear. He mentioned the Soviet Six."

"And that's why you went to see Gena Danchenko."

Levin already knew he'd seen Gena; there was no point in hiding that now. But Peter didn't intend to reveal how much

Gena knew. "She told me the Soviet Six had escaped from Perm. And that Yuri was killed. Yuri and Maria Petrovskaya. Since then I know Pinsky died."

"And Subolev. He's been killed, too."

Peter took the news calmly this time. It wasn't unexpected. And there had been so much death! He was numb to shock and pain.

But now there were only two left. The urgency returned. It sharpened.

"Did Gena tell you why they were killed?" Levin asked.

"She doesn't know, beyond the obvious answer: they were killed eluding recapture. But I know it has something to do with Korcula. I know Korcula is a hoax, from the Soviet side at least. The Soviets lied when they agreed to the meeting. I don't know why, but I assume that's what Steve was trying to tell me." Peter paused, then added, "Arthur Compton is a friend of mine. I think Steve was trying to reach him through me."

Levin almost laughed. "That's not quite what Steve had in mind, but we'll get to that later. What you've guessed is pretty much true, except for one thing. Korcula isn't a hoax, not the way you mean it. The Soviets entered into the negotiations in good faith. Premier Sukhov is committed to it as you are. But the Foreign Minister is unalterably opposed to it."

"Miloslavsky?" Peter was astonished, disbelieving. "That can't be true. He and Compton created Korcula. They negotiated the agreements."

"*Compton* created Korcula," Levin said. "Miloslavsky went along because he had to. The Premier and the Council of Ministers were unanimously behind it. He could not afford to let them know how he felt. Let me tell you what I know, what Steve would have told you if he'd lived to do it. It's the reason Steve called you to meet him that night. And it's something you aren't going to hear around the State Department, because most people there don't know it, and the one who does won't believe it."

Levin pushed himself up out of the chair, thrust his hands into his pockets, and started to pace the room. Peter followed him with his eyes. He felt something stirring inside, a sense of excitement. The truth, at last.

Or was it a sense of dread?

"There are two factions at work in the Soviet government," Levin began. "On the one side, the Premier and most of the people who run things at the Kremlin. They fear the threat of confrontation as much as we do and are dedicated to strengthening détente. On the other side is Miloslavsky, who has consolidated his power with the KGB. I know—publicly, Miloslavsky is an advocate of détente. It's an image he's cultivated to preserve his position with the current regime. Prevailing winds. Among other things, he's a master politician. But whatever he says in public, he's really a hard-liner of the worst kind. His faction wants to destroy détente. They're philosophical purists, Marxist of course, who want to go back to Lenin's original goal. World revolution. And this time they intend to make it work."

Peter looked back at him skeptically and opened his mouth to object, but Levin raised a hand to stop him.

"You've heard this before," he said. "The radical right has been arguing this kind of threat for years. It's kid stuff. Naive. Well, I don't care about that. I only care that they exist, that they're organized, that they intend to try. You can guess how they feel about the Korcula meeting. Even the date, in October—when they celebrate the October Revolution—it's an insult to them. It's no wonder they've chosen Korcula to make their strike."

Peter's skepticism vanished. "Assassination," he said.

"That's right."

"But why? Just to destroy the meeting?"

Levin shook his head. "Korcula itself is the last straw, the event that spurred Miloslavsky to act. It's a secondary goal. Premier Sukhov is the real target. Briefly, Miloslavsky's faction plans to kill him and create chaos at home. A sudden political vacuum, catching everyone else off-guard. Miloslavsky intends to seize power—and remember, he has the support of the KGB."

"A coup?"

"Not quite. Because no one will know there's been one. The transition is all set to go. By Soviet standards, it will be a model of smoothness. And then...*then*...Christ! It won't matter if Korcula happened or not. Every inch of progress toward improving human rights over there will be undone in a second. Utterly wiped out. Miloslavsky will take over and make us wish we had Stalin back. That's bad enough, but there's more to it, because they intend to kill the President first and make it look as if *he* was their target. Sukhov's death will appear to be an accident, an ironic twist, since subsequent evidence—manufactured, of course—will prove that *Premier Sukhov himself ordered the President killed*."

Levin stopped pacing and swung around to face Peter, his eyes blazing, his hands clenched into fists. "Think about that for a moment," he said. "A Soviet plot to assassinate the President of the United States. An *official* plot, conceived at the highest level. Successful. And then revealed. Just imagine the public reaction! Can we count on our own leaders to stay cool in the face of that? And what about Miloslavsky? It's hard to guess how he would play the 'discovery' of that evidence. He might use it to purge his government of the old Sukhov loyalists, which is hardly a move we would welcome. Or he might decide he doesn't need an excuse and let it lie there, a challenge, a dangerous provocation, leaving us with two choices—to lose face or retaliate. And that would be the ultimate no-win situation."

Peter's eyes had grown steadily more incredulous. Now he stared at Levin, horrified. His mouth opened. A question emerged slowly. "Can any of this be *true*?"

"It's all true, I assure you."

"How do you know? How *can* you know?"

"Because I have Steve's word for it. If he'd lived longer, you would too. If he'd lived longer. . . . But they didn't let him."

Levin's hands dropped wearily to his sides, and Peter thought he saw defeat in his eyes. It came as no shock. If half of what he had just heard were true, there was reason to feel defeated. What surprised him was his own reaction to the look on Levin's face. It scared him. He needed the man who owned the gun in its holster across the room. And he realized he was counting on Levin. He started to count on him back in the park when he said he had worked for Steve.

But then Levin pulled himself up and walked back to his chair. He sat down and picked up his beer. "Actually," he said,

"Steve and I worked on this together. It started when we found out about the escape of the Soviet Six. The CIA was behind it. Did you know that?"

"Yes."

"That alone was enough to make us suspicious. I don't know, maybe they were on to the same thing we discovered. Whatever, we started to piece it together between the two of us, with a lot of legwork, a lot of questions. I've always stayed in close touch with the Soviet underground, and much of what we found out originated there. The dissidents, for example, have long suspected that Miloslavsky isn't what he seems to be. They put me in touch with some people who claimed to know, but most of them were afraid to talk. Obviously, I made several trips into the Soviet Union. Then, about a month ago, Steve went there himself. He managed to make contact with a high-level informant, someone close to Miloslavsky, someone Miloslavsky trusts. Jackpot. This man confirmed everything we suspected and filled in the rest. I don't know myself who it was, because Steve never told me, but I think I can make a good guess—Boris Levitsky, the head of the KGB."

"*Levitsky*! But you said Miloslavsky controls the KGB—"

"He does. Levitsky may be in Miloslavsky's position— unable to do what he wants to because it's not what he's *supposed* to do. And the KGB is more than one man, even when it's the chairman. Or I could be wrong. Maybe it's not Levitsky, but I can't think of anyone else, short of Miloslavsky himself, who could know what Steve's informant knew—including a way to prove everything I just told you."

Peter sat forward. "Jesus! *Proof* exists?"

"In Miloslavsky's own voice. On tape."

On tape! Peter's face went pale. All of it fit together. "The tape Yuri and the others were killed for," he said.

Levin smiled crookedly, but he didn't look surprised. "I see you know more than you've told me," he said.

"A little, but not much. I only know there is a tape, that the dissidents are trying to smuggle it out of the country. But I don't know what's on it." Peter looked at Levin across the table between them. "Do you?"

"Yes," Levin said, nodding slowly. "I know. It's a record of the preliminary Korcula meeting between Compton and Miloslavsky."

Peter frowned. "I don't understand. What kind of proof is that?"

"It's no proof, but there's something else on the tape. As I told you before, Miloslavsky went to that meeting because he had to. Maybe he hoped he and Compton wouldn't succeed. I daresay he probably raised every problem he could without being obvious. But when he began to realize the negotiations were going to work out and lead to a summit agreement, he called another *separate* meeting of his own. The assassination conspiracy was planned right there, in the same meeting room late at night, after the official talks were over. What Miloslavsky didn't know was that someone among his chosen group disapproved of the plan. Steve's informant was present—and horrified when he understood what Miloslavsky was planning. He activated the tape system. The conspiracy was recorded, and it's there now on the Korcula tape."

"Did Miloslavsky ever find out?" Peter asked.

"I don't know. But I do know Levitsky was there among the conspirators. He could be the informant." Levin dismissed the point with a gesture. "It can't matter now. Since Steve died, I have no way of making contact. There's no help for us there. I'm afraid we're on our own."

"On our own!" Peter's eyes filled with disbelief. "Are you crazy? This isn't something you and I can take care of. You've got to go to the FBI! Or the Secret Service."

"Steve did better than that. He went to Arthur Compton."

"*What?*"

"He went to Compton two days before he died and told him what I've just told you."

Peter groaned as he sank back against the couch, closing his eyes, remembering that moment with Compton when he had mentioned Steve's name. To Compton it was familiar! *Oh, yes, I remember him now.* One more lie. One more *lie!*

"And what did he say?" Peter asked, not able to look at Levin, not really wanting to know.

"He said Steve was imagining things, creating a whole new problem where plenty already existed. He promised to beef up security at the conference, but a lot of good that will do. Steve told him so. The assassins are going to be part of the Premier's security team!" Levin shook his head. "All right, to be fair, it's a wild story to swallow. But Steve said Compton wouldn't listen; he didn't want to believe it. Korcula is a blind spot with him."

Peter laughed dryly. He understood the feeling. He'd been there himself.

"Compton told him to come back with proof," Levin said, "and that's why Steve called you. He needed your help to get it."

Now Peter looked up. "What proof? How could I help? The tape is in Russia."

"But there's another one here." Levin leaned forward. "The meeting between Compton and Miloslavsky was recorded on tape, by a special system installed by the CIA and the KGB together—a highly technical system that produces not one tape, but two. If you play either one alone, you get what they call white noise—real *noise*, pure tone, nothing more. But if you play both together on the proper decoding equipment, human voices emerge. Compton's voice. And Miloslavsky's. A record of the points they agreed to at the preliminary meeting.

"The point was to have a record that couldn't be made public except by joint action of both governments. When the meeting was over, Compton and Miloslavsky took the tapes, one each, back to Washington and Moscow, not realizing what they had. The agreements *and* a conspiracy to destroy them. Proof. That's what Steve died for—both tapes together—and that's why I need you now. I can't go after the Soviet tape; the underground has to do that, and they assure me they can. What I have to get is the Washington tape, and that's where you come in." Levin leaned back. "I want you to steal it for me."

Peter was openly shocked. Incensed. He knew what was coming, and he didn't want to hear it, but he couldn't take his eyes off Levin's face.

"Compton has the tape," Levin said. "And I think he has it at home. I know it's not in his office."

Peter stared at him, confused. Then slowly he began to understand what Levin was saying. "You actually *searched* Compton's office?"

Levin didn't reply. He didn't have to. The blank look in his eyes was the clearest possible answer. He finished his beer and put the can back on the table. "I said you wouldn't approve of the way I work."

At least he didn't try to soften the truth.

"How did you get in?" Peter asked him.

"Up the fire stairs, down the corridor." Levin shrugged. "An office building is easy, even the State Department. Two or three thousand people work there, and a few hundred more go in and out every day. But you can't lose yourself in the crowd in a private home. And Compton has a security system that would baffle Houdini. I know. I tried to break it and failed. That won't be a problem for you."

Peter shook his head firmly. "I won't do it."

"You have to do it."

"No!" Peter pushed himself angrily up off the couch. "I won't. I can't. I'll talk to Compton, but I will not search his house."

"Fine, you go talk to him," Levin said. "And after you do, I think you'll come back to me."

Peter glared down at him, torn by doubt, filled with fury. "I won't listen, damn it! Why should I? I never saw you before tonight. I don't know if you ever met Steve. I don't know who you are. Why should I believe any of this is true?"

"Because what I've said makes sense. Because it fits with everything else you know. It has to, because it's true. And anyway, if you don't believe me, maybe you'll listen to Steve."

"Steve is dead."

"True. But he left me a message for you."

Levin got up and left the room, and when he came back he was carrying a small cassette tape recorder. He put it down on the coffee table, glanced briefly at Peter, and then pushed the button to start it.

Steve's voice filled the room:

> Peter, I'm making this tape in case something happens to me and I can't talk to you myself. By now you will have met a man named Eric Levin. I can't mention the things he will tell you here. I can only say believe him. He works for me. You can trust him. He'll tell you what I would have told you. Please do what he asks—if not for him, then for me. Or if not for me, then do it for the man who once saved your life.

* * *

Steve's voice, and then silence, broken only by the soft whir of the tape as it ran on through the machine. Peter stood where he was, not moving, too full of anguish to speak. His hands and face had gone damp with perspiration, and a tightness gripped him inside. For a moment he couldn't breathe. It was true! It was all true! Doubt vanished with one more message from Steve.

"Well?" Levin asked.

Peter turned to face him. "You were right. I don't have a choice. I'll let you know when I've found it."

26

Nina Kovalyova had to smile. Here she was, surrounded by the faded elegance of a first-class railroad car, even as she escaped from the Soviet Union. She had never traveled first class; she'd never had the money for it. Her eyes scanned the compartment, pausing briefly to admire the curved brass door handles, the burgundy-colored drapes at the window, and she thought of a time long past, the Russia of the czars, of Tolstoy.

Or Dostoevsky?

Nina's smile faded as reality took hold again. Dostoevsky himself might have traveled this way. He, too, had known the pain of exile in his own land. He had served five years at hard labor, here, in Siberia. Nina's year at Perm was less difficult, and yet somehow more, because nothing had changed. Power shifted. One tyranny rose up to replace another. Life went on.

Nina was alone in the compartment, and grateful for that. At least for now she didn't have to pretend to be something she was not. Someone she was not, a false person, created for this purpose, escape.

Nina hadn't given much thought to the reasons behind her escape. She didn't know exactly who had planned it, or why. The Americans, so it seemed. At least it was an American who had made these arrangements for her, who insisted she travel first class. (Because the *cheka* won't expect to find you there.

They will look for you, if they know where to look at all, among the hard-seat passengers in the rear of the train.) It was the American who supplied the clothes she was wearing— dress, stockings, warm boots, a coat with a thick fur collar— all designed to convey the impression of some (not too much) affluence.

It was the American who gave her the coupons for the train, and traveling papers that identified her as the daughter of a middle-level bureaucrat assigned to a post at Khabarovsk, near the end of the long Trans-Siberian Line. Nina, the dutiful daughter, working in Moscow, was on her way home because her father was ill. That, too, was part of the American's plan. Worry would explain the lines in her young face, the pale tone of her skin, the fear that might spring unexpectedly into her eyes.

Nina wasn't afraid. She was terrified—not for herself, but for Vladya.

She had lived with fear for so long, it seemed absurd to let these feelings surface now. But she couldn't *see* Vladya. She didn't know where he was, or if he was safe—or hungry, or cold. Maybe he'd even been captured!

No, she wouldn't let herself think that. Of course she couldn't see him now. He was hundreds of miles from here, following his own escape route. The American insisted they had to separate. It was harder, he said, to trace one person than two, let alone six. It was safer this way, for Vladya, for all of them. But Nina didn't feel safe. The train was typically over-heated, like all Russian trains in the winter, but she felt coldly alone.

She turned her face to the window. Dusk was starting to settle over the open fields beyond. The train had crossed the Urals and the continental boundary, had left Europe behind. Mountain forest gave way to plains as the vast expanse of Soviet Asia, Siberia, unfolded in deepening darkness, like the endless steppe, to an uncertain horizon still two days' journey ahead. Nina closed her eyes. Her own life seemed as distant as the farthest edge of Siberia. Her days at the university were only a memory now. But it was only four years.

Four years since she finished her degree and was named a Lenin Scholar. She had achieved that distinction, no matter how fiercely they scratched her name from the lists. No matter how often they denied her a post on the faculty or the chance to go on for an advanced degree. They could not take away her pride in what she had done.

Instead, they had taken her freedom. For one reason. Because she loved Vladya. Because she applied to go with him when he wanted to emigrate.

She had seen Vladya only once in all the months between arrest and escape. She never saw him at Perm, where they were put into separate camps with no official lines of communication. But there, at least, she had known that he was nearby. And alive. Secret messages could be passed from time to time. Now she knew nothing, only that Perm was behind them. Whatever happened, Perm was behind them now.

The train jerked over a stretch of uneven siding, and Nina looked up again. The past no longer mattered. The passing scene on the other side of the window roused no more sense of belonging than cinema pictures of some foreign land. She loved Russia once, but now she only loved Vladya. She closed her eyes, and this time she slept.

She slept for an hour or more, until a subtle change in the motion of the train set off an inner alarm. She looked out the window. A small town lay just ahead, and she wondered where they were. Then, quickly—remembering what the American had said about the dangers of *cheka* surveillance along the railroad route—she turned away, raised a hand to shield her face, and picked up a paperback novel.

Somewhere up front, brakes were applied more sharply. The train began to shudder against its own decreasing speed, then jolted to a stop. A light was shining on the station platform just beyond Nina's window. The words on the page before her streamed past, unabsorbed. She heard voices, saw moving figures at the edge of her vision, but she was afraid to look. The movement soon disappeared, was replaced by the sound of footsteps at the end of the car.

New passengers, she told herself.

She turned a page. A door opened and closed. Another door, and another. Each one closer to her than the last.

That's all, just new passengers looking for space.

Then the footsteps paused at the door to her own compartment.

Nina watched in terrified silence as the curved brass door

handle moved slowly inward. The door opened. The figure of a uniformed man filled the frame. She dropped her book, jumped to her feet, backed away to the window. The man came forward as tears rose up in her eyes. She tried to speak, but no sound emerged. There was nothing, *nothing*, to say.

She stared at the man, afraid that he might disappear. It was *Vladya*! Yes, it *was* Vladya!

Nina threw herself into his arms.

Vladimir Levitan was twenty-nine years old, a composer and pianist, a winner of the Tchaikovsky competition, and an enemy of the Soviet state.

He was a criminal. He had been expelled from the musicians' union and banned from the state-approved list of soloists and teachers. His deferred draft status had been revoked, making him eligible—indeed, a prime candidate—for ten years of service in the army. They might as well have cut off his hands.

But here he was, in the very same sort of uniform he might have been forced to wear if he hadn't been sent to Perm before the army got its chance. He held Nina at arm's length, searching her eyes, absorbing the details of her face. He smiled at the mixture of astonishment and relief he saw there. Astonishment and relief. Love and fear.

"What are you *doing* here?" she asked.

"The same thing you are. Escaping."

"But you're not supposed to be here."

"Why not?"

"Because! It's not safe!"

"Safe! I've forgotten what it is to be safe." He raised a finger against her lips to silence her protest. "I'm safe where you are," he said. "That's all I care about now."

He lowered her onto the seat and sat down beside her, holding her close, saying nothing. Questions and answers could wait. For now it was enough that they were here, together.

He had made the decision quite suddenly—not to go to Murmansk, where he was scheduled to leave the country two days after Nina. The uniform and the papers he carried were designed for his own escape, but soldiers were a common sight in this part of the country, so close to the Chinese mainland.

Border clashes frequently went unacknowledged, and so did the soldiers who fought them. He hoped he would not be asked any questions at all—or at least that bravado would supply the difficult answers.

He'd made the decision quickly, even rashly, without ever stopping to let himself think what would happen if he failed to catch up with Nina. He'd been able to manage only a glimpse at her papers during the brief time they'd had together after Perm. If he'd made one mistake—if he'd misread the dates or the route, if he'd miscalculated the time he would need to backtrack—he would have been left here alone, without Nina or the slimmest chance that he would see her again.

But now he knew that he'd made the right choice, the only choice. He had found her. They would both escape by the route set up for her. Then he would have his music. She could study again, or teach—whatever she wanted. They would have a new life on the other side.

And if they were caught, at least they would die together.

Boris Levitsky was alone in the stationmaster's office at Taishet, in Siberia, more than six thousand miles from Moscow. He stood by the window watching the light dust of snow as it covered the trees and neighboring rooftops, and the old cossack fortress that stood in the distance, barely separate from the black night sky. Permafrost would grip the land here later, as winter deepened to the subzero months ahead. But now it was barely cold by Siberian standards, merely ten degrees below freezing. Levitsky pulled up his collar, though the office was said to be heated. Siberian standards, he decided, were not for him.

He turned at the sound of a knock from the outside door. "Yes?"

The door opened with a gust of wind, and a man entered, brushing snow from his coat, closing the door behind him. He crossed the room to the place where Levitsky was standing, brought his heels together, raised one hand in a salute. "The situation is better than we expected," he reported. "Kovalyova hasn't left her compartment. She's been joined there by a companion."

Levitsky frowned. "A companion?"

The man permitted himself a small smile. "Vladimir Levitan. He boarded the train at Achinsk."

Levitsky stared back, incredulous. He couldn't believe his good luck. The best of CIA plans done in by a pair of moonstruck young lovers! It was almost as if the CIA wished him well.

"We have agents throughout the train and at every station from here to Khabarovsk," the man told him.

But Levitsky dismissed the words as unimportant. He knew where his agents were; he cared more for where they were not. "Maintain surveillance," he said. "Beyond that, do nothing—unless you receive additional orders from me."

The man raised his hand in a final salute, then turned and left the same way he had come.

Alone again, Levitsky laughed out loud. There was plenty of time, and hardly a chance for failure. He reached into his pocket to reassure himself that the tape was still there. Then he brought out his train-coupon book and glanced through it. A first-class passage, like Nina Kovalyova's.

And now Levitan was there, too.

Perhaps they could all share the same compartment!

27

MRS. ROSS, THE housekeeper, opened the door, as Peter expected her to.

"Is Nicole home?" he asked. The words stuck in his throat as he spoke them. He didn't like using Nicole's name, but he couldn't think of another way to get into the house on his own.

"I'm sorry, she's out."

"Could I come in and wait?"

"Certainly."

Mrs. Ross closed the door behind him and showed him into the library. "I don't know how soon she'll be home, but of course you're welcome. Would you like some coffee?"

"No, thanks."

Peter did not know how soon Nicole would be home—or at least how long she would be out. She had a long class this morning, and Compton was tied up in meetings most of the day. Peter had time for a good start on what he had to do.

Later he would think of something to tell Nicole, to explain why he'd come here and then left before she arrived. Later. Something. He wished that were the only explanation he would owe her.

"Don't let me keep you from whatever you need to be doing," he said.

Mrs. Ross disappeared upstairs. Peter sat down and picked

up a magazine; he skimmed through it without much interest. Then he heard the sound of a vacuum going on an upper floor.

He stood up and let his eyes scan the room. Where in this house would Compton have hidden the tape? A safe was the most likely place. Or maybe it wasn't. Maybe it was the least likely because it was the most obvious. It didn't matter. Safe-cracking might be Levin's style, but it wasn't Peter's. He wouldn't know how to start.

Where else?

In the office, of course. It had to be in Compton's private office.

Peter knew where to find the button that opened the book-shelves to the private rooms downstairs; the shelves swung open, revealing a flight of stairs. A simple latch worked the door from the inside. Peter closed it behind him. Let Mrs. Ross think he'd grown tired of waiting and left.

Compton's office was just past the wine cellar, across from the exercise room. It was cluttered with mementos of his ca-reer—photographs, paperweights, a gavel from a former House Speaker, presidential pens used to sign various bills and trea-ties, souvenirs of the countries where Compton had served when he was in the foreign service. There were file cabinets built into one wall, and a desk with four drawers in it.

Peter studied the room, while his heart gave a tug at his conscience. What was he doing here, lying his way into the home of his oldest friend, preparing to rifle his office like a thief? He knew what he was doing. He was compromising his honor. And Arthur's. And Nicole's. They trusted him; if they didn't, he would never have gotten free run of the house. He was compromising the principle he valued most, trust in its absolute form. Compromising, hell! He had thrown it away. And the knot of guilt in his stomach was no less severe for the fact that Compton had lied first.

Compton had lied for a reason, however misguided, how-ever blind. He had lied to save Korcula, to bring the world a step closer to lasting peace, to close the gap between his dream and reality. He had lied to keep Peter from meddling, but it was too late for that. Peter was going to meddle. He had no choice.

He had to find that tape.

He sat down behind the desk and went to work. None of

the drawers were locked, nor did they need to be. The house itself was inviolate. Eric Levin could have testified to that. Peter felt one more twinge of guilt. Compton hadn't thought to secure his home from friends who were always welcome.

First the desk, then the filing cabinets.

There were hundreds, thousands, of papers here, correspondence and personal notes on every international issue over the last twenty-five years. Material for Compton's memoirs, yet to be written. Peter paid no attention to them; they were off limits even now. He flipped through the files quickly, glancing at subject headings, feeling for the bulk of a tape that might have been thrust down between them.

Nothing.

He was getting nowhere. Thirty minutes passed. Another drawer searched, snapped shut; another drawer pulled open. C through E. F through H. I through K. . . .

Korcula.

Peter's hands seized the file and spread it open on top of Compton's desk. A few pages of notes. He read through them quickly—and sadly. These were old notes, Compton's earliest thoughts on the concept of Korcula, based largely on Peter's own suggestions. The start of a dream that would turn into a nightmare. Peter stood there a moment, remembering. Then he closed the file. There was nothing here; the tape wasn't in it.

Then, from behind, came the sharp sound of glass breaking. Peter dropped the file and spun around, his defenses aroused by the memory of KGB killers still fresh in his mind. He raised an arm to strike out, to defend, but then pulled it back quickly.

"Nicole!"

She stood motionless in the doorway, her face ashen, her eyes wide with shock and disbelief. A bottle of wine lay broken at her feet. Peter's eyes met hers, and his voice failed. There was nothing for him to say.

Nicole's face softened to sadness as tears came up in her eyes. "Dear God, Peter," she cried. "Anyone else—but not *you*!"

Peter stared into empty space as he paced the length of the library. Anything to avoid looking at Nicole. Her professor had picked a hell of a day to go home with the flu.

Explanations. Peter hadn't bargained on this one.

Nicole watched him in silence. There were no more tears after the first rush of shock. Now her eyes were accusing, full of reproach. She was furious—and, Peter knew, deeply hurt. What a mess he'd made of this! He should have told her the truth from the start—his doubts, his fears, his suspicions. It was easy to see that in retrospect. Now it was probably too late.

What could he say to undo what he had done, to soften the shock of what she had already seen, to make her understand why he'd done it—to make her believe him, and trust him, even against her own father. Trust, obviously, came with no guarantees. He loved Nicole; she loved him. It was no wonder nations couldn't get along.

At least she had loved him an hour ago. Now Peter wasn't so sure.

He turned around to face her. "I know you're upset," he said. "God knows, you have reason to be."

"I don't need you to tell me how I feel," she said coldly. "All I want from you is an explanation. What were you doing here, sneaking into this house, going through my father's personal files?"

"I didn't sneak in. I rang the doorbell."

"On the pretext of seeing me. Damn it, that was a lie. You knew I had a class this morning. You knew I wouldn't be home."

Yes, a lie. Like Compton's lies, motivated by expedience, without regard for who got in the way. "There's a lot I haven't told you," he said.

"That's painfully clear."

"A lot. It's a long story."

"I don't care if it takes all day. I want to know all of it. Everything. And I want to know right now."

Peter smiled. Nicole was her father's daughter, and never more so than when she was angry. Too late or not, he could only tell her the truth.

He crossed the room, closed the door. Then he sat down across from her. "I was looking for something," he said. "A tape. Your father has it, and I have to find it."

She looked back at him defiantly. "Then why don't you ask him for it?"

"He wouldn't give it to me. It's a classified document, far beyond my own clearance."

"Peter, my God!" Nicole stared at him, disbelieving. A secret document beyond his security clearance, and he was trying to *steal* it from her father's house.

But Peter went right on. "I need it to prove a conspiracy," he said. "A plot to assassinate the President and the Soviet Premier."

"You're not serious."

"Completely. It's going to happen at Korcula."

"At Korcula? I don't believe it."

"Neither does your father."

"I don't understand." Disbelief remained in her eyes, but Peter thought he saw a small edge of doubt. At least she was listening to him.

"Well, I understand," he said, "but it took me long enough. It's what everything has been leading to. Steve Katz and Jovan Kersnik were both trying to tell us. Investigate Marco Polo. Destroy Korcula. And they were both murdered because of what they knew."

"Kersnik wasn't murdered. He died of a heart attack."

"Yes, but it was drug-induced." He told her about the cable from Belgrade, the autopsy results. "And that's not all," he added. "Last night after I left here, someone tried to kill me."

A flicker of emotion passed through Nicole's eyes. Her face softened. Her voice dropped to a whisper. "Oh, Peter, I knew it. What happened?"

"I was in the park, over by Pierce Mill. I went there to think, for some time alone, and someone started shooting at me." He told her the rest—how he'd been trapped in the creek by two gunmen who were speaking Russian. He left out no details; if he wanted Nicole to believe him, she had to hear it all. He told her about Levin.

When he was finished, she closed her eyes and covered her face with her hands. He knew she wanted to come to him, to hold him, to let him hold her. But he also knew she wouldn't. There was too much yet to explain.

"You're confusing me," she said. "I don't know what to believe."

"The proof is on the tape."

"But if Daddy has it—"

"He doesn't know what's on it."

"Then you've got to tell him."

"I can't tell him. Steve tried, and your father didn't believe him. I have to handle this my way. I'm going to work with Levin."

"But that's insane! Not only insane, it's dangerous! If someone *is* planning to kill the President and the Premier—"

"Not someone," Peter broke in. "Miloslavsky." He explained what Levin had told him about the conspiracy, where it was planned, by whom, and how it had come to be taped.

Nicole's expression changed from dismay to shock, and then fear. Her voice was barely a whisper. "Peter, dear God, you can't handle that yourself. Are you mad? You have to tell Daddy. If you don't, I will."

"I can't tell him, and neither can you!" Peter pushed himself up and started pacing again. "Oh, Christ, I don't know which is harder—saying it, or saying it to you."

"Saying what? What are you talking about?"

"Your father." Peter stopped and turned back to face her. There was no way to soften it, no way to keep it from hurting. "I can't tell him because I don't trust him. Your father already knows."

Nicole only looked confused for a moment. Then confusion gave way to astonishment; she was stunned. "Are you saying that my father is *part* of this conspiracy?" She jumped up from the couch. "You bastard! You ungrateful bastard!"

Peter took a step toward her. "Nicole . . ."

"Don't touch me! I want you to go."

"But you've got to listen. You have to let me explain."

"I don't want to hear it. I've had enough explanation. I want you to leave *now*." She was glaring at him, full of hatred, but tears welled up in her eyes.

Peter grabbed her shoulders, held them firmly when she tried to back away. "You're going to listen," he said quietly.

The tears spilled over onto her cheeks as she strained against his tight grip, trying to push him away. Peter stayed where he was, didn't budge, and finally she quit fighting. She lowered her eyes, let her shoulders go limp, made no effort to wipe the tears away.

Peter was engulfed by a sense of sadness and loss. For a moment he forgot about Compton and Korcula, and the Soviet

Six, about Levin and Miloslavsky. He forgot the tape, the conspiracy. Forgot everything but Nicole.

He wanted to hold her in his arms, to comfort her, to comfort himself. But instead, he let her go.

"Your father doesn't have anything to do with the conspiracy," he said. "Of course he doesn't. I never believed that. I never could. But he does know about it. Steve told him before he died."

"How do you know?"

"Levin told me. And there was a taped message from Steve. Your father didn't believe him. He told Steve to bring him proof. That's why Steve called me. The proof is on the tape."

"If that's true," Nicole said, "then all you have to do is tell Daddy. He'll listen to you. He'll play the tape . . ."

Peter shook his head. "It isn't that simple. There are two tapes, each a part of the same recording. One alone isn't enough. I need both of them."

"Where's the other one?"

"In the Soviet Union. The Soviet Six are trying to smuggle it out. That's why they're being killed. Four of them *have* been killed."

"Peter, *tell* Daddy!"

"I told him. It was after I went to New York to see Gena Danchenko. I told him. And he lied to me. He lied about the escape and the CIA. He lied about his intentions. He lied about Steve."

"I don't believe that. He wouldn't lie to you."

"It's not an open question. He did lie. I've seen documents that prove what he told me was false. He even suggested that I should take a vacation. He actually wanted to get me out of the way."

"Why would he do that?"

"Because I'm on to something that could destroy his dream. He must have forgotten it's my dream, too. Damn it, Nicole, he's *too* wrapped up in Korcula. He's blinded himself. He won't listen. He won't risk Korcula. He's hell-bent on seeing it happen, and when it does, it's going to tear him apart."

Nicole's tears had stopped. Now she looked only numb. "If you believe that," she said, "then you ought to go to someone—the President, *someone*."

"No, I don't want to do it that way. In the first place, there's

no guarantee the President would see me. Or believe me. In
the second, whatever you think, I'm not an ungrateful bastard.
Your father means more to me than anyone in the world but
you. I won't go around him to someone else. I want the proof
for him, so that *he* can act on it. I want to let him correct his
own mistake. Otherwise, it will destroy him."

Nicole shuddered and turned away.

"I need that tape," Peter said.

She didn't reply.

"Will you help me find it?"

"How can you even suggest it!"

"Because I need your help. Your father needs your help.
At least give me some time. Don't tell your father. If someone
has to tell him, let me do it."

"I don't know."

"Will you think about it?"

"Yes."

"And call me?"

"I'm not sure I can do that," she said. "I want you to leave
now."

"Nicole, I love you."

"Please, Peter. Please go."

28

A PHONE WAS ringing behind a closed door as Peter stepped off the elevator in his apartment building. *His* phone. He looked both ways down the corridor to make sure there was no one there. Then he unlocked his door and made a dash for the phone.

But it wasn't Nicole; it was Levin.

"What do you want?" Peter said.

"I'm checking to see if you've made any progress."

"I told you I'd let you know." Peter hung up before Levin could ask any questions. He would call him back later. At the moment, he didn't want to talk about it, didn't want to explain that the tape might as well be in Russia, with the other one, for the access he had to it. He didn't want to say why. He wasn't ready to face the fact that he had lost Nicole.

He looked through the apartment, then poured himself a drink and sat down. What was he supposed to do now?

Another sharp sound—not the phone this time, but a visitor. Someone was buzzing him from downstairs. He got up slowly, crossed the room to the intercom. He didn't let himself hurry; he tried not to let himself hope.

He pressed the button. "Yes?"

"Peter?" A woman's voice, tinny through the small speaker. "Yes."

"Thank heaven you're home. This is Gena. May I come up?"

Peter's heart sank. Gena Danchenko. He wasn't surprised; he felt only disappointment. He pressed the button that unlocked the door downstairs. Once again, it wasn't Nicole.

Nicole hadn't moved from the library, though the afternoon sun was going down, throwing shadows across the room. For hours she had simply sat and thought.

She had been over everything in her mind, from one view and then another. She had been back and forth, up and down, torn this way and that by her own conflicting emotions. Despair, anger, hope. Love, concern, fury. Disillusionment.

Despair.

An empty place ached inside. None of the feelings could fill it.

Because Peter was gone. She had sent him away. Her own fault, her own doing. No, it was *his* fault. How could he think the things he'd said? After all these years, how could he turn on her father? How could he let anything be more important? An assassination attempt. Yes, of course that was important. If it were true. If it were really going to happen.

The President—my God!—and the Soviet Premier. *Was* it true? Was Peter right?

And her father. Had he lied? Had he lied to Peter?

No, he wouldn't do that. But then, Peter wouldn't turn against him, either. And yet he had.

Nicole sighed. Tears came again. In all the world, there were only two people she loved, and now she had to make a choice between them. An impossible choice, one that left her empty and aching. She wished now that she'd never come back to Washington, that she'd stayed where she was, safely absorbed in a world where trouble ended two thousand years ago. Yet she knew even as she thought it that she couldn't have stayed there forever. The past was only a plaything, a puzzle with missing pieces, a riddle without a known answer, a challenge to the mind, not the heart. It gave her enormous satisfaction to discover a long-buried facet of human existence, to dig into the lives of ancient people. But she also needed a life of her own, and she thought she had found it with Peter.

Now Peter was gone. She had made her choice. She could not go against her father, not now. He was too close to achieving what he wanted. He was too busy, too pressured; he was under too much tension. The effects of it showed in his face and his behavior. He was tired, at times edgy and short-tempered. On the surface, nothing had changed, but Nicole knew him too well. Underneath, he wasn't the same. He was feeling the strain. He was too wrapped up in Korcula.

Peter's very words! Dear God, had she made the *wrong* choice? She closed her eyes, trying to remember exactly what Peter had said. Her father was too wrapped up in Korcula. He had blinded himself, wouldn't listen. He was hell-bent on having his dream, a dream that would tear him apart.

Was she blinded too, by a sense of loyalty that was more instinctive than reasonable? Did she love her father too blindly? And what about Peter? Had she given him a fair hearing? Didn't he deserve loyalty too?

A fair hearing. What if Peter *was* right?

Nicole glanced at the telephone on the table at one end of the couch. Idly she picked up the remote-control switch beside it, pressed a button. Nothing happened. The electric train was broken, and somehow that seemed appropriate. Should she call Peter? Or did she only want to?

Or should she look for the tape herself?

She sat there a moment more, feeling terribly alone. More than that, terribly lonely. Then she put the switch back and turned away from the phone. Not yet. Not now. She needed more time to think.

"I've been trying to reach you," Gena said. "I finally decided to get on a plane and come here."

Peter nodded. "I haven't been home much."

"Nor in your office."

That was true. Peter hadn't been in all day. Given his present mood, he wasn't sure he would ever go back there again.

"I'm sorry you had to go to the trouble," he said.

"It doesn't matter, I had business here anyway. But I'm glad I found you at home."

"Why, has something happened?"

"I'm not sure. Could we sit down?"

"Of course."

Gena leaned back in her chair. "How well do you know Daniel Ravage?" she asked.

Peter stiffened. It wasn't a question he had been expecting from her. "I don't know," he said vaguely. "Pretty well."

"What kind of job does he have?"

"He's in charge of arrangements for the Korcula meeting."

"I know, but is it a sensitive job? Does he handle classified material? Does he have real influence on policy?"

"Some. What are you getting at? I didn't know you knew Dan."

"I don't. I never heard his name before last night. Do you know about his background?"

"The gist of it," Peter said. "He was in Warsaw when the war broke out. His family was killed. He was stuck there for a long time."

"Are you sure of that?"

"Of course I'm sure." Peter was starting to feel annoyed, defensive, and he didn't like the feeling. "Why?" he asked. "Why do you want to know?"

Gena ignored the question and went on with one of her own. "Do you think it's likely that there might have been two families named Ravage, two American families trapped in Poland by the war, each one with two children, including a boy named Daniel, and that the two Daniels would have been the same age?"

Peter laughed uneasily. "That does strain the imagination."

"I thought so, too. That's why I'm here. Eleanor had a visitor yesterday, a man named Ravitch who came here from Warsaw looking for a cousin he still hopes might have survived the war. Her name was Sarah Ravage. Her parents immigrated to this country from Poland. She and her brother were born in New York. Like your friend, her family was visiting Warsaw when the war broke out; they were trapped there. And guess what her brother's name was. *Daniel.*"

Peter's jaw tightened. "So what? Maybe she's Dan's sister. He had one, I think."

"I daresay he did."

"Maybe this man is Dan's cousin."

"That's impossible."

"Why?"

"Because that Daniel Ravage was killed in 1943. Ravitch told Eleanor. He's sure, because he saw it happen."

Peter closed his eyes as the truth swept over him coldly. Levin had warned him—a traitor inside his own office. Peter didn't want to believe it, not then and not now. He shook his head, rejecting what Gena was saying.

"It's an old KGB trick," she said softly. "Quite a few Americans were trapped in eastern Europe by the war. Many of them were killed, and often there was no record, no proof whether they lived or died. The Soviets use those people's names, especially the people who left here as children, because no one can remember much about them. The KGB researches records here and creates a new person to fulfill existing facts. A Russian *becomes* an American and comes home. An authentic American, with no ties to the Soviet Union, above suspicion, free to work."

Peter shook his head. "Not *Ravage*. It can't be Ravage!"

"Then ask him. Find out if he had a sister. Find out what her name was."

"I'll do better than that," Peter said. He picked up the phone and called Mary at the office. "I need to know something," he told her. "I want you to get Dan Ravage's personnel file."

"Now?" Mary asked.

"Yes."

"It may take a minute."

"Then just look something up for me. I want to know if he had any brothers or sisters. And if so, their names."

If Mary found the request odd, she didn't say so. Peter waited in silence until she was back on the line.

"Here it is," she said. "One sister. Name, Sarah."

Peter's hand tightened on the phone. "Are you sure of that?"

"It's here in his own handwriting."

Peter's face went blank as anger welled up inside, and he slammed down the phone without saying good-bye. Now he knew where the Kersnik cable had come from. He knew where the manipulation had started. Ravage! His whole life was a lie!

He looked up at Gena. "I want to talk to Ravitch," he said.

"You can't. I tried to reach him at his hotel, but he'd checked out. He left for Warsaw last night."

Peter turned away. It didn't make any difference. Gena was right. Levin had warned him. A traitor inside his own office! Dan Ravage was Miloslavsky's spy.

Nina awakened suddenly, uncomfortably aware of the stranger's eyes watching her from the other side of the compartment. But as she looked up, his eyes shifted to the window.

He *knows*, she thought. He knows who we are. He knows what we're doing!

She glanced quickly at Vladya, who was sitting stiffly erect in the seat beside her, an anonymous soldier. When they talked now, it was with the mild interest of two people who had chanced to share a compartment on a train. They could no longer touch, because they were not alone, but their eyes met often.

Had the stranger noticed?

Nina lowered her gaze. Then she, too, turned away to the window. She didn't trust herself even to look at Vladya.

The train was descending a mountainside that rose sharply on one side of the track and fell away to a ravine on the other. They were making their way through pine forest, climbing or descending ever since Taishet, where the stranger had joined them.

Nonsense, Nina told herself. The man knew nothing. He couldn't know who they were. Beyond saying hello when he came aboard, he had paid little attention to them.

But now he turned back to face her across the aisle. "I believe we're approaching Nizhneudinsk," he said. "It's a good place to visit."

Nina forced a smile, politely. "I believe I'll stay on board," she said, and glanced out the window. Yes, there was a small town ahead, nestled against the slope of the mountain.

Vladya seemed to sense her apprehension and picked up the conversation, giving her a moment to collect herself. "Is there time to get off at Nizhneudinsk?" he asked.

"It depends on whether you want to get back on," the stranger replied.

Vladya laughed uneasily.

The stranger was looking interested now. "Are you assigned to duty in this part of the country?" he asked.

Vladya nodded vaguely.

"And what are your orders?"

"I'm not allowed to say."

The stranger nodded, as if he understood. He glanced at the window briefly. Then he turned back to Vladya and studied the regimental markings on the sleeve of his uniform. "I wouldn't have thought to meet you here. I'd have guessed you might have been on your way to Murmansk."

Nina felt Vladya stiffen beside her. She looked up at him, then across at the man, who was smiling benignly. He produced a wallet, held it open across the aisle.

Nina wanted to scream, but something held it inside. She felt weak with despair, and yet fortified by hatred. She recognized the name on the card in the wallet. It was whispered with loathing at Perm and throughout the Gulag. This stranger, smiling benignly, was first among the secret police! He was Boris Levitsky. He *was* the KGB!

Suddenly Vladya was no longer sitting beside her. He lunged at Levitsky, grabbed him by the collar, shoved him back into the seat. Then his hand found Levitsky's throat and tightened around it.

Levitsky struggled against him, tried to push him away. "Stop it, you idiot," he gasped.

Vladya's face reddened with strain. His eyes turned cold. His fingers dug into the thick neck. Levitsky's face was scarlet.

Nina jumped up and grabbed Vladya's arm, her own eyes full of terror. "Don't kill him," she cried. "Vladya, my God— we'll never escape!"

But Vladya didn't hear.

Levitsky tried to pry the hand loose. Then he reached up, groping, grabbed an ear, and twisted it sharply. Vladya cried out in pain. He pulled back, and Nina's arms closed around him. She felt only relief. Not that she cared what happened to Levitsky! She just couldn't let Vladya kill him.

Levitsky leaned forward, choking, rubbing the tender skin where the pressure of Vladya's fingers still showed in an ugly red handprint. He pulled himself up, raised the window, and breathed the cold air into his lungs. Then he straightened his coat and swung back to face them.

He shouted an order.

Nina looked around as the corridor door burst open. Then her shoulders sagged and her knees gave way. Four armed guards blocked the corridor. There was no way out. No hope. The escape had failed. The long journey was over.

Nicole dialed Peter's number. He answered straightaway.

"I think I know where the tape is," she said. "If you want it, come now, before I change my mind."

29

NICOLE OPENED THE door as Peter ran up the front steps, and the look on her face told him everything he needed and wanted to know. There was love there, fear, and sorrow— anticipation, the first signs of relief. He took her in his arms and held her. Things were going to be all right between them. The rest could be resolved, but the rest would have to wait.

Nicole leaned back and looked up into his eyes. Her face was pale, her makeup smudged by tears. "Darling, forgive me. I didn't mean the awful things I said."

Peter smiled. "I'm afraid I deserved them. I should have been honest with you. I should have told you everything much sooner."

"It's just that I was so shocked..."

"I know. I've been shocked once or twice myself in the last few days."

"That's all the more reason why I should have listened. Peter, I'm still confused. I don't know what I believe now. But Daddy *has* been under a lot of pressure."

"And it may have affected his judgment. I worry about that. I get torn between caring about him and..." Peter stopped abruptly, not wanting to jeopardize what he'd almost lost. Nothing was worth the risk of losing Nicole again.

She touched his face and smiled. "We can't avoid talking

about it. We have to finish it now. You get torn between caring and hating him because you think he may have betrayed your trust. I understand that. I'm not going to choose between you because I can't. If Daddy betrayed you, he must have had a reason, and I want to know what it is. If he didn't betray you, then there's even more to find out. And that's why I'm going to help you."

Peter pulled her close again; his lips brushed her eyes and her hair. This trust, at least, was solid. This love was sure; it would last.

But the simple contentment he was feeling couldn't last. There wasn't time for it now. Nicole was right; what was started, they had to finish. They had to find the tape.

"Where is it?" he asked.

"Come with me."

Nicole took his hand and led him into the library, where she picked up the remote-control switch from the table at the end of the couch. "It's broken," she said, and handed it to Peter. "At least it *appears* to be broken, and it has been for several weeks."

Compton's electric train, with its track built into the molding around the ceiling. Four buttons—forward, reverse, a whistle, real steam. Peter tested them; nothing happened. He remembered trying to work the train a few nights ago, the night they went to the opera, the night Kersnik died, and Steve. He had tried, but it didn't work then, either.

"It's not like Daddy to let these things go unrepaired," Nicole said. "I think the tape is hidden up there in the train."

Peter looked up. Light fixtures set into the molding threw a soft glow onto the ceiling, but there was no sign of the train. "Where is it, then?" he asked.

"That's the point, it's in the tunnel. And with the remote switch not working, there's no way to bring it out."

"*No* way?"

"No obvious way. There's a manual switch up there somewhere. I don't know where it is."

Peter's eyes shifted to the tunnel that ran along the top of one wall, over the bookshelves that hid Compton's private stairs. A smile spread slowly across his face. "You're brilliant," he said.

"Not brilliant. I only live with the man. He's done this before, hidden things in the train, when he goes out of town and has to leave the house vacant. There's a boxcar with doors that slide open and shut. It's not quite big enough to conceal the family silver, but it is big enough to hold a small reel of tape."

Peter studied the overhead molding. Then he pulled up a chair and climbed up for a closer look. "Knowing your father," he said, "it shouldn't take me more than two days to figure this out."

But it didn't.

The track was nailed to a board that lay flat where the molding adjoined the wall. Ballast filled the spaces between the ties, and shrubbery sprouted along the side of the track bed, all of it done in miniature, done to scale. Peter poked and prodded, looking for something movable, for the manual switch. One of the track ties was loose. It shifted at Peter's touch, and inside the tunnel the engine came to life. Peter almost expected to hear a conductor shouting.

The train charged out of the tunnel, whistling and puffing smoke, hissing with real steam. Peter let it go once around the track, around the four walls of the room. Then he switched the track tie back to its original position. The whistle sounded one last time; the train slowed down with a last shot of steam and came to a stop where he stood.

The boxcar with the sliding doors was three cars back from the engine. Peter opened the doors, peered inside. There was something there. His heart started pounding faster as he reached for it with an unsteady hand.

A moment later, he was holding the Korcula tape.

An ordinary reel of tape. Nicole studied it, frowning, as she threaded it into her father's tape recorder. She glanced up at Peter. "How do we know it's what Levin says it is?" she asked. "How do we know it is the Korcula tape?"

"By what we hear on it."

"Daddy talking?"

"No."

Peter started to explain, but Nicole raised a hand to stop him. The tape was unwinding onto the take-up reel. He reached for her hand and held it as they listened. There was silence.

Silence. Then a piercing sound erupted into the room, a shrill whistle that soon descended to a low-pitched hum. The hum ran on for another ten seconds or so and then lapsed into silence again. This time the silence was punctuated by a series of small beeps, so soft that they were almost inaudible. Peter timed them; they were coming at regular intervals, on the second. The tape continued to unwind, but there was nothing more on it.

Peter shut off the machine. It was noise. It was just as Levin described it.

Nicole leaned back, her eyes on the tape; she was puzzled. "That's all there is?"

"That's only the start," Peter said. "It takes both tapes. You have to play them together on the right kind of equipment. Beyond that, I don't understand myself. I'm going to see a man I know at the Smithsonian; he does all of their records and tapes. Maybe he'll know more about it."

"And after that?"

"I don't know."

"Are you going to give it to Levin? Do you trust him?"

"Besides you, he's the only person I do trust."

But Peter wasn't sure that trust was enough anymore. He picked up the tape and held it in his hand, saying nothing. The issues it represented were staggering—war and peace, life and death—and so was Peter's responsibility for them. It was an enormous burden. An enormous risk.

But one Peter couldn't duck. He had to see it through, and for that he needed Levin. But he didn't intend to *give* the tape to anyone.

He looked up at Nicole. "What I need is a place to hide it for now, an electric train of my own."

Nicole smiled. "I have an idea," she said. "Let me tell you about it."

The equipment in Carl Whitney's studio in the old Smithsonian castle on the Mall was as baffling to Peter as the blueprints for an ICBM. There were turntables and tape decks, amplifiers, mixers, and filters, all wired for sound by a system that looked more intricate than the inside of a telephone. In the whole room there was only one thing Peter thought he could manage without a book of instructions, the coffeepot on a table under the arch-shaped windows. But Whitney already had that going, too; it belched now and then to prove it was perking.

Whitney was the Smithsonian's director of sound technology. He was a big man with graying dark hair and a boyish smile that took years off his age. Peter no longer remembered where or how they had met; it was years ago. But if anyone in Washington could tell him how the tape worked, it would be the man who was master of all this equipment.

Peter handed it to him with no explanation and only one question. "What can you tell me about this?"

Whitney turned the reel over in his hands, frowning with obvious interest. What looked ordinary to Peter and Nicole apparently wasn't to him. He unwound a short length of tape and examined it with his fingers, held it up to the light, turned it over. "I've never seen anything like it," he said. "It's not a commercial brand. Where did it come from? What is it?"

"I was hoping you could tell me."

Whitney's frown deepened.

"It's supposed to be a record of a meeting," Peter said, "but when you play it, all you hear is noise."

"Noise?"

"It starts with a sharp whistle; then it goes to a humming sound and from that to a series of beeps. Play it yourself. I'd like to know what you think."

Whitney sat down behind his desk and wound the tape onto a small desk-model recorder. Then he pressed the play button and listened. The sounds emerged from the speaker and finally faded to silence. Whitney looked up. "Is there anything more to it?"

Peter shook his head.

"All right, then let's hear it again."

Whitney rewound the tape and leaned back in his chair, eyes closed, face tense with concentration. When it was finished, a moment passed in silence. Then he got up and crossed the room, taking the tape with him.

"Could it be a hoax?" Peter asked. "Is it possible there's nothing more on the tape?"

"I don't think so," Whitney replied over his shoulder as he

headed the tape into a different machine. "But frankly, I'm puzzled by it. Let me try something here; then I'll tell you what I'm thinking."

Peter walked over to the windows and looked out on the Mall, where the trees were at their peak of fall color. The carousel below was closed down for the season, but the children had found a new place to play; they were scaling the giant triceratops near the entrance to the Museum of Natural History. The day was warm for October. People filled the gravel paths that ran the length of the Mall, from the Washington Monument all the way to the Capitol. Some were walking, some running, some riding bicycles. And some were stretched out in the grass to enjoy the sun before it gave way to the damp chill of another Washington winter.

Peter's city. Routine and familiar. He wondered if he would ever again spend a lazy summer Sunday here, with nothing more to worry about than the tourist crowds or the line at the hot-dog vendor. He lit a cigarette, tossed the match into an ashtray by the coffeepot, and turned away from the windows.

Whitney was at his desk once again, holding the tape and gazing at it intently, as if it might reveal its nature to him by osmosis or telepathy. After a moment, he put it down and looked up at Peter. "What you have here doesn't exist," he said.

"I beg your pardon?"

"Well, of course it *exists*," Whitney added, with a gesture for the physical object before him. "It's here. I can see it and touch it. I can hear what it's trying to say. And I know what it is. There's only one problem: the technology doesn't exist yet, the hardware to create it. What I think it is is impossible, but I can't think of another way to explain it."

Peter pulled up a chair and sat down. "What do you think it is?"

"A digital tape recording in micro-mini form. Sound converted to binary digits and left that way, undecoded, with quantization error controlled by white noise to offset distortion."

"What the hell does that mean?"

"It means I can't bring out what's recorded on this tape." Whitney leaned back and let his eyes scan the equipment that filled the room. "Everything here is analog," he explained. "Conventional recording equipment. By analog method, you get an actual waveform, continuous sound—music, talking, whatever—engraved into a disc or in magnetic patterns on tape. The same principles Thomas Edison developed a hundred years ago, and they haven't changed fundamentally in the meantime. Until now. Digital sound. It's the hottest new thing in the music-recording business."

Peter drew on his cigarette. "But you said it didn't exist . . ."

"The process exists," Whitney said, "and to some extent it's even available to the public. Playback equipment for digital disc recordings is on the market now in sizes designed for consumer use, though they're still much too expensive. But the taping part of the process is another matter. It's a computerized operation that requires a data-handling system composed of at least three modules, each about the size of a refrigerator and worth at least a year's salary—if you're well paid, that is. And digital tapes are much larger than this one. The R-and-D people at half a dozen companies are working on integrated circuitry, trying to miniaturize the process, like the kind of thing that happened with digital watches and calculators, but right now there's no such thing as a transistorized digital tape deck."

"What if I told you the people who made this tape don't acknowledge the word impossible?" Peter asked. "What if I said they've got access to vast sums of money, enormous electronic expertise and technical services that simply aren't available in the private sector? Would that make a difference?"

"Are you talking about the CIA?" Whitney let out a slow whistle.

Peter shrugged. "Something like that."

"It certainly would make a difference. They could be years ahead of the industry, especially with a tape like this one—talk instead of music—since the signal is much less complex and they wouldn't have to worry about precise sonic fidelity. As a matter of fact, if they wanted to keep a secret on tape, I can't think of a safer way to do it."

Peter could. If one tape based on "nonexistent" technology was secure, then that tape split in half, with the halves maintained on opposite sides of the world, would be inviolate.

"Let me ask you something else," he said. "Can you tell if this tape is complete? Is it possible that it's only a part of the original recording?"

"Not only possible, but entirely likely," Whitney replied.

"Digital recording involves ultrahigh frequencies, millions of cycles per second, much higher than human hearing. That's why, when I play this tape on my analog equipment, we can't hear what's recorded on it. So what are the sounds we do hear? The first sounds, your whistle and hum, are manifestations of white noise that's programmed in to help minimize a certain kind of distortion. But the pulses that follow are something else. They've been added by an electronic beeper. They're precisely timed and can have only one purpose—synchronization, lining up this tape with another. All of which means there are at least two tapes designed to be played together, for whatever reasons. I can't say whether they're both parts of one original recording. One could be background music for voices on the other."

"But the tape could be divided?"

"Yes."

"Is it possible that one tape played, even on digital equipment, would be meaningless without the other?"

"Certainly. Remember this, digital recording is a computerized process. You don't edit digital tape by the old splicing method, for example. You talk to it. You program it. You *tell* it what to do. Two tapes could be programmed to produce sound only when they're played together. There could be a third tape that tells the equipment how and when to synchronize the other two. Or they could be programmed to work only on a specific tape deck that accommodates both tapes at once. If you're talking about something secret, that kind of programming would do it. I doubt if anyone could play those tapes except the people who made them, or someone with access to their equipment."

"If I had both tapes, could I play them?" Peter asked.

"Damned if I know how. *I* couldn't. You can't buy that kind of equipment in a store. But maybe they've got a lending library at Langley."

Peter laughed.

But maybe they did. Maybe Beth Grant could help him.

"One more question," he said. "Can you make me a copy of this?"

"What, just your whistle and hum?"

Peter nodded.

"The tape itself would be different," Whitney said, "but only an expert would know that. Of course, none of the original material will transfer to the copy. But yes, I can make you one."

Compton wasn't an expert, and Peter wanted the copy to replace this one in the train. "That's good enough," he said. "How fast can you do it?"

"When do you need it?"

"Right now."

Thirty minutes later, Peter left the old castle building. He found a pay phone and called Levin to set up a meeting for later. Then he dialed the CIA.

"Beth Grant, please."

"Just a moment."

A man came on the line, and Peter asked for Beth again. There was a moment of silence.

"Well?" he asked. "Is she there?" He was slightly annoyed, but also apprehensive. Had they found out what Beth had done?

"No, she's not," the man said. "Could someone else help you?"

Peter didn't want to leave his name. "I'm a friend of hers. Do you know when I can reach her?"

Another long silence passed before the man spoke again. "I'm sorry to have to tell you this, but if you're a friend . . ." He paused and then blurted it out. "Beth was killed last night in an accident on the beltway."

30

NICOLE DROVE NORTH on Wisconsin Avenue, making her way through the rush-hour traffic and keeping an eye on the shop fronts on her right. She spotted the one she was looking for over a pair of sleek, mirrored doors: Barclay Interiors, Retail and Trade.

She had called ahead and found out the shop closed at five, but Olivia Barclay had said she was willing to wait; for the daughter of a client like Compton, whose house was one of her showpieces, she would probably wait until this time tomorrow morning. But Nicole was in a hurry herself. She had to finish her business with Olivia and get home in time to see Peter again before he met with Levin. Then she would take a long hot bath and try to undo the damage the emotion of the day had done to her appearance. She and Peter were going out.

And if being out for the evening was part of Peter's plan, there was no reason why they shouldn't have a good time.

But first, Olivia Barclay. Nicole turned into a side street and looked for a place to park.

It was seven o'clock when Peter walked into the Great Hall of the Library of Congress, where a pair of marble staircases rose to a recessed colonnade that housed the library's permanent exhibitions. The main reading room was still open, but at this hour few people came to see the Gutenberg Bible or the contents of Lincoln's pockets when he died. It was a good place for a quiet talk.

A private talk. Levin had already proved he knew how to get somewhere without being followed. And anyone following Peter would find it hard to remain unobserved from the upper level.

Levin was there and waiting when Peter came up the stairs. His dark eyes and beard were reflected in a glass display case, superimposed over a manuscript that appeared to absorb his attention. He looked up as Peter approached him. "Have you found the tape?" he asked, his voice low, his tone anxious.

Peter nodded.

"Thank God! Where is it?"

"I don't have it."

A look of worry crossed Levin's face and was mirrored back in the glass. Peter glanced at the reflection. Then his eyes shifted focus to look at the manuscript, a rough draft of the Declaration of Independence in Jefferson's own handwriting, with marginal notes by John Adams and Benjamin Franklin. Unalienable rights, self-evident. The course of human events hadn't come very far in the meantime.

He looked back at Levin and steeled himself for the reaction. "I have the tape, but I didn't bring it with me. I'm not going to give it to you."

"What are you talking about?" Levin said. "Of course you'll give it to me!"

But Peter shook his head. "It's a government document, classified. There's the law, for one thing, and my own responsibility to my job. I can't give it to anyone. I have to be there when the two tapes are played. I want to hear for myself what's on them."

"Oh, Christ!" Levin shoved his hands into his pockets and turned away in frustration. He moved closer to the balustrade overlooking the Great Hall. A guard was crossing the floor below, his footsteps echoing up through the chamber. Levin watched him in silence, from behind one of the marble pillars. Then he turned back to Peter, who had come up beside him.

"All right," he said, "I understand how you feel. You've got a right to hear them, and I'll try to arrange it. But I can't let you keep that tape. It's too dangerous. If our friends from the park even suspect you have it, they'll come down on you so fast, so hard, you won't even see their faces."

"That's a calculated risk," Peter said.

"That's suicide! If you're intent on risking yourself, that's your business, but I can't let you sacrifice that tape."

What Levin was saying was true, and Peter knew it. He hadn't forgotten the experience at Pierce Mill. He hadn't forgotten how many people were dead because they had come too close to Miloslavsky's plot—including, possibly, Beth Grant. But all of that only strengthened Peter's determination.

"I don't plan to sacrifice it," he said. "It's in a safe place, and it's going to stay there. We have to do this my way."

"Why?"

"I told you."

"No, there's more to it." Levin suddenly looked alarmed. "Have there been any more incidents like the one in the park?"

"Nothing like that," Peter assured him. "And it's not that I don't trust you. You worked with Steve, and that's enough for me. But I trusted Arthur Compton, and he lied to me. I trusted Dan Ravage, and he doesn't even exist. I may be naive—I'm not very good at double-dealing—but right now the only person I really trust is me."

Levin studied Peter's face in silence for several seconds, his eyes veiled in darkness, the thoughts behind them unclear. "Is there any way I can change your mind?" he asked.

"None."

"Well, I think you're dead wrong, but I guess you don't care about my opinion."

Peter smiled. "I wouldn't put it that way."

Levin returned the smile briefly. Then he started to walk slowly along the balustrade toward the other staircase at the opposite end of the hall. "There's one problem," he said. "I'm not going to get the other half of the tape for at least another forty-eight hours. By that time, you'll be on your way to Korcula."

Peter followed along beside him. "Why is that a problem? You can bring it to me there. After I've heard them, we'll go to Arthur Compton."

"That's cutting it pretty close."

Peter shrugged. "Until you have the other half, there's nothing you can do anyway."

Levin conceded the point. "But there's still the matter of the equipment we'll need to play the tapes."

"A transistorized digital tape deck?" Peter asked.

Levin frowned. "Did I tell you that?"

"No, I've been doing some research."

"I see you have." Levin chuckled; he was impressed. "Maybe I've underestimated your natural bent for an undercover job."

"I doubt it," Peter said. "That's all I know, except that it's not the kind of thing you can buy in a store. I was worried about it."

"Well, don't be. I've already got the equipment. Steve got it somewhere, probably from his informant. I was only thinking about how I would get it to Korcula. But never mind that. I'll take care of the tape deck. *You* take care of that tape. If anything happens, if you have the slightest suspicion that someone knows..."

"I'll let you know right away," Peter promised.

"Be sure you do. I'm not happy about this at all."

"I'm sorry."

Levin shrugged. Then he said, "Who's Dan Ravage?"

They had reached the other staircase. Peter glanced down. A bronze statue stood in the spiral of the banister at the foot of the stairs. Marble cherubs were set into niches in the wall. The guard had vanished. The Great Hall was empty.

"I was going to tell you," he said. "You warned me about a Soviet agent working in my department. That's who Dan Ravage is."

Levin looked at him, frowning. "Are you sure?"

"I'm sure." Peter told him what he'd learned from Gena and Ravage's personnel file. "There's hardly room for doubt," he said. "He's the last person I'd have suspected, because of his background, but that's the idea, I gather." He laughed dryly. "Right background, wrong person."

Levin's eyes turned sympathetic. "I know how you feel, but Gena is right. It is an old KGB trick. What's his job?"

"That's the problem," Peter said. "He's in charge of all the arrangements for the Korcula conference."

Levin looked horrified. "Is he *going* to Korcula?"

"Unless we can think of a way to prevent it. I don't know how. Normally, I'd go to Compton, but—"

"I'll take care of it. Where does he live?"

"On Virginia Avenue." Peter was suddenly worried. "What are you going to do?"

"Nothing permanent. That's not my style."

Peter swallowed hard and lowered his eyes. Ravage *had* been his friend. No, that was wrong. Friendship was a pretense; manipulation was real. Ravage never existed; he didn't exist now.

And anyway, Levin's duties for Steve could not have included murder.

Peter glanced at his watch. "I have to go," he said. "I've got a date."

Levin nodded. They were finished. Then he reached out to touch Peter's shoulder. "I want to thank you for what you're doing," he said. "I know this is tough on you, but Steve was right when he said I could count on you to be with me. I'm glad we're on the same side."

Peter smiled. "I am too. I've been glad since the moment you appeared in the park."

"Forget it," Levin told him, and his hand dropped away. "Just take care of yourself. And for God's sake, take good care of that tape."

Peter stopped by his own apartment and took a careful look at the arrangement of it—the position of the towel he'd left lying on the bed; the exact location of books, ashtrays, pictures; the angles of rug to couch and of couch to chair. Then he placed a thread in the doorframe, locked the door, and went to pick up Nicole.

When he came home four hours later, the thread was gone. He knew the door had been opened, his apartment entered, as he had expected it would be. Still, he was impressed. Nothing was out of place, not a glass or a handkerchief. Everything was exactly as he left it.

Except the thread was gone. Levin had been here. He was by his own admission a spy and a thief. He didn't like the position Peter had taken. He could not have resisted the urge to do it his own way.

Peter smiled. Levin had been here; he tried. But he couldn't have found the tape because it wasn't here. It never had been.

Peter had put the copy Whitney made for him in the electric train. And then he gave the Korcula tape to Nicole.

The next morning, Daniel Ravage left his apartment building and walked across Virginia Avenue to the drugstore in the Watergate, where he bought a copy of the Washington *Post*. There was a coffee shop in the back. He sat down at the counter, exchanged a few words with a waitress whose name he couldn't remember, and ordered his usual coffee and Danish. Then he opened the paper and started to read.

A few minutes later, a man sat down beside him. Ravage looked up, nodded, and moved his paper to the other side of his plate.

The man ordered tea. When it came, he reached across Ravage for the sugar.

"Excuse me," he said. "Oh, sorry!"

His hand had bumped Ravage's coffee cup and very nearly spilled it.

"It's all right." Ravage turned back to his newspaper.

The man drank his tea quickly. He dropped a quarter on the counter, took his check, and left, heading for the cashier at the front of the store. Ravage watched him go, frowning slightly. Then he picked up his coffee and continued to read.

It was several minutes before he began to realize something was wrong. His vision was starting to blur; the lines of newsprint ran together, moved apart. He shook his head to clear it, but that only made his head hurt. A pain rippled through his left temple.

He looked up, trying to focus, trying to find his waitress, trying to remember her name.

Then the pain returned, more harshly.

His face was flushed. He felt feverish, hot and cold. He dropped the newspaper and clutched the edge of the counter with both hands. Thank God, the waitress had seen him. She was coming this way, hurrying. . . .

Standing over him now. "Are you sick?"

Ravage tried to speak, but his tongue had grown thick. He could only groan.

The waitress looked up, called for help. An ambulance!

Ravage clung to the edge of the counter as his head started to spin. He felt weak; he was starting to shiver, and there was a bitter taste in his mouth. Then, for a moment, his vision cleared. He saw the coffee cup, half-empty, and remembered the man who had come to sit down beside him. His lips tried to smile; laughter emerged from his throat as a gasp of air. But for that moment his mind was clear, and so were the circumstances.

He had been discovered! He had known it would happen, had been waiting for it for years. And now his death had been ordered from Moscow!

He fell forward, knocking the coffee cup to the floor. The waitress screamed.

Betty, he thought. The waitress's name was Betty.

It was the last thing he remembered for several days.

Levin waited outside in the Watergate plaza until he heard the siren coming near. Ravage would spend a few days in bed, and that was enough to stop him from coming to Korcula.

After Korcula, Levin planned to meet up with Ravage again. But that would keep.

He smiled. Then he hurried away as a crowd began to form.

Nina's hands whitened on the armrests of her seat as the plane touched down in an undisclosed location. Terror rose in her throat. She *knew* where they were, where they had to be! Near Moscow. And their next stop would surely be KGB headquarters. Lubyanka.

She knew it, though no one would tell them. Levitsky had said almost nothing since they left the train at Nizhneukinsk. He wouldn't say where they were going, or why. But Nina knew, and the knowledge was paralyzing.

The plane shuddered against its own forward momentum as the pilot applied the brake. Nina slipped her arm through Vladya's, leaning against him for comfort. He was outwardly calm, his eyes blank and staring, but she knew he was torn, as she was, by fear and longing. Wherever they were, these could be their last moments together.

Their last moments! Her fingers dug into his arm. His hand covered hers, held it tightly. They were rolling past a series of small gray buildings, but Nina didn't see them. Across the aisle, Levitsky unfastened his seat belt. The four agents who had accompanied them from Nizhneudinsk got to their feet and made their way toward the front of the plane. There were no other passengers on board.

Nina tried to force the fear from her mind. She studied Vladya's face, memorizing, though she already knew it by heart. She tried to recapture the joy she had felt when she saw him on the train, to store up a sense of his presence, to treasure this moment, not thinking about the next one. But the fear refused to be brushed aside. It clung to her, as she was clinging to Vladya.

Then the plane stopped near one of the gray buildings, and a fuel truck pulled up alongside it. Steps were rolled into place. The four agents got off. Levitsky stood up and put on his coat, taking his time, carefully fastening each button. Nina held her breath. Orders to them would be coming now, anytime. She clutched Vladya's arm. Now, in these last moments.

"I'll be leaving you here," Levitsky said.

He was standing over them in the aisle, smiling, his hand extended, offering a small package. Nina stared at him, not moving.

His voice dropped to a whisper. "Yuri Danchenko gave you a tape to take with you out of the country. That tape is a blank. This is the one he wanted you to have. I'm trusting it to you, along with my own identity. Keep it safe. You'll be met at your destination."

Nina took the package he thrust into her hands, her eyes meeting his, astonished and bewildered.

But Levitsky said nothing more. He turned and walked off the plane.

And then they were moving again, backing away from the building, swinging around on the runway, picking up speed for liftoff.

Keep it safe. You'll be met at your destination.

Met by whom? Met where?

Nina looked at Vladya, scarcely daring to hope. Then she started to laugh and threw her arms around him. They were in the air and alone, except for the crew in the cockpit. Alone and alive. Together.

Together!

And on their way to freedom.

31

THE PRESS POOL was waiting for Compton when he boarded the plane at Andrews Air Force Base. An aide had briefed them already; it would be the usual backgrounder, with no direct quotes from the Secretary.

"Ladies and gentlemen," Compton began in a voice edged with excitement, "you know I'm a careful man. But I believe that what we have in the making may be the most important international development of our time. Future generations will thank us for the journey we're starting today. They may owe their very existence to the outcome of this quest for peace. . . ."

As Compton went on, the big jet moved into position for departure. Its passengers were the forty-nine members of the American delegation, who would travel by air to Dubrovnik and continue from there by passenger steamer up the Adriatic coast to Korcula.

As the ranking member of the Soviet delegation, Miloslavsky was seated in the forward section of the plane, impatient to take off. Levitsky had already boarded and was sitting four rows behind him. More importantly, he had raised his hand in a signal. The tape had been delivered.

Miloslavsky was anxious to go. And now, at last, they were moving away from the terminal building toward the runway.

The Deputy Foreign Minister was sitting across the aisle. He looked up, smiling broadly. "Comrade," he said, "I believe our cause is about to take a major step forward."

Miloslavsky grinned. "Possibly. Quite possibly."

Then he leaned back and closed his eyes. A major step forward, yes. The tape had been delivered. It, too, was on its way to Korcula.

Levin hailed a cab near DuPont Circle and directed the driver to Dulles International Airport.

"Hurry," he said. "I'm late for my plane."

Then he reached into his pocket and produced his airline tickets. He glanced through them, found everything in order. From Dulles he would fly to London, and from London to Dubrovnik. And from there he would travel by car and ferry to his destination.

Andrei Voloshin was waiting in Pan Am's VIP passenger lounge at Dulles, a glass of Scotch in one hand, a newspaper in the other. The American press were very nearly unanimous in supporting the Korcula summit, and the Washington *Post* was no different. An unusual front-page editorial in this morning's edition lauded the goals of the meeting and stopped just short of deifying Arthur Compton. Voloshin smiled. Then he looked up as an airport official approached him.

"Your flight is just about ready to leave," the man said. "If you'll come with me, I'll escort you through customs."

Voloshin finished his Scotch and got up to go to his plane. He did not take the newspaper with him.

Nicole took in a sharp breath of air as the steamer rounded a curve in the shoreline and Korcula came into view. "Oh, Peter," she said, "it's absolutely exquisite!"

Peter agreed. The island rose out of the Adriatic in the midday sun—mountainous, thickly wooded, deep green. At the point closest to them, a cluster of white stone buildings, with red-tiled roofs aging green in the sea air, sat on a circular promontory still surrounded by Venetian walls. The old town of Korcula, a medieval fortified city. It was solid. Enduring. Tranquil.

Peter looked at Nicole, who was leaning against the rail and smiling serenely into the wind and sea spray. The lines of worry had vanished, all trace of lingering fear. It was almost as if the last week had never happened.

But of course, it had. And the last thing that happened was Daniel Ravage's sudden unexplained illness. He'd been hospitalized at George Washington University, where the doctors were still trying to diagnose his symptoms. But they were optimistic about his recovery, and part of Peter was relieved to hear it. Another part was relieved to know that Ravage wasn't there.

"And to think," Nicole said, still absorbed by the view, "the Greeks called it Korkyra Melaina—*black* Korcula—because of the dense forests. They were so wrong! The first thing that strikes you is color."

Peter looked at the island, inching closer to them as the steamer progressed toward the passenger quay. For a moment the sunshine paled and gave him a different view.

Maybe the Greeks had had a premonition. Black Korcula. Peter shivered and turned away.

Nicole fell in love with Korcula Town the moment she stepped off the steamer onto the quay, but Peter persuaded her to go first to the hotel, which was located in the newer part of the city that rose above and south of the old town walls. They checked in and got their bearings, their location in relation to the Bon Repos Hotel, where Compton was staying, and the seaside villa where the meetings were going to take place.

Now it was late afternoon and they were back at the main gate to the old town, with time to spare before the first session, a dinner for both delegations. Tomorrow the talks would begin in earnest, and Peter wouldn't have much free time. But he had the feeling Nicole wasn't going to care. The island of Korcula had been inhabited since the beginning of recorded history. He didn't think she'd have trouble filling her time.

In fact, looking at her now, he wasn't sure he could coax her back for dinner.

A stone bridge led them through the gate and the Venetian walls to a labyrinth of narrow, crooked streets close-packed with houses. Small-scale Renaissance palaces and Gothic mansions—some derelict, some abandoned and never reclaimed since the plague. Everywhere, there were fascinating details—balconies overrun with bougainvillea, colonnaded doorways, a cartouche of arms for a family long extinct—an air of elegant emptiness and extraordinary charm. Nicole was delighted with it.

But she was struck by the absence of people in the streets. A man with a broom, and a woman scrubbing the steps of a guild church. A group of sightseers from the Soviet delegation. No one else.

"Where are the people?" she asked. "Doesn't anyone *live* here?"

"The people who live at this end of the island have been moved off to the mainland," Peter told her.

Nicole was astonished. "For heaven's sake, why?"

"Security." He shrugged. "The Russians insisted on it."

"That seems a little excessive."

"I agree, but I don't intend to make it an arguing point." He smiled. "City Hall is there on your left if you want to lodge a complaint."

Nicole turned to look at the old town hall, entranced once again by the charm of the physical setting. A banner was hanging across the Renaissance loggia, welcoming visitors to the island in English and Russian. It was made of natural canvas with red letters, maybe ten feet long and half as high, and was held in place by a rope across the top. It looked out of place here, Peter thought, like a cardboard sign tacked up on the Acropolis.

Or maybe it was the bright color of the letters. The old town looked different now, in the late afternoon, than it had when they first saw it from the steamer. Golden light muted the color of red-tiled roofs and mellowed the white native stone to a shade of amber, like a sepia-washed photograph. It seemed to change the texture and tone of the buildings and deepened Peter's feeling of history abandoned, as if the plague had come back and sent the townspeople fleeing to the mountains. He took Nicole's hand and walked on.

"These streets were laid out by the Greeks," she said. "The buildings have changed, but the layout is intact from ancient times."

If so, Peter thought, then the Greeks had proved their skill as city planners. The old town was built in an odd herringbone pattern, like the skeleton of a fish, with side streets evenly spaced at an angle, and slightly offset where they met at the central spine. An ancient energy-conservation measure, designed to deflect winter wind and summer sun. It still made sense today.

"Are there any ancient sites here?" he asked her.

"Not really, but there was a tablet found on the island. It dates to the fourth century and lists the names of the original Greek settlers."

Peter listened as Nicole explained the history of Korkyra Melaina. Her enthusiasm was infectious and relaxing.

The main street, Glavna Ulica, rose in a series of steps to the town square, where a cathedral bell tower dominated the old town. Nicole stopped to study the carved figures around the main door, and Peter stepped across the piazza for a better view of the building.

The cathedral was typically Korculan—cramped to fit limited space, a mixture of Gothic and Renaissance, oddly lopsided. But nice. A traceried rose window was set into the front wall. Peter studied it briefly, admiring the four heads set into the rim, then cut back across the piazza to Nicole.

"Look what I've found," she said. She was standing at the corner of the cathedral, gazing into the adjoining side street. "It's the house where they say Marco Polo was born."

Peter followed the direction of her eyes. The Marco Polo House—a tall, narrow building with a watchtower on top and a balcony at the second-story level. It wasn't particularly interesting architecturally, especially here, where it had so much competition. Not very interesting, and not very accessible, either. A sign on the door prohibited trespassing and announced that the house was closed down for repairs.

The Marco Polo House, a reminder of Steve and Jovan Kersnik, of four Soviet dissidents who would never be freed. Peter looked at Nicole, and her face changed. Enthusiasm vanished; worry showed in her eyes.

"What do we do now?" she asked.

"Nothing." Peter put his arm around her waist and turned her away from the house, glad to escape it himself. "All we can do now is wait for something to happen."

32

NOTHING HAPPENED. At least, not for three days. Peter spent his time in the meetings, and Nicole rented a car to explore the island.

On the third day, she set out along the coast road to the eastern tip of the island, stopping at a medieval church and a stone quarry that had been supplying Dalmatian builders since antiquity. She had lunched at a café in the village of Lumbarda and sampled the local wine.

She had taken dozens of pictures and a sample of rock from the quarry—not because it had any real value, but more to make use of her sample kit, which she'd brought along because she never went on a trip without it. And for other reasons this time.

A pleasant day. It might have been possible to believe that there was no intrigue going on here, no conspiracy, no threatened assassination—except for the fact that time was passing too quickly. In another forty-eight hours, the President and Premier would be here. But nothing had happened. There had been no word from Levin. They knew nothing more than they did when they arrived.

Now it was midafternoon, and Nicole was on her way back to the hotel, anticipation of an evening with Peter uppermost in her mind. To her left rose the slope of a hillside, terraced and cultivated. Olive groves. Orange and almond orchards. To her right, the view offered long stretches of white sand and blue sea. Small islets jutted up out of the water. Most of them were too small for habitation, bits of moorland and bare rock, of practical use only to gulls and seals. Still, they were lovely to see. And the water was inviting. . . .

A sign caught her eye at the edge of the road—handpainted on brown paper and taped to a low stone wall that surrounded a seaside cottage. *Boats for Hire.* The same message in English and Russian, like the welcoming banner in the old town. Someone knew full well what visitors were on the island. Such enterprising business sense, she decided, should be rewarded. Besides, a boat ride would be almost as nice as a swim.

She pulled off the road, locked her camera bag and sample kit into the trunk of the car, and made her way to a path that led past the cottage to a stone quay, where a half-dozen motorboats were tied up to the pilings. A man emerged from the cottage as soon as she appeared. He was somewhere past seventy, but not yet a hundred. Beyond that, Nicole couldn't guess his age.

"*Dobar dan*," he greeted her formally, but smiling from under the wiry mustache that was as white as his hair.

Nicole smiled back. "Do you speak English?"

"Certainly," he replied with assurance, as if she'd asked him if he could name his own children. "But not very well."

His modesty was misplaced, his English excellent under a heavy accent. Nicole asked him the cost of a boat for an hour or two. Ten dinars, he told her, and the price included the fuel. He went on to tell her his name, which was Andric, and his life's occupation—he had been a shrimp fisherman since he was a boy of eight. Now he ran this little operation to supplement the income from his retirement pension. And he'd lived on the island of Korcula all his life.

"Then you should be able to tell me where to go," Nicole said with a gesture toward the sea.

Andric shook his head. "The best trip is no longer allowed."

"Not allowed?"

"Badija. It's one of the larger islets. There's a monastery there, lovely woods, beautiful flowers. But now it's closed to the public. The soldiers will tell you so."

Nicole frowned. "Soldiers? They've turned a monastery into a military post?"

Andric shrugged. "No one knows. At least, no one says."

He dismissed the subject abruptly and produced a rental form which Nicole filled out with her own name and the name of her hotel. Then he took her money, selected a boat, and showed her how to operate the motor.

It was really quite easy, but Nicole had done it before: press a button here, pull a cord there, and the motor was running smoothly.

Andric pushed the boat off from the quay. "Take your time," he said, "but be sure you're back before sunset. The islands can be dangerous for someone who's not familiar with these waters."

"I'll be back before that," Nicole shouted over the sound of the motor. Then she waved to him and turned to face the sea.

The water was incredibly calm, incredibly clear. In the distance somewhere lay the island of Lastavo, where legend claimed the nymph Calypso held Odysseus captive for seven years. Nicole didn't wonder why it took him so long to escape. The scene all around was enchanting, tranquil, inviting, like the call of the Sirens.

She guided the boat among the small rocky islands, an intruder where nature reigned. Gulls swooped off the rocks, crying abuse as they circled overhead, waiting for the intruder to move on. A sleepy seal stretched out in a patch of sunshine looked up, caught her eye, and then slipped back into the sea.

Nicole glanced over her shoulder. Korcula was mellowing now as the sun dropped lower in the sky. Andric was no longer visible on the quay. There were no people at all, only the slope of the hills, where terraced land mingled with cypress and pine woods, and snatches of barren rock where only scrub would grow. She was alone in an ancient world.

The island ahead now was larger than any of the others she had seen, larger and densely wooded. She brought the boat within thirty yards of its shore, then swung away to the right, starting to make a broad circle around it. Yes, this was Badija. The cloister Andric had mentioned was visible here. A few yards farther on, she found a clear view, and she realized the church was an imitation of the cathedral in Korcula Town. She started to move in for a closer look.

Then suddenly, from nowhere, a soldier appeared on the shore. He called to her in words she couldn't hear.

Nicole called back. "I'm sorry. I don't understand."

But the soldier made himself clear, waving his arms in an unmistakably inhospitable gesture. She was unwelcome, even at this distance. There were only soldiers here now.

Nicole brought the prow of the boat around; she was more than happy to leave. But as she did, she saw something—no, not something, but someone—and for a moment she was brought up short. Where had she seen that face before? Why was it so familiar?

Then she remembered and was more puzzled than before. What was *he* doing here? What possible business, or right, could he have on a Yugoslavian island taken over for some unspoken military goal?

The soldier was still waving his arms, and now he slipped a rifle off his shoulder. Nicole didn't really believe that he intended to use it, but suddenly she wanted to be anywhere else but here. She gave the boat its full throttle and headed back to the shore.

Peter unlocked the door of his hotel room, and what he found there no longer caused him to be shocked. The room had been searched thoroughly. Dresser drawers were left hanging open; one was on the floor. His suitcase had been emptied onto the bed, where sheets had been stripped, the mattress pulled away. His clothes in the closet had been torn from their hangers, sleeves and pockets turned inside out. Even the wastebasket had been overturned, its contents examined and left on the floor.

The same sort of scene greeted him in the bathroom. A can of shaving cream had been emptied into the sink and discarded. Towels were pulled from their racks. His shaving kit had been slashed open, apparently with his own razor.

Peter wasn't shocked, he was furious. This wasn't the same as when Levin searched his apartment, almost by invitation. This was heavy-handed and blatant. Whoever did this didn't care what he destroyed.

Was Levin right? Had someone else found out he had the tape?

Nicole!

Peter picked up the phone, called her room, got no answer. Then he checked with the desk clerk and found out she hadn't come in, that she hadn't picked up her key. He sat down on the lopsided bed. That, at least, was a relief.

Or was it? She should have been back by now. Where was she?

Exploring. Peter told himself not to worry. He stood up, spent some time putting the room back into order. Then he took a shower and changed.

And picked up the phone once more.

Still there was no answer. He let it ring ten times, fifteen, but Nicole wasn't there. Now he was worried. He put the phone down, crossed the room, and opened the door.

Nicole unloaded the car, slung her camera bag over one shoulder, her sample kit over the other, and made her way into the hotel. She stopped at the desk for her key.

"Mr. Lucas was trying to reach you," the desk clerk said.

"Oh? Where was he calling from, did he say?"

"His room. I believe he's still there."

"Good. I'll call him. Thank you."

Nicole took her key and climbed the stairs to the third floor. Peter's room was just down the hall. She started toward his door but decided to leave her bags off in her own room first.

She fit the key in the lock, pushed the door open. Then her mouth dropped open and her eyes opened wide in dismay. Her room was a shambles. A wreck! Someone had been here!

She stepped across the threshold, too stunned to do anything but stare. A moment of silence, then a soft rustling sound came from behind the door. But the warning was too late.

Nicole started to turn, to run, but a hand came down across the back of her neck. A scream formed in her throat, but the sound was cut off before it really happened. A sharp pain, and then blackness. Her bags slipped off her shoulders. She fell to the floor, unconscious.

33

PETER KNOCKED AT NICOLE'S door, calling her name. His voice was made sharp by instinct. He was sure she was in her room, and terrified that something had happened to her.

On the other side, Nicole heard him vaguely, through mist, in a dream. Then slowly she opened her eyes. The pain at the back of her neck had become a dull, throbbing ache, and she wasn't sure where she was. But after a moment it all started fitting together. Her room, searched. Someone waiting behind the door. Peter calling to her. Peter was calling *now*. She got up and let him in.

Peter took it all in with a single horrified glance—the room, Nicole's face, her hand at her neck, her bags on the floor— and he knew exactly what had happened. The rage he felt in his own room was only a prelude to the fury that gripped him now. If the intruder was here, Peter thought he might kill him!

But his hands were gentle as he reached for Nicole and closed his arms around her, holding her head softly against his shoulder. "I'm so sorry I got you into this," he said.

"You didn't. Someone was here when I came in."

"Don't try to talk. You'd better lie down."

He led her across the room to the bed; like his, it was stripped to the mattress. He found a pillow, a blanket to put around her.

"I'm going to call for a doctor," he said.

Nicole shook her head, wincing as the movement set off new pain. "Just get me some aspirin, please. There's a box in the bathroom."

The bathroom was in the same state as Peter's. Cosmetics were strewn everywhere. Containers of any size had been opened and emptied, but the tin box of aspirin was there intact. He shook two out in his hand and ran a glass of water. Then he returned to the bed and helped Nicole raise her head to drink.

"I really think you should see a doctor," he said. "You could have a concussion."

Nicole smiled. "You worry too much. It's only a headache—not half as bad as the time I fell off the mountain at Nimrud Dagh, and I didn't have a concussion then."

Peter laughed—Nicole *made* him laugh—and the tension began to ease out of him. And yet someone had hit her. Someone had actually *hit* her!

Nicole leaned back against the pillow and closed her eyes. "Damn it, I didn't even see him. He must have heard me coming. He was waiting behind the door." Then suddenly her eyes popped open. "Peter, my sample kit! I had it with me!"

She started to sit up, but Peter eased her back down and tried to explain.

She clutched his arm, too anxious about it to listen. "Get it for me, please! Let me see it."

Peter retrieved the bag from the floor just to calm her. She unzipped it quickly, reached inside.

He tried to tell her. "The tape isn't there—"

"It must be!"

"—because *I* took it out."

Nicole looked at him, not understanding.

And Peter smiled. "Don't worry. The tape is perfectly safe."

Nicole pushed the bag away and sank back against the pillow. "You might have told me," she said, but she was more relieved than angry.

The sample kit was Nicole's electric train, a rush order from Olivia Barclay, who created the gadgets for her father's house. The bag itself wasn't new; the leather of it was scratched and softened by age. It was the same one she'd been carrying around for years, a part of her, expected and unobtrusive.

The bag wasn't new, but the false bottom in it was—a sufficiently good hiding place for the tape as long as it remained inside Compton's house, good enough for the trip over. But not good enough, Peter thought, to fool a professional thief.

"I was afraid this would happen," he said. "I took the tape out the first night we were here and hid it somewhere else."

"Where?"

"I'm not going to tell you."

"Peter!"

He reached for her hand. "Will you please take it easy?" he said. "This isn't the time for an argument."

"I don't want to argue. I just want you to tell me."

"I'm sorry, I won't. Look what happened tonight."

"So instead, you'll keep the tape and get yourself hit on the head."

"Better me than you."

"Why? Do you think I'm not as hardheaded as you are?"

Peter smiled. "I never said that. Anyway, I don't have it. And it's not in my room. I've hidden it somewhere else. But I'm not going to tell you where, so you might as well relax and get some rest."

Nicole sighed.

"Are you feeling better?" he asked.

"A little. I'll be fine in a while." Peter looked skeptical, but Nicole paid no attention. "I've got something to tell you," she said. "You'll never guess who I saw today—Michael Baker."

Peter frowned. "Senator Harvey's husband? The computer man from Yale?"

"The one who believes in famine as a means of population control."

Peter laughed. "I don't think he's quite as bad as that," he said. But he remembered his conversation with Baker that night in the President's box. Some people sacrificed now for the long-term good of society. Solutions produced by computer, because machines were dispassionate; they didn't flinch from the truth.

Maybe Baker had a point. Peter knew he'd been doing a lot of flinching lately. He'd flinched from the truth about Compton, because Compton was his friend. He'd flinched from the truth about Korcula, because Korcula was his dream. But he only flinched. He hadn't let painful reality prevent him from doing what he had to do.

But none of that had anything to do with Baker's presence at Korcula. He was surely not an official guest; they had taken all the hotel rooms, and half the population had been removed off the island in the name of security. Nicole must have been mistaken.

"Are you sure it was Baker?" he said. "Where did you see him?"

She told him about her boating expedition, the island of Badija, what Andric had told her and what she had seen for herself. "That soldier was perfectly serious," she said. "He didn't want me near the island. Yet, there was Dr. Baker walking into the monastery unhampered."

"It couldn't have been him. It must have been someone who looks like him."

"No, Peter, it *was* Michael Baker. I saw him. It took me a minute to remember who he was, but once I did, there was no doubt at all in my mind."

"Very strange." Peter lit a cigarette. "You don't suppose he's defected!" The suggestion seemed ridiculous. Melodramatic.

But Nicole didn't take it that way. "Even so," she said, "why would he be here?"

Peter didn't have an answer and couldn't think of one. He walked over to the window, which looked across the sea to the mountainous gray spine of the Peljesac peninsula, ominous in the fading light. He was worried. Too much was happening that he didn't understand. Too much and too little. On the surface, things were calm, and yet there were forces convening here that didn't fit anyone's notion of what was supposed to be happening. A human-rights summit. Treachery and deceit. Where did Compton fit in? And now Baker?

There wasn't much time now, two days. Peter drew on his cigarette. Where the hell was Levin?

The boat came ashore under cover of darkness near the coast road that ran between Korcula Town and Lumbarda. A man and woman stepped out of the boat and were met by another man, who hurried them into a waiting car. Twenty minutes later, they were traveling by foot across the stone bridge to the old town.

They made their way up the steps of the Glavna Ulica, to the town square, and into a dark street that angled back alongside the cathedral. This street, like the others, was deserted. It was after midnight; no one was out for a walk. Nonetheless, the man who was the escort looked around carefully before he stopped at the door of a tall, narrow house and knocked.

He knocked twice, then twice again. The door opened. The man and woman from the boat were drawn inside, and the other man disappeared into the darkness.

The front room of the house was large, but vacant except for ladders and drop cloths, paint cans and brushes. The two people looked at each other. Then a door opened at the rear of the room and another man entered. He was tall, dark, bearded.

Nina's eyes weren't yet accustomed to the bright light of the room. She moved a step closer to Vladya.

But the man who came toward them was smiling behind his dark beard. No, not smiling. Beaming.

"My name is Levin," he said, extending both hands in welcome. "You're safe here. This is Korcula. Yugoslavia. You've left the Soviet Union."

34

PETER AND NICOLE were leaving the hotel dining room after lunch the next day when they saw Levin strolling across the lobby. Literally strolling, hands in pockets, face completely relaxed. Peter felt almost weak with relief. But Levin looked at him, then past him, and walked straight out through the door.

What the devil!

Peter started after him, but Nicole placed a hand on his arm. "I don't think he wants to see you here," she said. "Why don't you see if he left a message for you."

Peter hesitated. But he knew Nicole was right. He forced himself to relax and walked up to the desk.

The man on duty was pleased to see him. "A man asked me to give you this," he said, and pushed an envelope toward him.

"Thank you." Peter picked up the envelope, took Nicole's arm, and headed for the doors.

Outside, Levin had vanished. They crossed the street to the car and got in, with Nicole behind the wheel. Peter tore the envelope open and read what was inside.

"What does it *say*?" Nicole asked.

He handed the message to her.

The twins want to be reunited tonight. Meet me at the cathedral at nine. Levin.

"And he talked to *me* about cutting it close," Peter said. "The President and the Premier are going to be here tomorrow morning!"

He took a cigarette from his pocket, and Nicole pushed in the lighter for him.

"That's still enough time," she said. "You can talk to Daddy yet tonight. Even if they're already on their way, their planes can be rerouted."

"And the pact won't be signed." Peter turned away, bitterly disappointed. But of course the assassination came first. It had to be stopped. Human lives were no less valuable because they were heads of states.

Nicole reached for his hand. "Don't be discouraged, darling. Daddy can set up another meeting. The pact *will* be signed, only later. Or maybe once he knows what's on those tapes, there will still be time to destroy the conspiracy, to stop the assassins. . . ."

Peter turned back to face her, half-smiling. "Maybe. We'll see." He reached across her for the lighter and held it against his cigarette.

"What are you going to do?" she asked.

Peter leaned back. "The only thing I can do. I'll meet Levin."

Peter got out of the car in front of the villa and disappeared inside for the afternoon session. Nicole watched him go, put the car back in gear, and started to pull away; she was thinking about her own plans for the afternoon. Then another car pulled up behind her, and Arthur Compton got out.

She leaned out the window. "Daddy?"

A smile spread slowly across Compton's face. He walked over to her, bent down beside the window, let his hand come to rest on her arm. "Hi, sweetie. Are you having a good time? Found any ancient tombs?"

Nicole hadn't seen him so cheerful in a long time. "Not yet, but I'm looking. How are you?"

"Busy."

"It figures."

"But I'm glad to see you," he said, and gave her arm a squeeze. "Maybe I can get some time off later and we can have a drink."

"I'd like that, but I think you'll be a lot less distracted once we're back home."

Compton grinned. "You're probably right. Anyway, Peter might not approve. How's he doing, by the way? I haven't seen him alone since we got here."

Nicole was purposefully vague. "He's almost as busy as you are, which is why I'm on my own this afternoon." She shrugged. "I don't mind. It gives me time for contemplation, and that's good for the soul."

"Is it, now? Maybe that's what I need."

"No, Daddy, what your soul needs is waiting inside that villa." She leaned up to kiss him. "There's a world to save. Go do it."

A flicker of emotion passed across Compton's face and disappeared into the familiar smile. "You've got a point," he said. Then he patted her arm and turned away to the villa.

Nicole sat there for several minutes after he'd gone inside. He *was* in good spirits, and she was delighted to see it. But she was also uneasy.

No, what she felt was fear. It had little to do with a threatened assassination. It was less specific than that. She wasn't sure why, but she was afraid *for* her father.

Andric was working on one of the boats as Nicole came down the path toward the little stone quay. He looked up and saw her, and greeted her as a friend. "*Zdravo!*"

Roughly translated, it meant "Flourish. Be well." Nicole accepted the compliment with a wave and a smile.

"Are you back for another outing?" he asked as she came up beside him.

"Yes, indeed. It was so lovely yesterday. But this time I thought I might try something different. Do you rent scuba equipment?"

"Scuba?" Andric frowned, not comprehending.

"*Diving* equipment."

"But of course." Andric beamed. Then his face grew suddenly serious. "Diving is something you have to know how to do. It's not like the boat and the motor. I can't show you how to use the equipment in one simple lesson."

Nicole smiled. He still didn't understand that she knew how

to use the boat and the motor, even without a lesson. "I've been diving many times," she said. "I'm an archaeologist. Ancient artifacts are often found in the sea."

Andric wasn't convinced. He gave her a long appraising look.

"You show me the equipment," Nicole said, "and I'll show you what I know."

"Fair enough." He gestured for her to follow him into the cottage.

Ten minutes later they were back on the quay, and Andric was loading the diving equipment into one of the boats—an air tank with attached mouthpiece and hose, fins, a rubber face mask, and a black rubber wet suit to protect her from the cold. Nicole had worn a bathing suit under her clothes; she would change in the boat. She stepped down into it now.

Andric untied the knot that held the boat to the piling. Once again he was frowning. "You won't go to Badija today," he said.

Nicole didn't answer directly. "I had the feeling I wasn't quite welcome there."

Andric shook his white head. "I was troubled by what you told me yesterday. And I think I ought to tell you for your own good. Stay away from Badija."

"Why?"

He hesitated, raising his eyes to look out across the sea. Then after a moment he lowered them to her. "They're only rumors, of course, but they've been repeated often. If they frighten you . . ." He raised his hands in a gesture and left the words unspoken.

"What rumors?" Nicole asked him. "Are you trying to scare me?"

"The soldiers at Badija—I've heard it said they're not ours. They wear uniforms of Yugoslavia, but the language they speak is Russian."

35

IT WAS TOO late to turn back. Nicole *was* frightened, but she intended to carry through, to find out why the soldier had been so pointedly hostile, and, if she could, why Michael Baker was here. She tied the boat up to a sharp jutting rock on one of the tiny islets. From here she could see Badija in the distance, but she'd purposely chosen an approach that was shrouded, from there, by trees.

She slipped off the slacks and shirt she was wearing and folded them in the boat with her shoes. Then she untied the scarf around her neck and folded that neatly, too. The scarf was a gift from Peter—a subtle, unusual mixture of muted color, unlike any other scarf Nicole had seen. She held it in her hand for a moment. Then, on an impulse, she put it back on and knotted it at her neck. If she ruined it in the water, Peter would have to forgive her. She needed it now. A talisman.

She pulled the black wet suit on over her bathing suit and slipped over the side of the boat into the water. It was cold, but not cold enough to impede movement. She reached into the boat for the air tank and slid it on over her shoulders, fit the mouthpiece in place, loosened the valve that released the air, and checked to make sure the equipment was all in order. Then she put on the face mask and dived under the surface of the sea.

The water was deep and clear. Rays of sunshine angled down through it, giving off a glow of soft light. Fish that darted away when she first splashed into the water came back now to swim along with her, as if she were a breed that belonged here—a mild curiosity, worth no more than a glance from the flat, staring eyes. Breathing through the mouth, always awkward at first, was coming naturally now. The silence was wonderfully calm and deep, unlike any silence that ever occurred on land.

There was nothing else as peaceful as this, she thought with a blissful sense of detachment. She found herself watching for the sudden appearance of a stone column or a carved marble face from the past. This was timelessness in its absolute form. Urgency had no place here.

But it couldn't last. Within a few minutes the darkness of a landmass began to emerge ahead. Nicole rose to the surface, got her bearings, dived under again. The water grew more shallow where the rocky shore of the landmass descended into the sea. She swam on until her feet could touch bottom. Then her face broke through the surface; she scanned the thickness of trees.

Dense pinewood covered this part of Badija. There were no signs of human life, no soldiers patrolling this part of the beach. Nicole went ashore. She pulled off the mask and fins, slipped the air tank off her shoulders, and hid them in the scrub that grew at the edge of the forest. Then she set off through the trees.

Pine needles stabbed her bare feet, but they also cushioned the sound of her movement. The black wet suit faded into the darkness, where no sunshine broke through. But then the trees began to thin as she neared the clearing where the cloister stood.

The west front, all she could see from here, was indeed a replica of the cathedral in Korcula Town, a mixture of Venetian Gothic and Renaissance, though not as well done as the other. A walk led up to the entrance where she'd seen Dr. Baker the day before. There were gravestones on both sides of the walk, old stone, their edges eroded by time and sea air—gravestones, and, there among them, a soldier in uniform. He was looking away through the clearing where the cloister showed from the water, but he didn't show any signs of planning to move on.

Nicole backed away from the spot and moved around through the trees until she found a side entrance that didn't seem to be guarded. She stood back, waiting and watching. Her heart was pounding inside her chest, her hands trembling at her sides. She squeezed her hands into fists, then released them and rubbed them together. She would not give in to fear.

A moment later, the door opened and two people came out, a man and a woman, both wearing white lab coats. They were talking to each other. Nicole strained to hear, could not discern words, only knew they were speaking English. The man and woman were as American as she was.

What were they doing here?

At the same time, another soldier appeared, moving easily, arms at his sides, unworried. He appeared from the back of the cloister and stopped, not twenty feet from Nicole. He lit a cigarette, tossed the match away, and moved on.

If the one in front had a stationary assignment, this one, she decided, was making regular rounds. She waited until he appeared again and guessed it had taken him ten minutes to make the circle. Yes, the island cloister was guarded, but not as closely as she had feared it would be. Like the kings at Mycenae and Troy, these people seemed to believe that an isolated location was security in itself.

The guard walked on. Ten minutes.

Nicole moved forward quickly and quietly. The side door wasn't locked. She opened it, looked in. A long corridor, dark and empty. She stepped inside and closed the door behind her.

Several interior doors opened off the corridor. All of them were closed but the one at the distant end, through which she could see a high altar in the base of the campanile. She moved toward it and stopped, her back flat against the wall.

Voices came to her, some speaking English, others a language that might have been a Yugoslavian dialect or Russian. What surprised her more was the general level of sound. *Busy* voices. And there was the steady soft clacking of fingers on typewriter keys, the hum of equipment in use. She might have stumbled into a corporation office, or the State Department, where dozens of people worked in a single huge subdivided room.

She had to see what this was.

She moved forward, her bare feet making no sound on the cold stone floor, keeping close to the wall, as if somehow it might protect her. She stopped at the threshold, caught her breath, looked around. And what she saw left her stunned.

A church from the era of Marco Polo laid out in a cruciform plan, a central nave with transepts and side bays. Statuary remained in place in niches carved out of the walls. Figures of saints, a madonna, all in their proper places, smiling vaguely, detached from the scene they surveyed. The pews in the sanctuary had all been removed to make way for something quite different. This was some kind of *communications center*. Ultramodern. Highly technical. The cloister at Badija was full of computers!

It was also full of people. Men in business suits, neatly dressed women, some of them wearing lab coats like the two who had left while Nicole was outside watching. And there, directing the traffic, clearly in charge, was Dr. Michael Baker.

Nicole was more frightened by this than by threats of assassination! She didn't know precisely what she was looking at, but she did know one thing. She had to get out. She had to go back and tell Peter.

Then suddenly a hand grabbed her arm from behind and yanked her back into the corridor. Another hand covered her mouth, stifling the scream that rose in her throat. She was thrown up against the wall and held there, helpless.

Fear deepened to terror as she saw the eyes of the soldier who was her captor. Cold eyes, without feeling. She bit his hand. He jerked it away, but then swung it back. He slapped her.

Nicole glared at him, her face stinging, the ache throbbing at the back of her head. Now he had a gun and was pressing it into her neck. With his free hand he pulled her harshly away from the wall. Nicole stumbled. Tears burned her eyes, but she held them back. She was terrified! But she pulled herself up and went with him.

36

THERE WAS A knock at the door. Miloslavsky looked away from the other two men at the table. "Yes?"

A fourth man entered the room. "A message for Chairman Levitsky," he said.

Levitsky turned around, took the envelope that was held out to him, and dismissed the man with a gesture. He tore it open, read the message inside and was clearly startled by it.

"What is it?" Miloslavsky demanded.

"A woman has been captured at Badija. She says she's Nicole Compton."

Miloslavsky's expression froze as he stared at Levitsky, absorbing this unexpected news. Then he leaned back in his chair. "Well, now, this *is* interesting. Was she inside the monastery?"

Levitsky nodded.

"How much did she see? And why was she there at all?"

"Not for any reason her father would approve," Levitsky said. "But she saw enough. One of the soldiers found her in a diving suit. They've taken her to the guardroom and are waiting for orders from me."

"I see." Miloslavsky's forehead creased into a frown, and he stroked his chin thoughtfully. "This could be a problem for us," he said. "Or it could be an opportunity. The question is, what should we do with her now?"

Dmitri leaned forward against the table. "Let her go. Let her go to Lucas."

Miloslavsky's eyes rested on him briefly. Then he looked back at Levitsky. "Does anyone else know about this?"

"No one. As chief of security, I was informed directly. No one else knows she's there, not even the people who work in the monasteries. We have the leeway to make a decision, if that's what you're asking."

"It is. And we might let her go, as Dmitri has suggested. However, another plan has occurred to me at the moment. Time is so short. We might use her for ransom."

"Against Compton?" Dmitri asked.

"No, against Peter Lucas." Miloslavsky pushed back his chair. "Bring her here, Boris. We'll see what happens tonight, and then we'll know if we need her."

Peter wandered through the old town with no particular destination. It was only seven o'clock, two hours before he had to meet Levin. He was killing time and avoiding Nicole. He didn't want her along tonight, because he didn't know what was going to happen.

He found himself in the piazza, looking at the cathedral as darkness closed in on the narrow streets. The sky was clear, the moon bright, and there were streetlights burning around the square. But evening only deepened the emptiness of the old town. As far as Peter could tell, he was alone.

He crossed over to the cathedral's main entrance. The doors were unlocked. He stepped through them.

Inside, it was dark and a little gloomy. The only light came from votive candles burning in the side bays and two larger ones flanking the crucifix on the altar. Peter stopped to let his eyes adjust to a different level of darkness.

The architects of the cathedral had done what they could with this limited space, but the sanctuary was oddly off-balance, an irregular shape, as if the corners didn't line up at right angles. Aisles ran down each side of the church to the altar. To Peter's right a sarcophagus lay on a catafalque near a Byzantine madonna. To his left were the baptistery and a small chapel.

He made his way down the left aisle to the chapel, where, from under a kneeling bench, he retrieved the plastic reel.

It was empty. There was no tape on the reel. Peter himself had taken it off and hidden it somewhere else. But the reel would be needed for playing the tape, and so he had saved it, hidden it here. He dropped it into his pocket. For now, he would leave the tape itself where he had put it.

A side door opened from the north wall of the church. Peter closed it behind him and stopped to light a cigarette. Then he stepped out into the street. The Marco Polo House was directly in front of him here, entirely dark, its watchtower silhouetted against the moonlit sky. An empty house, closed for repairs, in a town without people. It was lonely and foreboding.

And yet, as Peter stood there, the door slowly opened, throwing light out into the street. He moved instinctively, back into the recessed doorway of the cathedral, dropping his cigarette and covering it with his foot.

There were lights on in the house! But no trace of light showed until the door was opened.

Peter flattened himself against the church door as a man emerged from the house on the other side of the street. He looked both ways and then turned toward the piazza. The moonlight was clear on his face. And Peter's mouth dropped open. The man was Boris Levitsky!

What was the KGB Chairman doing here, at night, walking out of a house that was closed for repairs? Or was it? Was Levin right? Was this the man who informed on Miloslavsky?

Peter stayed where he was even after Levitsky had disappeared around the cathedral. He stayed there watching the house, deeply interested now. Shortly the door opened again, and two men emerged together. They paused a moment, talking quietly, their voices too soft to hear. Then they separated; one turned toward the piazza, the same way Levitsky had gone, and the other moved away toward the city walls at the opposite end of the street.

Levitsky's appearance surprised Peter, but now he went rigid. He froze where he was, his mouth open and gaping, his eyes staring, his features distorted by shock. He was paralyzed, unable to think, unable to see or feel. Manipulation! Christ, it had never stopped! *Nothing* was true! Nothing was *real*. Nothing. Except the nightmare.

Peter ran blindly—away from the house and cathedral, away from the men, through the streets of the old town, toward the passenger quay. He ran to escape, from the men and himself, to escape from the truth. He ran because he no longer knew who or what was the enemy. Because he recognized *both* men. The first was Miloslavsky. That was bad enough.

But the other one was Levin!

37

PETER RAN UNTIL he was gasping for air, and then he went on walking, in a daze, not thinking, not caring, not knowing what he wanted to do. Knowing only one thing: he wanted Nicole.

"Mr. Lucas, could I see you a moment?"

He was crossing the hotel lobby on the way up to her room, but now he turned to the sound of the voice. The concierge, a large gray-haired woman, was studying him. She looked worried.

But Peter didn't care. "I'm sorry," he said. "Not now. I—"

"It's urgent," she insisted gently. "I must see you now in my office."

Peter glanced at the stairs, drawn to them, but the woman's eyes pulled him back. She was worried, but it was more than that. She was looking at him with compassion.

He went with her to her office.

"Sit down, please," she said.

Peter remained standing. His mind was starting to clear, to focus on her and the look of her face. Something was wrong. Terribly wrong. He could feel it! Urgency broke through the numbness. An old feeling. Survival.

"What is it?" he asked sharply.

"It's about Miss Compton."

Not *his* survival, Nicole's! Peter panicked. He grabbed the woman's shoulders. "Where is she? What's happened to her?"

The woman looked back at him calmly. "We don't know. We had a call from a man named Andric who rents motorboats to tourists. She was there today for a boat and diving equipment. When she wasn't back by sunset, Andric went looking for her. He found the boat, empty. There is no trace of her."

"No!" Peter cried. "No, damn it, you're lying!" Anger erupted to cover the pain and fear that raged up inside him. A defensive shield, creating a moment of vacuum, letting mind and body take shock and absorb it.

The woman understood. Her face didn't change, though she reached for his hands and loosened their grip on her shoulders, even held them a moment before she let them go.

"The authorities have been notified," she said. "A search is being conducted. Everything possible is being done to find her. This could be just a scare. She might be perfectly safe on one of the small islands."

Just a scare! It might be—or it might not. Peter turned away, trying to maintain his composure. Nicole's survival *was* his survival!

But he was deeply frightened, and not just by thoughts of an accident or drowning. He knew, though she hadn't told him, why Nicole went diving today. She had gone to Badija, on her own. And whatever she saw there, she had not come back!

Oh, God—they had to find her.

"I'm terribly sorry," the concierge was saying. "If there's anything the hotel can do, please . . ."

Peter nodded.

"Of course, we have notified her father. And he sent you a message. He wants to see you as soon as you can come."

Peter raised his hands in a helpless gesture the woman could not have understood. He was torn by conflicting feelings, by uncertainty and need. He stood there in silence, not moving. Then abruptly he pushed past her and hurried out through the door.

Suddenly he wanted to see Compton, too.

Compton opened the door. "Peter! Thank God!" He pulled him into the room.

"Has there been any news?"

"None at all."

Compton's face was ashen and rigid with worry. He was badly shaken. Peter took a step toward him. Years faded as they embraced, and with the years, Peter's doubts. There was only this moment, like a piece of the past—their mutual fear. The woman they both loved was missing.

And something more, their own mutual feelings. The trust and respect of a lifetime could not be destroyed so easily.

Compton pulled away, still holding to Peter's arm. "I feel so damned helpless," he said. "But we're doing everything. We've got a search party out there. The Yugoslavian shore patrol is running it, but our security people are there, too. We could hear something any minute."

"Maybe we will." Peter's voice was hoarse with emotion. He turned away, crossed the room, and sat down.

Compton had a suite here in the Bon Repos, this sitting room and an adjoining bedroom. A bar was set up on a table with a room-service menu. The Scotch bottle was open; Compton was already drinking.

"Can I get you one?" he asked.

Peter shook his head. "I didn't come here to drink. I came to talk."

"Talk! About what? How much we both love her? How frightened we are?" Compton picked up his drink, took a stiff swallow of it. Then he looked back at Peter and said, "I'm sorry. It's good just having you here to share the waiting."

But Peter had something on his mind, something he had to say, so much to confess, so much he wanted to know. Whatever the truth, he believed Nicole had found it, had walked in on it. She knew. And that made her a threat to the same people who killed Steve, Jovan Kersnik, the dissidents. He believed she was in grave danger—if she was alive.

"I think there's more to worry about than an accident," he said. "Nicole wasn't diving for pleasure today. I think she swam out to Badija."

Compton's face registered no reaction beyond mild surprise. "To Badija? That's a Yugoslavian military installation."

Peter's eyes met his. "Is it? Then what is Michael Baker doing there?"

"Michael Baker?" Compton stared at him. "What are you talking about?"

"Nicole saw Baker at Badija yesterday afternoon. She also ran into a soldier who threatened to shoot her at thirty yards. But Baker was *on* the island. What's going on there, Arthur?"

"I haven't the slightest idea!" Compton brought his drink and sat down across from Peter. "What makes you think I would know?"

"There's nothing going on within two hundred miles of here that you don't know about." Peter sighed. "Or maybe there is. Including possibly . . . I don't know . . . an assassination attempt."

Compton didn't say anything for a moment. He sat there absently swirling the ice in his glass with one finger. His face looked tired now, older than his years. Finally he looked up,. laughed dryly. "So someone got to you," he said.

"Someone tried."

Compton took a drink and put his glass down on the table. "I know what you've been told. There's a militant faction involving the KGB. They're planning to kill the President and the Premier. Then they're going to take over the Soviet Union."

He had known all along! Peter stared at him, astonished. He knew he'd been wrong . . . wrong from the start! He should have *trusted* Compton.

"How did you know . . . ?"

"Your friend Steve Katz told me the same story. I told him then, it's not going to happen. It never was going to happen. He was being used by the adversaries of Korcula, and frankly, I think he found out. I think that's why they killed him."

"You *knew* he'd been killed?"

Compton nodded. "And then, obviously, they switched from him to you."

Peter swallowed hard. He was guilty. Used! And he'd fallen for it!

"Who are they?" he asked.

"A militant faction—oh, yes, there is one. A bunch of Marxist fanatics headed by Miloslavsky. But the only thing they intend to kill is the human-rights movement. They want to destroy Korcula. I've known about it for days, and so have the President and Premier. I wish you had come to me sooner."

"Arthur, I tried! And you lied to me!"

Compton didn't deny it. "I shouldn't have done it," he said. "I can see that now. But I did it because I didn't think you'd understand. The dissidents, for example. I led you to think I was planning to send the CIA back to get them. To free them. To bring them out. I wanted to give you a quick answer, one that would ease your mind. The answer I thought you expected. Something dramatic—because what I did intend wouldn't sound very exciting. I used a different approach. I appealed to the Premier through Voloshin; I asked him for leniency for the dissidents. I did it that way because we have a much stronger relationship with the Soviets than I think you realize."

"But I would have understood that," Peter said. "I would have accepted your judgment."

"Maybe so." Compton shook his head slowly. "Both of us should have been completely honest, the way we always have been." Abruptly he looked at Peter. "Have you told me everything now?"

"No." Peter reached for his cigarettes and lit one. "I could use that drink," he said.

Compton got up from the chair, and Peter watched him. He looked different, defeated; the bantamweight stride was gone.

A moment later, with a drink in his hand, Peter began to talk—about Levin and Miloslavsky, about the Korcula tapes. He told Compton everything.

Almost.

He didn't reveal he'd stolen the tape from the train; he didn't reveal that he had it or where he'd put it.

Compton stood still for a moment after Peter had gone, staring after him, letting it all sink in. Then he put his glass down and picked up the telephone.

"I want to see you now," he said, his voice tightly controlled, and hung up.

Voloshin appeared within minutes from his own room down the hall. He found Compton angrily pacing. "I know your daughter is missing, Arthur. I know you're upset—"

Compton turned on him and exploded. "'Upset' hardly cov-

ers the way I feel! I just found out where Nicole went today—
to Badija—and it seems she hasn't come back. Now, we agreed
to let *your* soldiers guard that island, because they're a little
less obvious here than a bunch of our GI's. But I'm telling you
something, and I want you to get it straight. If you don't find
out what happened to her and get her back here safely, I'm
going to charge that island myself with sixteen battalions of
the toughest Marines we've got, and then I'm going to land
a cruise missile right in the Premier's lap."

Voloshin nodded. "I understand. Let me see what I can find
out. I'll get back to you right away."

"Do that," Compton said. "Because there's one other problem."

Voloshin raised an eyebrow.

Compton told him. "It's Miloslavsky."

Nicole opened her eyes, trying once again to remember what
had happened just before everything went blank. Slowly it all
came together. The monastery. The soldier with the cold eyes.
The guard room....

She had been left alone there, a prisoner, but finally a man
came to talk. He was Russian. He wanted to know who she
was, why she was there. She turned her back on him briefly,
and that had been a mistake. Suddenly his hand was across her
mouth, and a needle was jammed into her arm.

After that, darkness.

At least she didn't have another headache, only the old one,
back now and throbbing painfully as she pushed herself up on
her elbows.

A different room from the one where she had been taken
before. Two windows, heavily curtained; walls covered by a
gray substance; a door, closed and presumably locked. A table,
some chairs. And two people sitting across the room, watching
her warily.

Two faces etched into her memory from the haunting poster
on Peter's office wall. Nicole looked at them and then back
at herself, absurd in the black rubber wet suit. She started to
laugh, but tears stung her eyes. She was laughing and crying;
frightened and yet relieved.

Nina Kovalyova got up and came over to her.

"I'll be all right," Nicole said. "It's just that I'm so glad to see you." She looked from one face to the other. "Does either of you happen to know where we are?"

38

NINA ANSWERED NICOLE in English. "A place called Korcula, in Yugoslavia. At least that's what we were told."

"Yes, well, I already knew that." Nicole smiled as Nina offered her a handkerchief. She swung her legs over the side of the cot and wiped the tears from her face. "It's an island in the Adriatic Sea," she told them. "There's a Soviet-American human-rights conference going on here now."

Nina and Vladya exchanged a look.

"I know," Nicole said. "It doesn't seem to be doing us much good. I gather we're not allowed to leave."

Nina moved back across the room and sat down beside Vladya. He took her hand. "We don't know how long we've been here," he said. "One day? Two days? We don't even know what time it is. They took our watches from us. The windows are sealed, and no sound passes through these walls."

Nicole got up and examined the walls more closely. The gray substance seemed to be a kind of plastic foam, probably applied in soft form and then allowed to harden. It ran up over the ceiling. Soundproofing, no doubt. Whoever was keeping them here was prepared in advance, and meant business.

"I don't suppose this can be torn away," she said.

Vladya shook his head. "We've tried that. And the boards on the windows are nailed fast."

Nicole stepped back from the wall and let her eyes scan the room. "Then I guess we're here to stay for a while, and we might as well get acquainted. I know who you are. My name is Nicole. . . ."

She told them who she was and why she had come to Korcula, and then explained why she was wearing the black rubber suit. But when she mentioned the monastery and the soldiers, Nina and Vladya both looked back at her in dismay.

"This isn't a monastery," Nina said. "And there weren't any soldiers. We walked through a town to get here. It was dark, but the moon was out. There were narrow streets, many houses . . ."

Korcula. The old town. Nicole realized she'd been moved—drugged first, and then brought here. But where?

"How did you get here?" she asked.

They told her about their capture on the train. About the plane trip—stopping, taking off again unexpectedly, and then landing at an undisclosed place. From there they had traveled by car and boat, car again, and finally on foot to this house.

"Which house? Can you remember anything about it?"

"There was a cathedral at the corner," Vladya said, and leaned down to trace a map on the floor with his finger.

Somehow Nicole knew before he finished the drawing. Somehow it all fit together, from Steve Katz to Michael Baker, from the President's box to this house, which claimed to be the birthplace of Marco Polo.

She shook off a chill, though she felt warm inside the wet suit, and sat down again on the cot. "Do you know who brought you here?"

They told her about Levitsky, and others along the way. "And then here," Nina said, "we were met by a man called Levin."

"Levin!" Nicole frowned.

"He was kind, gave us food, made us welcome. He told us we'd have to stay here until transportation could be arranged out of the country."

And perhaps he would discuss that tonight, Nicole thought, when he met with Peter. Then suddenly she realized what Nina was saying! Levin made them stay here; that made sense by itself—but locked up as prisoners?

Nina's face confirmed her fears. "We *thought* he was kind, but he was only pretending. He wanted a tape I was carrying. After I gave it to him, he locked us in here, and we've been here ever since."

"The tape," Vladya said, "was given to us . . ."

He went on, explaining. But Nicole didn't hear him. It was *Levin* who was holding them here as prisoners! And Peter was meeting Levin tonight at the cathedral, to play the tapes. . . .

She had to get out, had to warn him! Don't believe Levin! Don't give him the tape! Don't even meet him!

But how?

She jumped up from the couch, crossed the room to one of the windows, and threw the curtains back.

"We've tried to loosen the boards," Vladya said.

Nicole nodded. She was more interested in the type of wood that was here. Native pine, in two-by-four strips, arranged horizontally—soft wood, each board jammed up against the next one so that no light showed between them.

Native pine. It might well have come from Badija. If only she'd brought her sample kit, with its sharp scraping tools. They could carve out an opening in the wood and push a note through to the street.

But would anyone see it? Would Peter see it when he came to the cathedral?

Then she remembered something else. Her scarf! Peter's scarf!

She turned back to Nina and Vladya. "This wood is soft. We might be able to make an opening in it. Do you have anything small and narrow—like a comb or a mirror?"

"They took everything from us," Vladya said.

"Except this." Nina produced her lipstick.

Nicole took it from her and turned it over in her hands. Bless the Russians for their outmoded sense of marketing! No high-fashion styling here, nothing to rivet the eye to a display case on the counter of some capitalist emporium. This tube of lipstick wasn't made of sleek plastic, but old-fashioned metal, like something Nicole might have bought a dozen years ago. And the cap, removed, revealed a sharp edge.

"It might work," she said, and turned back to the window. She chose two boards at eye level and began to dig with the lipstick cap at the line between them. The cap filled with wood shavings. She emptied it, and started to scrape again.

In a little while Vladya took over, then Nina; they continued to work, taking turns, brushing the shavings out of view under one of the cots. Nicole, meantime, took the scarf from her neck, and using Nina's lipstick, wrote a message on it.

And finally they broke through the wood. Gray light showed through a small opening in the window.

Nicole's heart sank when she saw it. Gray light! It was *morning*! Peter's meeting with Levin was past. It was too late to warn him, to stop him. And Peter would have no reason for coming here now!

But it didn't matter, because there was glass in the window. Nothing could be pushed through.

Nicole closed her eyes, struggling to hide her bitter disappointment, feeling trapped, truly trapped. There was no way out. And no way to let anyone know they were here.

Then a sound came from the door. A key in the lock. It opened. Nicole's face went white when she saw who was standing there. She dropped the scarf and lowered herself slowly into a chair.

Miloslavsky came into the room.

He was carrying a small suitcase—a piece of Nicole's own luggage, taken from her hotel room. He had brought her a change of clothes! Nicole was too frightened to feel grateful, but she didn't want him to know that. She met his eyes with a level gaze, with defiance.

Miloslavsky noticed the scarf on the floor and stooped to pick it up. "Yours?" he asked.

Nicole tried to take it from him, but he held it beyond her reach. Then he read what she'd written on it.

Nicole's heart sank. Her talisman! Miloslavsky put it into his pocket.

39

PETER RETURNED TO the hotel at dawn. He had been out all night watching the rescue operation from the shore, but there was no sign of Nicole. Now he collapsed on the bed, weary beyond mere exhaustion, almost too tired to sleep.

But he did sleep. For how long, he did not know. He only knew that the phone by his bed was ringing; it *kept* ringing. He reached out to shut it off.

Then suddenly he sat up. The *phone* was ringing: it might be news, good news. Maybe Nicole had been found! Maybe she was calling....

He grabbed the receiver. "Yes? Hello?"

It was only the hotel desk clerk. There was someone downstairs to see Peter, a boy who said it was urgent; he had some kind of message.

Peter rubbed his eyes; sleep still fogged his mind. A boy? Who? What was this?

The desk clerk misunderstood his silence. He apologized. A mistake. He would send the boy away.

"No," Peter said. "I'll see him. Tell him to come on up."

A boy, maybe twelve, his manner shy, even anxious. He came through the door without speaking, reached into his pocket, and brought out a silk scarf.

The sight of it caused a twist of pain in Peter. Nicole's scarf, the one he had given to her. He snatched it away from the boy as her face came to life in his mind. Nicole, smiling gently yesterday afternoon, the last time he had seen her.

"There's writing on it," the boy said in English.

"Writing?" Peter opened the scarf in his hands. Words scrawled on it in lipstick: his name, the hotel, a reward. Suddenly he understood. Nicole was *wearing* the scarf in the picture that formed in his mind. She was wearing it when they said good-bye. But it wasn't there with the clothes she left in the boat. Peter's hand tightened around it as he looked back at the boy. "Where did you get this?"

"I found it."

"Where?"

"In the old town."

Peter grabbed him by the shoulders, too harshly. "*Where* in the old town?"

"In the street. Near the Marco Polo House."

Fear showed in the boy's face. Peter stared at him for a moment, then let his hands fall away. But Nicole had gone to Badija.

Or had she?

The Marco Polo House. Steve's message. *Miloslavsky!*

If Nicole were in the old town, had she dropped the scarf on purpose, her only way of trying to contact him? Or was this one more of Miloslavsky's tricks, an irresistible lure designed to bring Peter there?

The boy was standing still, hands in pockets, eyes downcast, face uncertain—as if he weren't sure whether to stay or escape.

Peter's face softened. "What's your name?" he asked.

"Sima."

"Well, Sima, you've got ten dinars for bringing me this. But I'll make you a deal. I'll double the money if you'll tell me the truth."

Sima still didn't look up. He just stood there shuffling his feet.

"Did you really *find* this?" Peter asked.

A long moment of silence. Then Sima shook his head. He looked relieved and embarrassed.

Peter touched his shoulder. "It's all right. Just tell me what happened."

"A man paid me to bring it here. He said it was a joke."

A joke, was it? "What did he look like?"

"He had dark hair and a beard."

Levin.

"An American," Sima added.

Yes, Levin—and Levin was with Miloslavsky!

Finally the boy looked up, eyes pleading. "Did I do the right thing?"

"Probably not." Peter smiled. "But thank God you did it." He dug into his pocket, counted out twenty dinars, overrode the boy's demurral, and sent him home. Then Peter hurried downstairs himself.

He had found the car where Nicole had left it, parked on the road near Andric's cottage, and the keys were under the floor mat. Now he was glad he had it; driving would cut ten minutes off the trip to the edge of the old town. He wasn't concerned about danger to himself—didn't think of it, didn't care. If there was a chance that Nicole was there, he had to go.

And if she wasn't? Then Miloslavsky wanted to see him. Okay. Peter wanted to see Miloslavsky, too. He got in behind the wheel and started the car.

The mellow color of Korcula stone had been washed away by the rising sun. The buildings inside the old-town walls were as bright as fresh snow under their red-tiled roofs. Peter glanced at the welcoming banner rippling gently against the rope that held it in place, and hurried on to the cathedral piazza. It was eight o'clock, the start of a new day—the day when the President and Premier would be coming here, the day when the pact would be signed. If it was signed. Right now the only thing Peter cared about was Nicole.

He stopped to catch his breath. Then cautiously he stepped around the corner.

The Marco Polo House was glistening white in the morning sun, as pristine as the others, as silent and empty-looking. Derelict. Foreboding. Peter wondered if there was another entrance besides the front door, perhaps a way in through the watchtower on the roof. But he knew that wondering was only a waste of time. He couldn't fight Miloslavsky on Miloslavsky's terms. They weren't evenly matched. To try it would be suicidal.

There was only one way to find out what was on the inside. Peter took a deep breath of air, then hurried across the street and up the steps to the door.

The sign was still there: CLOSED FOR REPAIRS. NO ADMITTANCE. He raised his hand to knock.

But the door opened before his hand made contact. Levin stood on the other side, smiling crookedly. There was no surprise in his face. Peter knew he had been expected.

He pushed past Levin into the house and then suddenly stopped, dismayed by the silence and emptiness of the room, where renovation was obviously under way. Work in progress. Ladders. Paint cans. Drop cloths.

Repairs! The sign wasn't a lie.

Then where was *Nicole*?

Peter swung around, grabbed Levin by the collar, his face distorted by a mixture of anger and fear. "Listen, you son of a bitch, if you've hurt her I'll kill you. I swear to God, I'll kill you! And Miloslavsky. And anyone else who even looked at her crossly. I'll kill the whole lying bunch of you—"

"Take it easy," Levin said, and he actually chuckled. "Don't worry. Nicole is fine."

Peter's hands gripped his shirt collar harder. "Then where is she?"

"Here."

"*Where*, damn it?"

"She's right here in the house. I can hardly show you as long as you keep me here."

Peter glared at him for a moment, then released his grip. "All right, take me to her. Now."

Levin straightened his collar, his eyes still on Peter's face. "Follow me," he said. He led the way through the house, through more hollow, echoing rooms and down a corridor to a set of double doors. He pulled the doors open and moved back to let Peter see past them.

Peter took a step forward. What the hell . . . ?

Beyond the doors lay a room that was grandly furnished
with tapestries and antiques, like a hall in the Doges' Palace.
A table inside was set for a feast, with melon and figs, sausage
and apples, strawberries and cream. Broiled trout, sturgeon,
shirred eggs, stuffed mushrooms and bacon.

They were having breakfast!

Peter's eyes took in the faces around the table. Nina Kovalyova and Vladimir Levitan—my God, *they* were here!
Miloslavsky. Levitsky. And Nicole. Her eyes met his, and he
saw no hint of fear.

Breakfast in the Doges' Palace, a mere pause for a late-
arriving guest. It was all so calm, so entirely respectable, except
for one jarring note. Miloslavsky sat at the head of the table,
sternly elegant in his pinstripes, holding a glass of champagne
in one well-manicured hand. In the other, he was holding a
gun.

And it was aimed at Nicole.

40

"WON'T YOU JOIN US?" Miloslavsky said.

Peter could feel an edge of tension in the words, in the room, but it didn't show in the faces around the table. Least of all, Miloslavsky's. The Soviet Foreign Minister was studying him with a kind of benign indulgence, the gracious host, apparently oblivious to the threat represented by the gun in his hand. Peter had never met Miloslavsky, but introductions hardly seemed in order.

On the outside, Peter was equally calm, but inside, his stomach was churning. He wasn't sure what he thought he would find when he got here—Nicole bound and gagged, at least locked up—and the dissidents, if he'd had any right to expect them to be here at all, should have been chained in stocks or sealed away in a dungeon. Something like that. Not this.

Breakfast!

Peter took a tentative step through the door, then hurried across the room to Nicole. She reached for his hand as he bent down beside her chair, as his arm moved around her shoulders.

The touch of her brought a wave of relief, easing a night of conflicting, tearing emotion. But now the waiting was over. She was here and alive; she didn't seem to be hurt or even frightened. As a matter of fact, she seemed no more than glad

274

to see him, as if she'd been off on an overnight trip and was back on schedule this morning.

Why *wasn't* she frightened?

"Are you all right?" he asked.

Nicole smiled. "I'm perfectly comfortable, if that's what you mean. The food here is delicious, and I've had plenty of sleep."

Peter knew her too well. No one else would have noticed, but there was something brittle in the tone of her voice, something stiff in her smile. Forced cheerfulness. And something more: a hint, not of fear, but of sadness.

"I know how you must have worried," she said, "and I'm sorry I put you through that. But really, I'm fine."

Peter's hand tightened on hers. Plenty of sleep—but not, he thought, of her own choice. He looked up at Miloslavsky, and anger flared inside. But the gun was still there, still aimed at Nicole. The danger wasn't over.

Peter sat down beside her. A place had been set there, for him of course, and a servant appeared to pour him a glass of champagne. But Peter's eyes remained on Miloslavsky. "What's going on here?" he said.

"At the moment, breakfast. I don't think you've met all my guests. Miss Kovalyova. Mr. Levitan. Chairman Levitsky. And of course you know Mr. Levin."

All right, introductions. Peter's eyes followed Miloslavsky's gesture. Levin had returned to his place near the end of the table, next to the KGB Chairman—Boris Levitsky, the same man Levin said was working against Miloslavsky! And now here they were, the three of them, as cozy as thieves, coconspirators.

But conspiring to do what?

And why were Nina and Vladya here? At another time, Peter would have been overjoyed to see them, but now he could only wonder. Why were they so calm? Like Nicole.

"*Guests*?" he asked, turning back to Miloslavsky. "Do you usually entertain your guests at gunpoint?"

Miloslavsky chuckled and set the gun aside, as casually as he would discard his napkin at the end of the meal. "A prop, nothing more," he said. "Miss Kovalyova, will you please pass the eggs to Mr. Lucas?"

Peter pushed his plate away, aware of the gun within Miloslavsky's reach, of the servant hovering somewhere behind him, of Levin sitting an easy few steps from the double doors through which he had entered the room. He didn't want food, but answers.

"I'm not hungry."

Miloslavsky gave a small nod of acquiescence. "As you wish. A pity, though. The trout is exceptional, and strawberries are hard to find at this time of year. I had them flown in from California." He picked up his fork. "I assume you won't mind if the rest of us go ahead?"

"I don't give a damn what you do. Just tell me what you want."

"To finish my breakfast. I don't believe in hurrying good food."

"Not even to get on with your assassination?"

The words had no outward effect on anyone at the table. Peter might have been talking about the threat of a thunderstorm. Miloslavsky took a bite of his trout, chewing it slowly, clearly savoring its taste. His expression showed nothing more than a vague, polite interest.

Then Peter produced his cigarettes and lit one. Polite interest faded to a look of clear distaste. But expressed disapproval of a breach of etiquette on the part of a guest was, apparently, a breach in and of itself. Miloslavsky said nothing. He signaled the servant to bring Peter an ashtray and resumed eating.

Peter wasn't about to apologize for his cigarette; he had never needed one more. Nor did he intend to indulge Miloslavsky with social conversation. "As you well know," he said, "the President and Premier are due to arrive this morning. You'll talk to me now, or else I'm leaving."

Miloslavsky only looked at him for a moment. Then he sighed and leaned back in his chair. "Very well, if you insist, though I'd think you would have guessed by now, there will be no assassination. None was ever planned."

Peter hadn't guessed. Compton had told him. "Why was I told there would be?" he asked.

"To supply you with the motivation to steal the Compton tape."

Peter glanced at Nicole, but she averted her eyes and reached for her coffee. The cup, he noticed, was trembling as she raised it to her lips. She steadied it with both hands.

Peter's jaw tightened. This scene was too hard to grasp. Surrealistic. Another kind of nightmare. An unlikely assortment of people all going through the motions of normalcy, except for the small signs of tension like Nicole's trembling hands. Only Miloslavsky seemed to be truly at ease with the situation. Sure of himself. In control.

But in control of what? What did he want? Why had he brought Peter here? Why *did* he want the tape?

Miloslavsky wouldn't be hurried. "The assassination," he said, "was a necessary falsehood created by Dmitri—I beg your pardon, Mr. *Levin*—to secure your cooperation. I gather it worked to a point, since the Compton tape is now in your possession. Unfortunately, Dmitri did not succeed in convincing you to turn it over to us."

No, and thank God. Peter turned to look at Levin, at the dark eyes set into the oddly shaped, moonlight-pale face. "So, it's Dmitri," he said. "No wonder you knew so much about Daniel Ravage. You're two of a kind!"

Levin hesitated, but Miloslavsky nodded and said, "Tell him the truth."

Levin picked up his champagne glass. It was crystal and fragile; for a moment Peter thought he was going to crush it in his hands. Instead, he took a drink and put it back on the table. His face didn't change; the dark eyes were void of expression. Like everyone here, he was calm. Too calm.

"Ravage and I were graduates of the same school," he said. "We did our American training at Gryazi, where illegal agents are taught the ways of American life. I was his control, and his contact with Moscow, for the whole time he was in the United States."

"*Was* there?" Peter asked. "Has he gone?"

"To recuperate from his illness in Moscow. He went shortly after the rest of us left to come here."

But it was Levin who had *caused* Ravage's illness! For Peter's benefit! That was clear now.

"And Ravitch?" Peter asked. "Was he an old school chum too?"

Levin smiled, the crooked smile, but it stopped just short of his eyes. "*I* was Ravitch," he said.

This was utterly unexpected. "*You* were Ravitch! You knew all along?"

"Yes, I was the man who went to see Eleanor Benjamin. In fact, I went there the day before I met you. At Gryazi we called that setting the stage. I knew Dr. Benjamin would repeat the story when she saw Gena Danchenko. I knew you were in contact with Gena. It was only a matter of time until the story reached you and you put it together with the doubts Ravage and I planted in your mind."

Peter stared at him as the pieces fell into place. Manipulation, one piece on top of another. He was *meant* to find out that Ravage was a Soviet spy, the traitor inside his own office, the physical presence of the forces whose treachery was outlined on the tape. He was *meant* to consider Ravage the threat, so that when Levin rendered him harmless, he would only trust Levin more. He was *meant* to trust Levin. From the start. From that night at Pierce Mill. A stage set! The killers had shot at him, not to scare him away, but to draw him in—to raise the curtain for Levin's entrance, to launch the final action. *His* action. And he had trusted Levin, because all of it came together on one well-designed stage.

"What about the Steve Katz tape?" he asked. "Did you manufacture that too?"

"No," Levin said, "the Katz tape was authentic. There was a man named Levin who worked for Steve. Of course, I'm not that man."

There was a man—*was* a man—meant to contact Peter if anything happened to Steve. But he hadn't made contact. He couldn't. Peter understood all of it now. This Levin killed that Levin and took his place. It was this Levin who killed Steve!

The anger inside swelled up into a fury. Peter started to push himself out of the chair, his eyes on Levin's expressionless face, his intentions entirely violent. But someone placed a restraining hand on his arm. Someone held him back.

Nicole.

"Peter, please. It won't do any good."

Her eyes were pleading, but gentle, and she no longer tried to hide the sadness that was there. Sadness and resignation. A look of despair. Of defeat.

"For God's sake, Nicole, what is it? What have they done to you?"

Nicole glanced at Miloslavsky; then her eyes shifted back to Peter. "He told me the truth. I believe him. You should listen and do what he says."

Peter stared at her, disbelieving and deeply concerned. What was this, hypnosis? Brainwashing? How had they made her come over to their side?

Peter's anger turned cold. "We're leaving here," he said to Miloslavsky. "And I don't think you'll try to stop us. I'm the only person who knows where that tape is hidden."

"Your courage is touching," Miloslavsky said. "Of course, I can't expect you simply to give me the tape. But Dmitri learned something about interrogation when he was a student at Gryazi, and I don't think you want to witness a demonstration of his skill."

Peter froze in his chair, the thought filled him with horror. They would use Nicole to break *him* down!

Miloslavsky laughed softly. "Don't worry," he said, "I have no intention of hurting Miss Compton. I've rather enjoyed her company. But she's free to leave anytime. As a sign of good faith, I'm releasing my best weapon."

Peter looked at him guardedly. "Why?" he asked. "If you don't want the tape, then why have you brought me here?"

"Because I want you to hear the tape, the two tapes together." Miloslavsky signaled the servant, who opened a door in a sideboard against one wall. He stooped down to lift something out and carried it back to the table. "Put it down in front of Mr. Lucas," Miloslavsky said.

Peter pushed away the dishes he hadn't used to make room for the box the servant was holding. A rectangular box made of light-colored plastic, with a darker inset showing through a clear window in the top. On the front was a web-covered speaker, maybe two fingers long and wide, and a series of buttons. *Search. Stand by. Synchronize. Play/Stop. Rewind.*

The whole thing was smaller than a conventional desk-model tape recorder, but larger than a cassette machine. It was sleek, clean-lined, contemporary, more advanced than anything in Carl Whitney's studio at the Smithsonian. And of course Peter knew what it was—a piece of equipment that didn't exist. A digital audio tape deck with fittings for, not one, but two micro-mini-size reels of tape. Peter could see through the window: one reel was already there, in place, only waiting for its partner.

"The Soviet half of the Korcula tape," Miloslavsky confirmed. "Delivered courtesy of Miss Kovalyova and Mr. Levitan—for which, as much as I hate to say so, they have earned their freedom. I suspect they intend to defect, and they're perfectly free to do so. No one will try to prevent them from leaving the house or the island."

"I don't understand," Peter said. "The tape was yours. You could have brought it out of the country yourself..."

"Ah, yes, but I chose not to. My credibility is somewhat lacking in your part of the world. I preferred a different source, Yuri Danchenko, working with your friend Katz. Dmitri, you see, *was* working with Katz, much as he's worked with you. We thought we could count on Katz to make the tapes public once he had them. But Danchenko was killed. And Katz became suspicious of Dmitri. He even went to talk to Arthur Compton and was planning to go back again. I had to prevent that. I couldn't let Compton find out what I was doing, which is why we've gone to great lengths to destroy your trust in him. The fact that *he* chose to mislead you only made that job easy for us." Miloslavsky raised his hands in a gesture, dismissing what he'd just said. "None of that matters," he said. "Time has run out. The pact will be signed today. I have no choice now but to trust you."

Peter's eyes had grown steadily more incredulous. "Surely you don't believe that I would consider *helping* you?"

"Like me, you will have no choice," Miloslavsky said. "We are on the same side, you and I, though for quite different reasons. You will understand that when you know the truth."

"What truth?"

"The truth of the Korcula meeting. I could tell you, as I've told Miss Compton, but I'd rather you hear it in Compton's own voice. He will be far more convincing. You have only to get your half of the tape, bring it here, and play them together. Then you, too, will be free to leave this house and to take both tapes with you."

Peter leaned back and drew on his cigarette, studying Miloslavsky's face across the table between them.

"How do I know this isn't another plot to get me to reveal where I've hidden my half of the tape?" He gestured toward Levin and Levitsky and the servant standing behind him. "What's to prevent your friends from taking it, once they know where it is?"

"You have my word on it," Miloslavsky said. "In any case, my friends, as you say, will be leaving here shortly to prepare for my own departure. I'm leaving the island this morning. I have urgent business in Moscow."

"Urgent business?" Peter smiled. "So urgent that you have to leave even as the Premier is arriving? Did Levin—Dmitri, whatever he's called—actually tell me the truth about that? Are you planning to seize power while the Premier is away?"

"What I do when I leave here is none of your concern," Miloslavsky replied coldly. "But on the chance that my word doesn't mean much to you, perhaps this will convince you that I do mean what I say." He picked up the gun beside his plate and looked at it for a moment. Then he handed it to Peter.

An automatic revolver. Peter checked to make sure it was loaded. He looked back at Miloslavsky and asked, "Do you have a telephone here?"

Miloslavsky frowned, but he nodded.

"And Nicole can leave first, with the dissidents?"

"Anytime she's ready."

Peter leaned forward to put out his cigarette in the ashtray. "All right," he said. "These are my conditions."

41

AN AIDE OPENED the door of Compton's suite at the Bon Repos. His mouth dropped open when he saw Nicole standing in the corridor outside. He stood there a moment, gaping. Then his face broke into a grin.

"Mr. Secretary, it's your *daughter*!"

Nicole pushed past him into the room, just as Compton got up from a table where he had been working on papers.

"Nicole!"

She rushed into his arms, clinging to him, never so glad to see him.

"Dear God," he said, "I've been *sick* with worry. Are you all right? Where have you been?"

"I'm fine, Daddy." There were tears in her eyes, tears in his, and that only made seeing him more painful. Because she knew. She had been to Badija. She knew what her father was doing.

And yet she still loved him. More than anything else, she wanted to protect him, but she couldn't. What he'd done, he had done to himself. She could only wait, and then be there for him.

She pulled away, wiping her eyes. "Isn't this silly?" she said, laughing, trying to cover the emotions she felt but didn't dare explain. Then suddenly she remembered the two people who had followed her into the room. She beckoned for them to come closer. "How rude of me! Daddy, this is Nina Kovalyova and Vladimir Levitan."

Compton couldn't have been more openly shocked. A strange look passed through his eyes. Nicole wasn't sure—was it fear? Or was it anger? Then his face softened, and he stepped forward to greet them.

"They want to ask for asylum," she said.

A moment of silence. She caught her breath.

But then Compton actually laughed. "They've picked a hell of a time and place," he said. "This could hardly be less auspicious."

"But you'll help them . . . ?"

"Of course, I will. Do you think I could say no?"

Nicole began to relax with the sound of his laughter and the look she saw on his face. Amusement, yes, but compassion too. *This* was her father—confronted by a twist of events he could not have foreseen, two Soviet defectors presenting themselves at a most inopportune time, threatening his life's work. He could laugh; he could welcome the challenge. But he couldn't turn them away.

"I'm not sure *how* I'll do it," he said, "since we don't have an embassy here. To start with, we'll have to find a safe place for them to stay."

He turned back to the aide, standing awkwardly at the table, trying not to intrude on the privacy of the reunion.

"In that case," Nicole said, "I think I'll go call Peter."

"Wait a minute, darling. You've got a lot to explain. I'm thrilled that you're safe, but my God, I thought you had drowned!"

"Oh, Daddy, I know. I'm sorry."

"Don't be *sorry*! Just tell me what happened. Where were you? And how in the world did the three of you meet up?"

Nicole's eyes met his, and she knew she couldn't lie. But she couldn't answer him, either. "I'll tell you all of it later," she said. "Right now, I have to call Peter. Could I use the phone in the bedroom?"

Compton hesitated. He was looking at her with a mixture of relief and concern, and a clear edge of anxiety. But he seemed to sense the distance that lay between them. To sense and accept it. He wouldn't press her, at least not yet. "Yes, of course," he said.

Nicole reached up to kiss him. "I love you," she said. "You know that, don't you?"

He nodded. He knew.

But she wondered if he would ever understand.

Peter and Miloslavsky were alone in the house when the telephone rang. Miloslavsky picked it up and listened for a moment. Then he handed it to Peter.

"We're at Daddy's hotel," Nicole said. "We're perfectly safe. The suite is full of people."

"And our three friends?" Peter asked.

"They're right where they said they would be. Ahead of the lunch crowd. They had no trouble getting an outside table."

She was talking about Levitsky, Levin, and the servant, who had left the house on Peter's instructions fifteen minutes after Nicole and the dissidents. They had gone to the café across from the Bon Repos, where Nicole could see them from the windows of Compton's suite. They would stay there for one hour, and if they should leave before that, Nicole only had to pick up the phone to warn him.

No interference.

It was what Peter wanted to know. "Good. Sit tight. I'll see you there later."

He replaced the phone with one hand while the other one felt for the revolver in his pocket. "All right," he said. "I'll need about ten minutes. Do you want to stay here or come?"

"Do I have a choice?" Miloslavsky asked.

"No. I want you with me."

Compton watched as Nicole escaped into the bedroom. She picked up the phone, gave the operator a number. Then she turned away, talking, her face to the window, her back to the door of the room. Obviously she had gotten through to Peter.

Yet Compton himself had been trying to reach Peter and knew he wasn't at the Marko Polo. According to the desk clerk there, he had been out since early morning.

Perhaps he'd come back?

Compton stood there a moment, thinking. Then he gestured

to one of the aides, one he trusted, and moved away to one side of the room, where they could talk quietly without being overheard.

"I want you to do something for me," he said. "When my daughter gets off the phone, call Peter Lucas at the Hotel Marko Polo. If he's there, tell him I want to see him. If he's not, check with the switchboard here. Get the number Nicole just called. Find out where it is and tell me."

The aide frowned but didn't ask any questions.

"Do it quietly," Compton added. "Under no circumstances should my daughter know what you're doing. Nor anyone else. Do you understand?"

"Of course, but isn't it time you were leaving?"

Compton looked at his watch. The President was coming across from the mainland by helicopter, landing in half an hour, and Compton was supposed to be there to meet him. "It's past time," he said. "I'm afraid he's going to have to land without me."

"The press will ask why. What should I tell them?"

"That I got tied up in a couple of last minute tangles. Nothing serious. Play it light." Compton's eyes narrowed, and he dropped his voice still lower, speaking tersely. "Then get a message to the President for me," he added. "Tell him I said we've got one hell of a problem. Marco Polo has been found out."

42

PETER TOOK MILOSLAVSKY the long way around, away from the cathedral, following the inner curve of the walls around the edge of the old town. He approached the town hall by way of an angled sidestreet and paused there, looking up the steps of the Glavna Ulica and the other way, through the main gate and across the bridge that led to the newer part of the city. There was no one to be seen in either direction. The street and the bridge were clear, the town silent.

Levin, Levitsky, and the servant were safely away from here, but Peter didn't know if Miloslavsky had other agents on the island. He had the gun in his pocket, holding it, ready to fire at the first sign of trouble. Now, for a moment, he released it and felt for his cigarette lighter. If he had to, he would burn the tape rather than let someone take it from him. The lighter was there. His hand closed again on the grip of the revolver.

Then he turned to Miloslavsky, smiling. "It's been here all along," he said, "almost in plain view."

Miloslavsky's eyes swept the buildings that lined the street. "Here? Where?"

"Well, it's not quite that simple," Peter admitted and glanced at the banner hanging across the Renaissance loggia of the town hall, twelve feet overhead. "Welcome to Korcula," he said.

Miloslavsky looked confused. "The banner? But we checked the banner—"

"For a reel of tape."

"Of course, for a reel of tape."

"I was counting on that." Peter produced the empty plastic reel. "That's why I took the tape off the reel."

Miloslavsky looked at him for a moment. Then he glanced at the banner and returned the smile coldly. "Very clever," he said.

Peter shrugged. "At least, sufficiently clever. It worked." He checked once more to be sure that they were alone; then he took hold of the rope that was hanging from one end of the canvas. "Grab that end as it comes down, will you?" he said.

They lowered the banner between them.

Two rows of heavy stitching ran across the top of it, forming a place for the rope on which it hung and leaving an extra hem, like the ruffled edge at the top of a shirred curtain. It was into that hem, hardly more than an inch in width, that Peter's fingers now probed. In a moment, he caught a loop of tape and began to pull it free.

They returned to the house, Peter holding Miloslavsky at gunpoint until he was sure no one had come here while they were out, that the house was still empty, that no traps had been set. Then he headed for the room at the back.

The tape deck was still on the table. Peter opened it and studied the fittings inside. Quite simple, really. One tape snapped into place alongside the other; the ends of them fed into two small slots from which they would wind automatically onto a pair of matching pickup reels.

In the meantime, he removed the tape from his pocket. He had wrapped it in clear plastic for protection against the rough canvas of the banner, a plastic wrap he had taken from Nicole's sample kit. Now he unwrapped it and began—slowly, carefully—to thread it back onto the reel from which it had come.

But then he frowned as he turned his attention to the switches on the front panel of the tape deck. "How does this work?" he asked.

Miloslavsky was at the head of the table again, watching Peter intently. "Press *Play* and then *Synchronize*," he said. "After that, the computer does it all."

There was no screeching sound, no hum, as the two tapes began to unwind together. Peter stood there a moment, watching. Then he pulled up a chair and sat down. The palms of his hands were damp with perspiration, and something heavy seemed to grip him inside. A sense of excitement and, with it, a deep sense of dread.

The truth, at last.

There was no stopping it now. Peter leaned back and closed his eyes.

A voice, speaking English:

This is the official record of agreements preliminary to the Korcula conference between the United States of America and the Union of Soviet Socialist Republics. Speaking first, for the United States, the Secretary of State, Mr. Compton.

Then the same voice, speaking Russian.

"An exact translation of the words you just heard," Miloslavsky said. "The next voice you'll hear will require no explanation."

No, it was clearly Compton.

Mr. Foreign Minister, we are prepared to confirm the points you and I have agreed upon in our meetings of the last three days. It is our purpose to bring about a firm arrangement between your government and ours to assure world peace and stability for this and future generations in the face of growing turmoil in the Middle and Near East, Central America, Southeast Asia and, indeed, the whole Third World. We seek to establish a regular means of guaranteeing that our respective governments are not drawn into confrontation of political or military nature by conflicts arising in other parts of the world.

Peter sat forward, frowning. He did not understand. He listened as Compton continued:

Toward this end, we acknowledge a mutual respect for the basic economic and military requirements, and national security needs, of our respective nations. We agree to establish and formally recognize new zones of responsibility, replacing the traditional system of spheres of influence and client states. We acknowledge that within these zones our respective governments will be free to operate to maintain stability, according to the confines of the principles set forth in Document Number Four—namely, one, notification; two, maximum local self-determination; and, three, minimum exercise of military power.

We further agree to a division of the world oil market, with two million barrels a day going to the Soviet bloc and fourteen million barrels a day going to the U.S. bloc, subject to annual reallocation as needed and as subsequently agreed to, and to market shares of other vital commodities, such as chrome, as detailed in Document Number Eight. We agree that within our separate zones of responsibility, first priority will be given to the maintenance of oil production in the existing producing nations.

Peter's frown deepened; he felt chilled, though the room was warm. What was Compton talking about? Market shares of oil and chrome? Zones of responsibility? What did any of this have to do with human rights? He glanced across the table at Miloslavsky, as thoughts started to form in his mind—thoughts not of the words he was hearing, but of the words he was not.

Peter tried to reject the thoughts, but they persisted in nagging him as Compton went on:

We agree that our commitment to these principles will be verified during a testing period, beginning with the conclusion of this meeting, by our noninterference in Soviet actions taken with regard to Norway and West Berlin. The Soviet government will verify its commitment to these principles in the same way, during the same testing period, by its noninterference with American actions in Cuba, China, and the Middle East.

* * *

Peter's body tensed as he shivered against the chill. China and Cuba! Norway! West Berlin! Ravage had laid it all out. Questions. Doubts.

But what *was* it? A testing period? For what?

Peter leaned forward, listening carefully. Compton was finally getting to the point, human rights:

> *We agree that the testing period will be concluded and that we will give formal agreement to these principles at a joint meeting to be held on the Yugoslavian island of Korcula, beginning October 7, concurrent with a summit conference on human rights.*

Here, at last. . . .

> *The human-rights conference will spell out certain agreements respecting individual freedom, as detailed in Document Number Twenty-seven, to which each side shall be bound to the extent that those agreements do not conflict with or jeopardize the requirements of this pact.*

What?

Was that *all*? As detailed in Document Number Twenty-seven?

Peter's heart sank. The human-rights conference was nothing more than a cover! Good only as long as it didn't conflict or jeopardize!

Korcula was a *lie*!

> *We agree that our respective zones of responsibility will be designated by use of the World Power Computer Model drawn up by a joint commission, headed on the part of the U.S. government by Dr. Michael Baker, and on the part of the Soviet government by Professor Ludmila Bunina. The model will incorporate such factors as border security, cultural heritage, historical tradition, availability of natural resources, etcetera, as outlined in Document Number Seven.*
>
> *A reassessment of our separate needs as related to the zones of responsibility will occur annually at a per-*

manent computer modeling center to be established under our joint direction on the Yugoslavian island of Badija, to which all future disputes arising out of this agreement will be referred.

Oh, my God! Peter leaned forward, listening intently.

We agree to recognize new zones of responsibility as follows. For the United States: All of Latin America, including the Republic of Cuba. All western European nations currently designated members of the NATO bloc, excluding Norway. All African nations having all or at least fifty-one percent of their territory on or above the zero parallel at the equator. All nations currently designated Middle Eastern, including the Arab Republic of Egypt on the African continent, but excluding Afghanistan, Pakistan, Syria, and Iraq.

Oh, my *God*! Norway! *Excluding* Norway!

Peter pushed himself up out of the chair. His palms were no longer sweating, but icy cold. He was trembling inside and out, chilled by revulsion and fury. This wasn't Korcula, but the total antithesis of it! No choice at all! Ever!

Because the United States and Russia were dividing up the world. This is yours, that's mine, like so many colored spaces on a game board! Dividing the world between them.

And they were doing it by computer!

For the Soviet Union: The western European nations of Norway and Finland. All eastern European nations, excluding Yugoslavia, which will be held under the joint protection of both parties to the agreement, but including East Germany and the city of West Berlin. All countries currently designated Southeast Asian. All African nations having all or at least fifty-one percent of their territory on or below the zero parallel at the equator. The Indian subcontinent, including India, Pakistan, Nepal. . . .

Peter stumbled against the table. He lunged at the machine, forgetting Miloslavsky, forgetting everything but the source of the words, wanting to shut them off. Shut them out! Make them cease to be real!

Norway, India, West Berlin—all theirs! Britain, France, China, Japan, Australia—ours! Germany, still divided. And Yugoslavia, so determined to be independent, a joint protectorate of *both* nations! The list was endless. And sickening!

Compton's masterstroke. *This* was what he had done to Peter's dream, to his own dream. He had twisted it into something else, something coldly, horribly frightening, something infinitely more terrifying than the nightmare. A world without any choice. A world run by computers!

Peter's hand found the machine and came down hard against it. The words ground to a halt. Silence fell over the room, a silence broken only by the sound of choking sobs—and in a moment, Peter realized that the sound was coming from him.

Norway, for God's sake! Why? Precious border security. Were the Soviets so damn worried about a bunch of arctic fishermen? Why hadn't the computers told them to *guard* their frozen border, or to move their base at Murmansk to a place where they could protect it!

Why West Berlin?

Why *any* of it?

Then suddenly he heard Compton's voice again: "Peter! Peter! There's so much you don't know."

Peter looked up sharply. The double doors, which he'd closed when they came back here, were standing open now, and framed in them was the figure of Arthur Compton.

43

THE THREE MEN stared at each other in the silence of the room—Peter anguished, Compton worried, Miloslavsky coolly arrogant, almost smug, because the victory was clearly his.

It was Miloslavsky who spoke into the silence, not to Compton but to Peter. "We have little in common," he said. "Almost nothing in common. We see the world from entirely antagonistic points of view. And yet, I have chosen to trust you . . ."

Peter hardly heard him. His mind was still whirling from the revelations of the tapes. He sat where he was, in a daze, his eyes riveted on Compton, who was still standing in the doorway. He had nearly forgotten that Miloslavsky was here.

But now the Russian's words began to penetrate shock and confusion and brought Peter back to the choice he was facing, a choice personified by the two men. His eyes shifted from one to the other, from enemy to friend, and he wondered which one he had *less* in common with now. The cold-blooded fanatic who attached no value whatever to human freedom? Or the peacemaker who valued freedom above all else but had knowingly turned his back on it? The Marxist who despised Korcula for the concessions it required of his side? Or the international diplomat who created Korcula without regard for its cost?

"I'm counting on you," he heard Miloslavsky saying. "I'm counting on you to do what you must, not for me, but for yourself and the goals you believe in."

Peter focused on him, glaring. "You've done what you came here to do," he said. "How much more do you want? My assurances? Go to hell!"

Miloslavsky smiled, and Peter turned away. His anger, his outrage, were all the assurance Miloslavsky needed. They had little in common, almost nothing in common. Only one thing, their separate reactions to the truth of the Korcula conference. Like Steve Katz and Jovan Kersnik, they had come to the same conclusion. Korcula had to be destroyed.

Miloslavsky nodded to Peter. Then, without another word, he got up from the table and walked out of the room, leaving Peter and Compton alone.

Alone with a gulf between them, too wide to be bridged even by years of devotion. And yet, Peter's anger was already starting to fade. He remembered how Nicole had looked when she sat here at this table, and now he knew what she felt. Not anger, but disillusionment. Despair. An overwhelming sense of loss.

Korcula was finished. He wasn't sure how he felt about Compton.

Peter got up and pressed the button to rewind the tapes as Compton stepped into the room.

"We need to talk," Compton said.

"Why?"

"You owe me that. A chance to explain. A chance to try to convince you."

Peter looked up. "Or a chance to take these tapes from me?"

Hurt showed in Compton's eyes. "I won't do that," he said. "I want you to *give* them to me."

Peter laughed but said nothing.

"Of your own accord," Compton added. "The least you can do is listen."

A moment passed in silence. Peter was torn by old feelings, old affection, old trust—between those and the truth that was on the tapes. And yet Compton was right; Peter owed him a chance. He nodded. "I'll listen."

A look of relief passed across Compton's face. "We can't talk here. I suggest we go for a walk."

"I've got a car," Peter said. "Let's get away from this part of the island." He removed the tapes and dropped them into his pocket with Miloslavsky's revolver. Then he picked up the tape deck and carried it under his arm.

The air outside was warming as the sun rose in the sky; it was midmorning, moving on toward noon. Peter glanced at Compton as they angled across the street to the piazza and started to make their way down the Glavna Ulica. Compton's jaw was firm, but his eyes looked tired. And why not? After all, he'd had a lot on his mind.

"Has the President arrived?" Peter asked.

"By now he's probably halfway to his hotel. But we have some time. The Premier was delayed. He's not due for another two hours."

"It's too bad they had to make the trip at all."

Compton turned to him sharply. "Are you that sure of yourself?"

"I'm that sure," Peter said.

"Well, we'll talk."

Peter nodded but said nothing more. They passed the town hall, where the rope that had held the banner in place was hanging loose from the loggia, and moved onto the bridge that led them out of the old town. The car was parked in a street around the corner. Peter put the tapes into the trunk, with the tape deck and the revolver. Then he got in behind the wheel, fit the key into the ignition, and turned to look at Compton on the other side of the seat.

"For Christ's sake, Arthur, *why*?"

Compton sighed. "Why? Do you have forty years to listen? Where do you want me to start?"

"How about Amsterdam. Or Paris."

"All right, let's start there. War. Six million people purposely destroyed, and that's not counting the soldiers who died on both sides, or civilians caught in the bombing—"

"Don't give me that," Peter broke in. "I was there, remember? Thanks to you, I survived it. I counted with you then, a two-year-old boy, and all the others like me. We mattered. We were *worth* trying to save."

"You still matter. You, and the others like you."

"Do we?" Peter started the car and pulled sharply away from the curb, tires screeching against the pavement. Then he took a deep breath, got a check on his feelings, drove on under better control. "Do we?" he said. "I don't think so. You've changed."

Compton shook his head sadly. "You'll never know how much you matter with me, even aside from our friendship. Can you guess how I feel when I look at you and know that you might have died? There's nothing I could ever do that would make me prouder than saving your life. Or that would give me more of a sense of self-worth. Your worth, my worth, every individual worth. All of it matters. It's *all* that matters. But how many more lives would have been saved if that war had never started?"

"So that's it." Peter chuckled. "It's a numbers game. Quantity versus quality. No wonder you've decided to turn the world over to Baker and his computers!"

"That's not what I've decided," Compton replied firmly. "I don't even like Baker. I think he's a son of a bitch, but he's also a genius. And we can't duck from computer technology. It's the backbone of our society, our defense systems, our war capability. Computers even design our weapons now. There's no reason why we can't use them to preserve the peace instead of making war."

"Try telling that to the Norwegians when the Soviet tanks roll in," Peter said. "Christ, if only we'd had Michael Baker back in the thirties, we could have been satisfied just *containing* Hitler! And would that have saved lives? Not as long as he kept his death camps and his Luftwaffe bombs safely off-limits, inside his own zones of responsibility!" Compton winced, and Peter knew he'd struck home. "On the other hand," he added, "Hitler wouldn't have had to worry about housing problems, would he?"

"It's not the same thing now," Compton said.

"Sure."

Anger flashed in Compton's eyes. "Don't be condescending," he snapped. "Are *you* willing to make war with Russia to close down the Gulag? Are *you* willing to risk the existence of all human civilization to protect the inherent freedom of the Soviet people?"

Peter glanced across the seat and found Compton staring at him. He turned away—his silence, alone an answer.

It wasn't the same.

"It's a lousy choice," Compton said quietly. "As a matter of fact, it's no choice at all. I don't have to tell you what the next war would be like. What kind of help do you think a nun's habit, or the walls of that orphanage would be against nuclear weapons? There's no help for people in that kind of war. No help and no hope. We can't let it happen. We've got to prevent it, and that's the purpose of Korcula. That's what we came here to do."

"That may be what you came here to do," Peter said, "but I came here to talk about human rights."

"And so you have. You heard the tapes. Those agreements are part of the Korcula pact."

"Only as long as they don't jeopardize the rest of the pact, the secret pact. Dammit, Arthur, you're making god-like decisions. If the idea is so wonderful, why do you have to lie about it? Why can't you tell the truth?"

"Because the world isn't ready to face reality."

"Which reality, yours or mine?"

"The only kind of reality that exists. Power politics on an international scale, based on military and economic strength. Look, Peter, I understand how you feel. Believe me, I've been there myself. And maybe you're right that I've changed, but my priorities haven't. I still want the same thing I always did— freedom for all people—but that's only a dream unless we can get control over the threat of confrontation between the superpowers. Because that threat is so final, and our defense against it so fragile, that we're paralyzed whenever it rears up. Remember what happened in Iran. Those hostages were at the mercy of a lunatic, but we couldn't move to help them. And the Iranian people, to the extent they were sincere about wanting their own form of government, free of intervention from the U.S. or Russia, never have had a chance. There they sat between us. The real issue wasn't freedom, but oil. Control of the Persian Gulf. It's hard to think about justice when you're worried about the potential collapse of the Western industrial nations."

Peter brought the car to a stop at an intersection. He took a cigarette from his pocket and held his lighter to it. Then he looked both ways and moved on. They had reached the far edge of the new town, on the street that became the coast road to Lumbarda. Somewhere to the south and west lay the island of Badija, where Baker and his computers were deciding the fate of the world.

"And so you figure the solution is taking all choice away from all people except the Russians and us," Peter said. "The rest of the world be damned!"

"On issues of war and peace, that's exactly what I think. God knows, we have major differences with the Soviets—cultural differences, philosophical differences—but we also have something very important in common. We are equally vulnerable to war with each other. To mutual destruction. If anyone is going to guarantee world peace and stability, we have to, and we have to do it together. No one else can. But to do it, we have to eliminate the small disputes that could set off the big one. Territory. Border security. Access to the world's natural resources.

"But *then*, once the threat of war is removed, we can concentrate on the issues of freedom and justice. Can't you see how we're better off making freedom secure in half the world than leaving it vulnerable everywhere? And, at the same time, establishing friendly relations with the Soviets, based on what we have in common instead of what divides us? Given time, we can soften their defensiveness, their mistrust of us, and vice versa, and possibly have real influence on their internal policies. Look at what we've accomplished already. The human-rights portion of the Korcula pact is no less significant for the fact that it's backed up by something stronger."

"Stronger! Good God! They release two hundred political prisoners, and we give them Norway and West Berlin! Do you really expect me to *like* that?"

Compton sighed heavily. "We have to give if we want to take," he said. "And you needn't worry about Soviet tanks in Norway. It will be a gradual process of influence shifting. Finlandization. As for West Berlin, that's been an artificial arrangement since its inception, impossible to protect, a constant source of danger. You know that's true. We've defended it on principle all these years. Now, under the guise of neutralization, it will fall under Soviet influence."

"Arthur, my God! I can't believe it's you talking! What about the people who *live* there?"

"What about the people who live in Cuba? They're free again. Or the people who live in the Middle East? World oil allocations will be absolutely secure, once the Korcula pact is signed; they will be removed as a point of conflict. Do you realize what that means? We can assure the continued existence of Israel, a peaceful existence, for no other reason than because it's right. We won't have to balance the freedom of the Israeli people against our own dependence on Arab oil. We can deal with the Palestinian question directly, because it should be resolved, and not because we're afraid of what will happen if we don't. In Latin America and Africa, the Soviets will have no reason to supply arms and advisers to revolutionaries or terrorists. They won't be seeking new territory. They'll have no one to terrorize. The sides are drawn. Third World nations will still be free to work out their own growing pains, but they'll never again be able to threaten the peace of the world."

"Because Washington and Moscow won't permit it! What kind of freedom is that? What about the Cambodians, for God's sake? Do we turn our backs on genocide and starvation just because Southeast Asia is theirs?"

"We abandoned Cambodia when we pulled out of Vietnam," Compton said. "And the Soviets, frankly, if they don't have to worry about preserving what they've got, may be tougher on maverick communists in Cambodia or Vietnam."

"Would that help you ease your conscience?" Peter asked. His hands gripped the steering wheel harder as he rounded a stand of pine trees and came out with a view of the sea. "People have to be free to make choices. And free to make mistakes. Tyranny is tyranny, regardless of good intentions."

"Is that such a bad thing?" Compton asked. "Look at the ocean, these hills, these trees. Have you ever seen anything more tranquil, more enviable, more worthy of protection? We've learned to cherish this kind of natural setting, for the *peace* we find here. And yet it's controlled by a tyrant. Nature. And man is a creature of those same natural forces."

"But man is nature's highest creature," Peter said. "We strive for peace *and* justice."

"We can and do," Compton said. "Listen to me, your reaction is precisely what I expected. It's why I've never discussed this with you before. But you must try to understand.

I'm trying to serve the same goal you are—justice, however imperfect, in a world we or the Russians could destroy. And I firmly believe that the most humane course to justice is, simply, for each of us to fight for the individual cause whenever and wherever we find someone in trouble. And then to hope that out of a million individual actions, a general state of peace and freedom will emerge. That's the road all of us should try to follow, all of us as individuals.

"But governments like ours, with life-and-death power over the whole human race, have another responsibility. We have to take the road that deals with power as it is, and not as we wish it would be. We have to try to shape events so that we can provide security and freedom for as many people as possible. We are forced at times to overlook, or ignore, the individual cause. I know you think that's heartless and cruel, and believe me, it tears my heart when we decide, as we have here, that a larger goal is more important than the freedom of one country or another. But, Peter, peace has to come first. The alternative is worse. At best, a stalemate—inaction, with two nuclear giants facing each other, terrorized by their own power to destroy. Or, at worst, extinction.

"Well!" Compton paused to catch his breath. "I'm sorry. I didn't mean to turn this into a lecture. It's just that it's so vital. We're almost there. We're so close. Now you're in a position to destroy everything we've accomplished. This is the most important thing I've ever asked you to do."

Peter felt sick. It almost made sense. Almost, but not quite. The price was too high. Freedom, of a kind, for half the world. Enslavement for the other.

"What are you asking?" he said.

"For you to give me those tapes."

Peter drew on his cigarette. "No," he said at last.

"You must," Compton said. "You can't make them public. The balance of world power is precarious already; this would blow it apart. Our allies would never trust us—"

"With good reason."

"But are you willing to let them know what it is? You have it in your power, Peter. You can bring down the Korcula conference, but you have to consider what else will fall with it—including, possibly, the Soviet Premier."

"Because of Miloslavsky?"

Compton nodded. "Now that he has your help, he has very nearly succeeded in destroying Korcula, but he's not content with that. He intends to place the blame for Korcula on Sukhov and then take control of the Kremlin. Think about it, Peter. Do you want Miloslavsky in charge over there? My God, human rights in the Soviet Union and every nation it dominates would be less than a dream, not even a vague hope. Détente would become a memory. He would *seek* confrontation—"

"No!" Peter slammed on the brake, brought the car to a sudden stop. "That's not *my* choice. I'm not the architect of Korcula. You are! *You* brought us to this."

"That may be," Compton said quietly, "but you have the tapes. The choice is yours to make."

Peter took a deep breath and forced himself to relax. Then he leaned forward to put out his cigarette.

"Well?" Compton asked. "What are you going to do?"

Peter stared at him for a moment, this man who was so much more than father or friend, this man to whom he owed his life. "I don't want to make the tapes public," he said, "and I won't if I don't have to. I'll keep them safe. No one will ever know I have them or what's on them. Unless—"

"Unless what?"

"What I do depends on what you do. Korcula must be stopped. I will do it only if you don't."

Peter eased the car forward. Then he swung it around, stepped down on the gas and headed back into town.

44

"It is therefore with deep regret," Compton said, "that I announce the failure of the Korcula meeting and my own resignation as Secretary of State."

Peter stood to one side of the room, watching the swell of shock as it passed from one face to another. The press, for once, had no inkling of what had been coming when Compton summoned them here. There had been no rumors, no leaks, and beyond Compton's absence when the President flew in today, no hint of a last-minute problem. There was only this stunning announcement.

Korcula was finished. Compton, too. And in this room, only three people knew why.

Peter glanced at Nicole, who was standing beside him, her gaze intent on her father, her eyes full of pride. Peter, too, was shaken by the reality of the announcement, irrevocable now, and his anger vanished. Like Nicole, he was proud of Compton's courage. It wasn't his fault that the dream remained elusive. He had advanced its cause and was leaving it now to others, his honor intact. Peter only wished there had been another way.

The press corps was stunned to silence, but it wasn't long to last. A barrage of voices erupted into questions, a dozen or more all at once.

"Mr. Secretary, when did you know this was coming?"

"Did the Soviets lie?"

"Is there any chance that the issues raised here might be raised again in the future?"

"Have the President and Premier met since they came here today?"

"Who made the decision to call it off?"

"Is your resignation, Mr. Secretary, an acknowledgment that the failure of the meeting is your fault?"

Compton's face showed no sign of emotion as he raised a hand for silence. His voice was completely calm. "It is my fault," he said, "to the extent that I misjudged our ability to overcome a long-standing tradition of hostility and mistrust. No one lied. We simply weren't able to work it out. Nothing happened here that hasn't happened a hundred times before. That's the point: nothing new happened. But that doesn't mean we stop trying. Of course these issues will be raised again, and again and again, until civilized people on both sides of the world come to realize that there's more to be gained from friendship than alienation. In the meantime, because my reputation has been so closely linked with these negotiations, I feel that my usefulness as Secretary of State is over. I hope to continue to serve my country and the cause of world peace in some other capacity, but what that might be, I can't say now."

"Is it true," someone asked, "that Foreign Minister Miloslavsky left Korcula rather suddenly this morning, and was his departure related to the failure of the meetings?"

"I don't know," Compton replied. "But I would like to say something about Premier Sukhov, whom I've had occasion to work with directly and have come to respect and admire. He entered into these talks with honor, in good faith, as I believe we have done. The Soviet people have every right to be proud of his efforts on their behalf. With leaders like him and the President I have served, I believe we can be optimistic about the prospects for our world in the future."

Compton paused for a moment, then added, "That's all the time I have now. The rest of your questions will have to be postponed." He turned to go.

But one reporter stood up and started clapping—one and then another, and then more and more, until the room filled with applause. It wasn't loud applause, but respectful, and Compton was clearly moved. He stood where he was, fighting to keep his composure. Then, with a wave, he walked out of the room.

Peter squeezed Nicole's hand. "Come on," he said. "I told your father we'd meet him in his room."

"Everything is arranged," Levitsky said, leaning closer to Miloslavsky to be heard above the engines as the jet descended toward Moscow. "Premier Sukhov arrives home tomorrow morning. He'll be met at the plane and placed under arrest."

Miloslavsky nodded slowly. It was difficult not to be anxious at this stage of the operation.

"And then," Levitsky added, "when he realizes the hopelessness of the situation, he will be offered a capsule."

"Do you think he'll accept it?"

Levitsky shrugged. "It's his choice—a life in exile, disgraced, or a state funeral with full honors. What would you do?"

"What I would do is beside the point," Miloslavsky said. "If he chooses the capsule, we have no problems. But if he chooses to fight..." His voice faded, leaving the thought unspoken. "What's the status of the Council of Ministers now?" he asked.

"They remain divided. Half for you, half for Sukhov."

Miloslavsky banged his fist against the arm of his seat. "That's not good enough! What if he refuses the capsule?"

"Then perhaps we will have to use force."

Miloslavsky sighed heavily and glanced up as Dmitri appeared from the rear of the plane.

"We've just received a radio report from Korcula," he said, and held out a piece of paper. Miloslavsky snatched it out of his hands as a light flashed on overhead. The seat-belt sign; they were coming in for a landing. Dmitri sat down on the other side of the aisle and buckled himself in.

Miloslavsky read the report and crumpled it in his hand. His blue eyes turned to ice as he turned to look at Levitsky. "Lucas did *not* make the tapes public," he said.

"What...?"

"Apparently he used them to force Compton's hand. The

United States has backed out of the conference, claiming in-compatibility, and Compton has resigned."

"That's all? Nothing more?"

"No, that's *not* all. Compton made a public statement *prais-ing* Sukhov. Tass and *Pravda* will have it by now. This will not help us with the ministers."

"No."

Miloslavsky's jaw tightened in anger. "He *must* choose the capsule!"

"Don't worry," Levitsky said. "I'm confident he will."

The suite was full of people, members of the U.S. dele-gation, more shocked by Compton's announcement than the press had been. And Andrei Voloshin, who was sometimes an adversary, sometimes a colleague, but always Compton's friend. Compton made his way through the crowd, smiling easily, shaking hands, brushing off concern and sadness with a promise or a light remark. Watching him, Peter smiled too. His presence still commanded the room; he made himself felt without effort. The State Department wouldn't be the same place without him. In spite of everything, he was going to be very much missed.

Compton caught Peter's eye, saw Nicole standing with him, and slowly made his way to them.

"Daddy . . ."

"It's all right, sweetie. I'll be fine." Compton hugged her, and then he hugged Peter. "You two may have your hands full, trying to keep me busy."

Nicole smiled. "Somehow I don't think so."

"I don't know. Maybe Peter can find a place for me in his office."

"I couldn't take the competition," Peter said lightly. Then his face grew serious again. "And I'm not sure I want to stay there myself after everything that's happened."

Compton's hand touched Peter's arm. "You have a great future," he said. "You mustn't be disillusioned. The President is well aware of your work and will want to advance you, even though I won't be involved anymore. As a matter of fact, I'm planning to make one last recommendation to him." Compton lowered his voice. "How would you like to go to Cuba?"

Peter frowned. "Cuba?"

"As ambassador."

Peter was truly astonished. His mouth dropped open and he stared at Compton, temporarily speechless. Then he said, "I...I don't know what to say. It never occurred to me. I hadn't thought about it."

"Well, I have," Compton said. "I've been thinking about it for weeks. I was only waiting until Korcula was finished. What do you think? Are you interested?"

"Of course I'm interested. More than interested!" Cuba. There was so much to be done there, so much to be undone. He was thrilled by the prospect of having a hand in that. And yet something held him back. "I don't know," he said. "I'm not sure it's a good idea."

"You think I'm setting you up before I leave. As a personal favor."

Peter smiled and shrugged.

"You should know me better. You are the perfect choice. You know we've been looking for someone who's known to have a strong interest in human rights."

"As a symbolic gesture..."

"No, more than that. Much more than that, especially now. We're going to have to work at it if we want to keep Cuba free. We don't want to make the mistakes we've made in the past. We want a strong alliance without imposing control. I'm not doing you a favor. We need you there."

Peter smiled and looked at Nicole. "What do you think? Would you like to live in Havana?"

She smiled back and moved closer to him. "I'd love to live in Havana, if Daddy will come visit."

"I'll be there," Compton said. Then he looked up and saw Voloshin leaving through the door. "By the way," he added, "a couple of friends of yours will be with us on the plane home."

Nicole looked at him anxiously. "Nina and Vladya?"

"I've worked it out with Voloshin. It's my consolation prize. There will be no interference from the KGB."

No interference. Peter thought of Miloslavsky and Levitsky. "Are you sure Voloshin can speak for the KGB?" he asked.

"I'm sure," Compton said. "They'll request asylum officially when we land in Washington."

"Oh, Daddy, that's wonderful."

"Yes, I'm pleased. I wish all six of them had survived. I wish it had been two hundred. But two people do count." A look of sadness passed briefly through Compton's eyes. "Well, I have to see the President now. Peter, let me ask you one more time. I'd like to take the tapes with me. The President and I want to see them destroyed. We want to destroy them ourselves."

The ultimate moment of choice. Peter knew what it had to be.

Compton's eyes caught his and held them. "Trust me," he said. "It's the only time I've ever asked for anything in return."

The first time. Ever. In all these years, Peter owed Compton his *life*. And now Compton was asking for payment.

Peter turned away. His voice was choked. "I'm sorry. I can't."

The jet touched down on a KGB airstrip near Moscow and rolled to a stop near a small gray building. Miloslavsky was out of his seat and at the door by the time the steps were in place. He took them quickly for a man of his age, in a hurry to reinforce his position, to make sure he would succeed.

But then, at the last step, he came to a sudden stop.

A uniformed man stepped from the gray building. Four others remained behind, near the door. All of them were armed and holding their weapons in firing position.

"Comrade Miloslavsky, it's my duty to inform you that you are under arrest."

For a moment Miloslavsky's mind went blank. The shock was too much to absorb. Then a rage rose up inside him. He glared at the man. "How *dare* you!"

The man said nothing, but his eyes shifted to a point behind Miloslavsky.

Miloslavsky turned around. Levitsky was standing at the top of the steps. Slowly he started down them.

"*Boris . . . ?*"

"I'm sorry," Levitsky said, "but this can't go on any longer. Your way is of the past, and we must look to the future."

Miloslavsky's anger vanished, was replaced by a feeling he'd almost forgotten. Deep hurt. "No," he said quietly. "Not you! I don't believe it."

"Yevgeni, you have no support. The Council of Ministers has never wavered from Sukhov. And I control the KGB."

"But you *agreed* with me . . ."

"About Korcula, yes. Korcula went too far. Otherwise, my loyalties are and always have been with the Premier. I am acting now on his orders."

Miloslavsky shook his head slowly. "I trusted you."

"Then trust me once more." Levitsky reached into his pocket. When the hand emerged, he opened it, palm up.

Miloslavsky stared at the capsule Levitsky was offering. A state funeral with full honors. Or exile and disgrace. No choice. He took the capsule and led the way into the building.

45

THE SIGNAL TO COMPTON had been Voloshin's departure. Compton left soon after, as quickly as he could, making excuses—a meeting with the President; no one could question that. He drove himself to a prearranged destination on the Lumbarda coast road. Voloshin was there with a boat and two Soviet soldiers, who piloted them across to Badija. They got out at the landing dock and walked up to the monastery, where they took an elevator to the second-floor conference room. Besides the two soldiers, who would soon be transferred to Sverdlovsk, no one had seen them enter, and no one would see them leave.

Compton dropped his attaché case on the floor and pulled out a chair to sit down. On the table was the usual assortment of notepads and pencils, freshly sharpened. A pair of rock-crystal ashtrays. A bottle of Russian vodka, a bowl of ice, and four glasses. Compton picked up the bottle and stared at it for a moment, the suggestion of a smile at the corners of his mouth. Then he got up again quickly as the door opened and two men walked into the room.

The President and the Premier.

Compton and Voloshin stepped forward to shake hands. Then the four of them sat down at the table.

"We've had a report from Moscow," Sukhov said. "Miloslavsky suffered a heart attack as he got off the plane. It was instantly fatal."

Compton lowered his eyes. He had not known precisely how Sukhov would deal with Miloslavsky. A heart attack. All right, let it stand unquestioned. It would be hypocritical for him to voice an objection.

He turned to Voloshin. "I guess it's official, then. Congratulations. I can't think of anyone who'd make a better Foreign Minister than you, but we'll miss you in Washington. *I'll* miss you."

"I suspect we'll still have occasion to see each other." Voloshin smiled. "Am I somewhere near the truth?"

Compton didn't confirm or deny what Voloshin was thinking. But of course he was right. Compton could not continue as Secretary of State. But Presidents used unofficial advisers. He would have his say.

"In any case," he said, "Miloslavsky is no longer a problem. If it weren't for the tapes . . ."

"You've seen Peter Lucas?" the President asked.

"I just left him." Compton smiled ruefully. "He wouldn't give me the tapes. I tried my best—I think I almost had him convinced. But in the end he kept them."

A look of concern passed across the President's face. He leaned back in the chair. "Did you ask him about Cuba?"

"I mentioned it to him. He's definitely interested."

"Good. I'll offer it to him as soon as we get back. The sooner he accepts, the sooner he'll be in Havana. And away from Washington."

Compton felt a small tug of conscience. But he hadn't lied to Peter. He did think Peter was the right man for the post, and he'd been thinking it long before it became a matter of expedience as well as good judgment. Peter and Nicole would be happy there. It was a good move, from everyone's point of view.

"Then we need only wait," the President said. "Since Lucas has the tapes, we can't act now. But in the future . . . during my next term . . . Who knows?"

Compton picked up his attaché case, unlocked it, and opened the lid. He removed two bound documents, gave one of them to the President, the other to the Premier. "I drew these up this afternoon," Compton said. "I think they reflect all our thinking. We can at least leave them for our successors—if nothing else, as a basis for an agreement that must inevitably come."

"What are they?" the President asked.

"Two copies of an *aide-memoire*," Compton said. "A summation of what's on the tapes, of what we came so close to achieving. A plan to keep the computer center downstairs in operation, though perhaps at a different location, so that when the opportunity comes to take up where we've left off today, we'll have immediate access to current accurate data and be prepared to move quickly. If that opportunity comes after all of us have left office, then we'll let our successors arrange the details. At least, when they do, and when the agreement is finally signed, our two countries will know where the idea started." He paused, and for the first time today, he looked happy. "Just sign them," he said. "By so doing, you will keep alive the concept of Korcula and, I hope, assure the eventual salvation of the world."

The President and Premier read what Compton had written; then the President picked up his pen and pulled off the cap. He looked at Sukhov. "Are you ready?" he asked.

Sukhov smiled and nodded.

Simultaneously, the two men signed the documents. Then they exchanged copies and signed their names once again.

Voloshin opened the vodka, poured four drinks and passed them around the table. "Arthur," he said, "no one has more right to speak at this moment than you do."

Compton sat there a moment, his thoughts hidden behind a sober face. Then he stood up and raised his glass in a toast.

"To peace," he said. "To Korcula. May it yet work."